The Roosevelt Presence

The Life and Legacy of FDR

The Roosevelt Presence

The Life and Legacy of FDR

Patrick J. Maney

UNIVERSITY OF CALIFORNIA PRESS
Berkeley • Los Angeles • London

University of California Press
Berkeley and Los Angeles, California
University of California Press, Ltd.
London, England

First California Paperback Printing 1998

Library of Congress Cataloging-in-Publication Data

Maney, Patrick J., 1946–
    The Roosevelt presence : the life and legacy of FDR / Patrick J.
Maney.
        p.   cm.
    Originally published: New York : Twayne, 1992, in series: American
biography series.
    Includes bibliographical references and index.
    ISBN 0-520-21637-7 (alk. paper)
    1. Roosevelt, Franklin D. (Franklin Delano), 1882–1945.
2. Presidents—United States—Biography. I. Title.
E807.M27   1998
973.917′092—dc21
[B]   98-16354
                                                                      CIP

First California Paperback Printing 1998

1   2   3   4   5   6   7   8   9

The paper used in this publication is both acid-free and totally chlorine-free (TCF).
It meets the minimum requirements of American Standard for Information Sciences—
Permanence of Paper for Printed Library Materials, ANSI Z39.48–1984. ∞

FOR ELAINE
AND FOR SAM AND MARION MERRILL

CONTENTS

ACKNOWLEDGMENTS

I have incurred many debts in the course of preparing this study. I owe more than I can express to Horace Samuel Merrill and Marion Galbraith Merrill who read most of manuscript and whose comments and criticisms were unerringly on target. When I attended graduate school at the University of Maryland, it was my great good fortune to acquire in Sam and Marion peerless advisers and friends for life.

I am grateful to John Milton Cooper, Jr., for offering me an opportunity to contribute to this series, for significantly deepening my understanding of Roosevelt, and for providing timely encouragement. Robert H. Zieger, whose friendship I have valued for nearly 25 years, read the entire manuscript and offered detailed criticisms that immeasurably improved the final product. Lawrence N. Powell and F. Robert Hunter went over the manuscript with care and offered countless helpful comments. Raymond A. Esthus read the chapters dealing with foreign policy and saved me from errors of fact and of judgment. Conversations over the years with my friends and colleagues, Bill C. Malone and Clarence L. Mohr refined my ideas and frequently lifted my spirits. James T. Patterson displayed uncommon generosity in providing helpful suggestions.

I am indebted to Samuel Singer, a student of many years ago whose chance comment during a lecture on the New Deal made me rethink some of my assumptions about Roosevelt. Thanks are also due to Leslie Parr who advised me on the selection of photographs and to Ted Tunnell, Gregory Smith, Kevin Fontenot, and Thomas Thompson who tracked down some elusive information. William R. Emerson and the staff of the Franklin D. Roosevelt Library went out of their way to make my stay in Hyde Park especially productive. Others who in various ways helped me in the preparation of this study include Radomir V. Luza, Wilfred M. McClay, Blake Touchstone, Anne Jones, Jacob Conrad, Barbara S. Malone, Michael Donaghue, James Lorence, Danton Kostandarithes, and Susan Rowland.

My deepest appreciation belongs to my family. As always, my parents,

Blanche and Thomas Maney, helped in every way imaginable, and my mother-in-law, Anita Cowie, provided welcome encouragement and hospitality. Son Kevin was a source of patience and understanding throughout. Words are inadequate to express my gratitude to my wife Elaine, who, in addition to pursuing her own career and helping raise our three boys, repeatedly rescued me from the brink of despair over having to complete a brief biography of FDR. Thanks, too, to sons John and Thomas who are still too young to understand how much I appreciate them.

INTRODUCTION

For over a half century, Franklin D. Roosevelt has served as the model for the modern presidency—the standard by which we measure our chief executives and by which they, Democrat and Republican alike, measure themselves. We even use Roosevelt's first one hundred days in office as a benchmark to assess the early performance of new White House occupants. Those who fail to achieve Rooseveltian feats during their first hundred days, we declare failures.

If any doubts remained about FDR's having achieved role-model status, events during the 1980s and 90s put them to rest. There was a time when Republican loyalists could hardly bring themselves to say his name. He was simply "that man." But no longer. President Ronald Reagan frequently and admiringly invoked FDR's memory, even as he was saying unkind things about the New Deal. Haltingly at first, but with more enthusiasm as time passed, other Republicans followed Reagan's lead, until, in 1994, Newt Gingrich, the first Republican Speaker of the House of Representatives in forty years, went so far as to declare Roosevelt the century's greatest political leader.

Democrats, meanwhile, were not about to let the GOP capture their party's legendary hero without a fight. Bill Clinton reportedly prepared for the presidency by reading all the Roosevelt biographies he could get his hands on. Once in office, he sought out scholars for advice on how FDR might have handled problems he himself was facing. When he visited Hyde Park, New York, where FDR was born, raised, and buried, Clinton acted as though he were on hallowed ground. He became "transfixed, his eyes wide, his jaw slack," a reporter noted. "I just love this," the president said."[*] The fiftieth anniversary of Roosevelt's death in 1995 and the long-delayed completion of the Roosevelt monument two years later led to another round of bipartisan paeans to the thirty-second president.

---

[*]Sidney Blumenthal, Rendezvousing With Destiny," *New Yorker* (March 8, 1993), 38–44.

It's not surprising that FDR still inspires awe and envy. After all, he was a great president. When he assumed office in 1933, in the depths of the Great Depression, his buoyant personality and life-affirming optimism infused a dispirited nation with self-confidence. During another time of peril, the Second World War, he oversaw the most successful military operation in the nation's history. Roosevelt dominated his times more fully than any president since Andrew Jackson; and, like Jackson, he became a richly symbolic figure who seemed to embody certain cherished American beliefs. Admittedly, he was also one of the most controversial chief executives in American history. People either hated him or loved him. But his admirers vastly outnumbered his detractors How else to explain his unprecedented four terms in the White House?

And who wouldn't envy Roosevelt's historical reputation? Since his death in 1945, historians have consistently placed him on a short list, with Washington and Lincoln, of great presidents. Although accusations of treachery at Pearl Harbor and a sell-out at Yalta still linger in the popular literature, most scholars long ago rejected claims that Roosevelt knew in advance about the Japanese attack on America's Pacific fleet or that he handed over Eastern Europe on a silver platter to Joseph Stalin. Historians take more seriously charges that he played a shameful role in the internment of Japanese-Americans during the Second World War and that he failed to do all that he might have done to save the Jewish victims of Nazism. But even these blemishes on his record have not significantly diminished his historical stature.

Yet, when one begins to think about Roosevelt as the exemplar of the modern presidency, at least three major problems arise. First, he did not actually do some of the things legend credits him with having done. He did not, for example, play as large a role in shaping the legislation of the New Deal as has been thought. Second, some of the things he actually did do, such as the way he treated critics of his foreign policy, set a bad example for his successors. Third, however much we might revere his memory, his record has offered surprisingly little help in resolving the most critical problems the United States has faced in the half century since his death, problems such as civil rights and Vietnam.

So what accounts for the durability of his stature as presidential role model? Longevity and popularity have much to do with it. But a third factor may shed the most light on why he has achieved role model status. To an unusual degree, people during his presidency and later projected onto FDR both their hopes and fears, imputing to him a mastery of events that he did not have, indeed that no person could have had.

The tendency to project personal feelings onto FDR was by no means confined to impressionable members of the general public. Consider the matter of FDR's supposedly complex personality. Before he became president, many who knew him well thought he was shallow. "All light and no darkness," one reporter said about him during the 1932 election, adding, "One expects depth and shadows in a great man." But once Roosevelt became president, he suddenly acquired *gravitas*. Observers practically exhausted the metaphorical possibilities trying to convey the complexity of his character. One presidential aide referred to his "heavily-forested interior," while others compared him to an ancient sphinx or a Tibetan Buddha. Historians and biographers echoed the refrain. Arthur Schlesinger, Jr., for example, described FDR's mind as "infinitely complex."**

Commentators have made too much of this aspect of his nature. Rexford Tugwell, a charter member of Roosevelt's Brain Trust, may have been closer to the truth when he noted that in FDR's case people tended to mistake privacy for complexity. After all, he belonged to a class and a generation that did not believe in the therapeutic value of baring one's soul, in private or in public. His parents had taught him that a gentleman kept his innermost feelings to himself.[1] So it's a mistake to suppose that his reserve in personal matters necessarily concealed turbulent inner stirrings. Humankind, by nature, is infinitely complex, and almost anyone subjected to the scrutiny Roosevelt was under would also exhibit bewildering combinations of personal attributes and behavior patterns.*** Indeed, Roosevelt had a strong religious bent and to the degree that his faith allayed self-doubt, he may actually have been less enigmatic than many of his contemporaries. In retrospect, he seems less complicated than the other great leaders of his time: Adolf Hitler, Joseph Stalin, and Winston S. Churchill. And he was less complicated than his wife, Eleanor.

The belief that Roosevelt's wall of reserve concealed vast complexities encouraged observers to search for the hidden meaning of practically everything he did. When things turned out a certain way, they said that Roosevelt had intended them to do so. For some, the very absence of any evidence of Roosevelt's involvement in a given situation was proof positive that he was directing operations. Roosevelt's enemies were no less apt than his friends, and historians no less apt than his contemporaries, to discern in him a maze of hidden intentions. This tendency to ascribe to Roosevelt an unusually complex nature and the concurrent tendency to see his hand everywhere exaggerates his control over events and obscures in the unfolding drama of his years in office the critically important roles of chance and circumstance, of broad historical forces, and of other key players, including the Congress.

Because FDR was less than, or at least different from, the man of legend,

**Milton MacKaye, "Profiles: The Governor—II," *New Yorker* (August 22, 1931), 28; Robert E. Sherwood, *Roosevelt and Hopkins*, 9; Arthur Schlesinger, Jr., "Origins of the Cold War," *Foreign Affairs*, XLVI (October, 1967), 22–52.

***It's worth noting that Edmund Morris, the official biographer of Ronald Reagan—whom few people have ever described as complex, described his subject as "the most mysterious man I have ever confronted." *New York Times*, March 13, 1991.

he is a somewhat problematic model for modern presidents. But to raise questions about his status as role model is not to deny his greatness. When he assumed office in 1933, his combination of attributes, especially his buoyant personality and irrepressible optimism, was just what the country seemed to need. The United States had abundant natural resources; ample industrial capacity; a first-rate educational system; a well-trained, although underemployed, work force; bountiful farmlands; and a stable political system. What the country did not have was the confidence to put its assets to work, and this Roosevelt helped supply. But in different times, people have different needs. If during the 1930s and 1940s, the country needed an infusion of self-confidence, at other times it may need to be shaken out of its complacency. Even during his years in office, Roosevelt's abiding faith in the future and his belief—reminiscent of Mr. Micawber's in *David Copperfield*—that something would turn up, sometimes caused him to procrastinate, to avoid facing up to problems, and to take actions without considering their long-term consequences. More often than not, something did turn up. FDR's successors have not always shared his good fortune.

1

PREPARATION FOR POLITICS, 1882–1910

Franklin D. Roosevelt's upbringing and education prepared him well for a career in politics. From home and school he acquired self-confidence and ambition, a sense of civic responsibility, and useful social and political connections. Moreover, in his dynamic fifth cousin, Theodore Roosevelt, young Franklin had a hero whom he sought to emulate. Above all, Roosevelt's inheritance endowed him with an extraordinarily sunny disposition and an abiding sense that all was right with the world. Conspicuous gaps remained in his political training, to be sure, and some of these he would have to fill by later experiences. Nevertheless, by the time he ran for his first elective office in 1910, at the age of 28, he had secured advantages that would serve him well during his long and spectacular political career.

Roosevelt was born on 30 January 1882 at Springwood, the family estate, on the east bank of the Hudson River, about two miles south of the village of Hyde Park, New York. During his youth, the Hyde Park area was inhabited by an unusually large number of upper-class families. Families of old wealth and impeccable pedigree, including the Roosevelts, mingled, uneasily at times, with families of new wealth and less august lineage. Archibald Rogers, an associate of oil baron John D. Rockefeller; Ogden Mills, a Wall Street financier; and Vincent Astor, whose family name was synonymous with high society, lived upriver from the Roosevelts. Another neighbor, Frederick W. Vanderbilt, grandson of Cornelius Vanderbilt, the famous shipping and railroad magnate, boasted the area's most elaborate mansion. With its 54 rooms, Italian Renaissance architecture, museumlike atmosphere, and $660,000 construction costs, the Vanderbilt mansion offended the sensibilities of some of Hyde Park's old-line families, including the Roosevelts, whose own red-clapboard, 17-room home, although spacious and comfortable, had an informal, lived-in ambiance.[1]

Franklin's parents, James and Sara Delano Roosevelt, had no need for ostentatious display, for they were immensely secure in their roots. Descended from seventeenth-century Dutch and English settlers in America, James, who was 53 when Franklin was born, led the life of an English country gentleman. At Hyde Park he raised fine dairy cows, hunted foxes, and presided over afternoon teas and formal dinner parties. Mr. James, as almost everyone called him, had a strong sense of civic responsibility, and over the years he took a turn as village supervisor, sat on the local school board, and served as vestryman and warden of St. James Episcopal Church. He had an equally strong sense of propriety. One time he forbade his wife to renew acquaintance with an old friend who had committed the unpardonable sin of divorcing and remarrying. As a defender of traditional standards, James shunned the gaudy displays of wealth that were so common during the industrial age. Once, for example, he declined an invitation from the Vanderbilts to dine in the grandeur of their estate. "If we accept," he explained to his wife, "we shall have to have them at our home."[2]

Yet when the spirit moved him, he was capable of defying convention. After graduating from Union College and the Harvard Law School, he practiced law for two years. Then, "preferring a more active life," as he put it, he plunged into the world of business, where he played for exceedingly high stakes.[3] He organized a series of highly speculative ventures, the success of any one of which would have brought him spectacular riches and world renown. One bold scheme involved the construction of a canal through Nicaragua connecting the Atlantic and Pacific oceans, this long before the building of the Panama Canal. But each time, just as he seemed on the verge of great success, a combination of economic hard times and just plain bad luck wrecked his plans. All was not lost, however, for he managed to shield the bulk of his inherited wealth in safer investments. The size of his estate, which was valued at about $300,000, paled by comparison with the fortunes of some of his neighbors, such as the Vanderbilts and the Astors. Still, in an era when most American families earned less than $500 a year, Roosevelt's holdings easily placed him within the ranks of the nation's economic elite.

On occasion, James took risks in his personal life as well. His first wife, with whom he had a son, died after 23 years of marriage. At that time, it was not unusual for an older man to marry a considerably younger woman, especially after one or the other of them had lost a spouse. Nevertheless, several years after the death of his first wife, James managed to raise a few eyebrows, when, at the age of 52, he married Sara Delano, who at 26 was young enough to be his daughter. Roosevelt's political affiliation also had a tinge of the unconventional. He was a Democrat, aligned with the conservative, sound-money wing of the party whose hero was fellow New Yorker and president, Grover Cleveland. But even that set him apart from most members of his class and region, who identified the Democrats with corrupt political machines and grasping, undesirable immigrants.

Sara Delano Roosevelt was strong, proud, intelligent, and supremely confident of the superiority of her values and her way of life. The first Delano in America had preceded the first Roosevelt. Sara's father, a daring businessman, made his fortune in the tea and opium trade in China and occupied the upper rungs of New York society. A staunch Republican, he was fond of saying that although perhaps not all Democrats were horse thieves, it had been his experience that all horse thieves were Democrats. As a young girl, Sara had experienced things that other children could only dream about. At the age of seven she had sailed halfway around the world on a clipper ship to join her father in China. She lived in Hong Kong for three years and later in France and Germany.

Tall, handsome, and dignified without being stuffy, Sara presented an imposing, even intimidating, figure. Within the family circle, however, she was warm, affectionate, and possessed of a self-effacing sense of humor. Like James, she displayed a strong sense of civic responsibility and compassion for humanity in the abstract, both of which she passed on to her son.

James and Sara gave their only child the best things that money and social prominence could buy. They furnished him with ponies to ride, yachts to sail, and governesses and tutors to look after and teach him. They gave him the freedom to explore their large estate, with its woods and streams, and to pursue favorite hobbies, such as collecting stamps and mounting birds. They introduced him to important people and ex-

3

posed him to different cultures and customs. By the time he was 10, he had met writer Mark Twain, members of European royalty, and his first president, Grover Cleveland. By the time he was 15, he had been to Europe eight times. James and Sara also tried to meet their son's emotional needs. They gave him their undivided attention and instilled in him an abiding sense of self-worth. "As a matter of fact," Sara later recalled, "I do not believe I have ever seen a little boy who seemed always to be so consistently enjoying himself."[4]

James and Sara gave much to their son, but they asked much of him in return. Like them, Franklin had been born to a superior station in life, and they expected him to conduct himself accordingly. "May you always bear in mind," James once lectured his son in his kindly, quiet manner, "that in the past—on both sides of your ancestry—they have a good record and have borne a good name." "Only tell Franklin to be good, to be a good man," James told Sara. To James and Sara, being good meant being devoted to God, family, and community. It meant living a life of moral rectitude and thereby setting an inspiring example for others. One time, after a particularly nasty divorce in the family's circle of acquaintances, Sara counseled Franklin, "In this age when the morals and principles of many people seem to consist in want of principle and [in] immorality, we must all do what we can to have a good influence and to keep ourselves unspotted from the world—but to do it without priggishness and yet always have the courage to stand up for what is right."[5]

Being good also meant avoiding flamboyant behavior of any sort. Franklin learned from his father that a gentleman kept his deepest feelings to himself and did not unnecessarily burden others with his personal problems. Nor did a gentleman flaunt his wealth or put on airs. "The best bred people and the most refined," Sara told Franklin, "are simple and not only please their own sort but never offend those beneath them in intellect or station."[6] Being good certainly meant doing good works, especially for those less fortunate than oneself; but even in the performance of good works, ostentatious display was to be avoided.

When his parents thought of the future, they imagined that Franklin would follow in his father's footsteps. Years later, when asked what ambition she had had for her son, Sara responded: "Very simple—it might even be thought not very ambitious, but to me, and to him, too, it was the highest ideal I could hold up before our boy—to grow to be like his father, straight and honorable, just and kind, an upstanding

American." The idea that he might enter public life seems never to have entered their minds, but neither do they appear to have ruled out a career in politics for their son. One time, Franklin told his mother that politics was a dirty business and that some men were too good even for high elective office. "I am thankful," Sara retorted, "that you are young enough to alter your mind many times. For instance that anyone could be too fine or well bred for the White House or any great position is a fallacy."[7]

In 1896, at the age of 14, Roosevelt left the world of his doting parents and attentive servants to enter Groton School, an exclusive preparatory academy near Boston. Groton's founder and headmaster, the Reverend Endicott Peabody, sought to rear his young charges in the tradition of elite English public schools, such as Eton and Harrow, which prepared the sons of the upper class to occupy positions of leadership in society. He emphasized character-building and physical and mental discipline. In a departure from their pampered upbringings, the boys led Spartan lives. They slept in tiny, sparsely furnished cubicles and followed a rigorous daily schedule. The curriculum, in the classical mold, was also rigorous. Roosevelt's courses over four years included Greek, Latin, French, German, English literature and composition, mathematics, science, and social studies.

Roosevelt compiled a respectable academic record. Obviously intelligent, he consistently placed in the top fourth or fifth of his class. Then, too, he acquired skills that would serve him well throughout his life. He developed a clear and uncluttered prose style, and, as a participant in compulsory debates, he received his first lessons in public speaking.[8]

He also received a healthy dose of Christian humanitarianism. In order to prick the consciences of his young wards, Peabody frequently brought in outside speakers to plead their special causes. One week, it might be urban reformer Jacob Riis describing the squalor of the tenements; the next week, an African missionary telling of his efforts to Christianize the natives. Whatever their cause, the speakers found a sympathetic ear in Franklin. "Last night," he once reported to his parents, "a Mr. Wilson came here and told us about the Nova Scotia coal mines and asked for money for his hospital. I think it is a really worthy charity and gave $2.00!" Inspired to do good deeds, Roosevelt joined Groton's Missionary Society, took part in a summer camp the school sponsored for underprivileged boys from Boston and New York City, and with the enthusiastic support of his mother, performed odd jobs for an elderly black woman who lived near the school.[9]

For Franklin, Groton was not an entirely happy experience. Like many an only child, he felt more comfortable in the company of adults than of his own peers. His combination of friendliness, deference, and obedience (he won the Punctuality Prize three times) quickly earned him the goodwill of his elders. Winning over that of his fellow "Groties," however, proved to be more difficult. For one thing, because his parents had been so reluctant to part with him, he had entered the school two years later than most of the boys in his class, and by that time they had already made their own friends and broken up into cliques. For another thing, his appearance and manner set him apart from the others. Tall and willowy, with smooth features that had not yet taken form, he looked slightly effeminate. Owing to his isolation at Hyde Park and to his frequent travels abroad, he also spoke with the trace of an accent, which may have struck his classmates as affected.

Roosevelt tried mightily to break down the barriers that separated him from others. One time, in order to dispel his priggish image, he deliberately misbehaved in class. "I have served off my first black-mark today," he proudly reported to his parents, "and I am very glad I got it, as I was thought to have no school-spirit before."[10] Sports being another possible path to acceptance, Roosevelt went out for football, baseball, hockey, and boxing. But he never advanced beyond the second team. His only athletic success came in a peculiar and physically risky competition called the high kick, which involved kicking a tin pan suspended high over the floor from the ceiling. His winning kick, after which he landed full force on the side of his neck, attested more to his determination to win the respect of his classmates than to his athletic prowess.[11]

While he was at Groton, three of his family members, in addition to his parents, came to play increasingly important roles in his life. Coming from backgrounds almost identical to his own, they offered vivid models of what he might or might not become in life. One of them was Franklin's half-brother, with the unforgettable name of James Roosevelt Roosevelt. Thirty years older than Franklin, Rosy, as everyone called him, was handsome, intelligent, and charming. Because of his own inherited wealth and because he married into the even wealthier Astor family, Rosy did not need to earn a living, a situation for which he was very grateful. Although he held several minor diplomatic posts in Europe and engaged in extensive charitable work, he devoted most of his time to the pursuit of leisure. He liked attending fancy dress balls, racing yachts, riding to hounds, and hunting grouse in Scotland. His favorite pastime, which came to occupy most of his waking hours, was the enormously expensive sport of coaching. Long after stagecoaches had become obsolete as a means of transportation, Roosevelt and other gentlemen of leisure on both sides of the Atlantic purchased expensive old coaches, outfitted them with teams of horses, then drove them back and forth across country roads. Rosy Roosevelt was a typical product of old wealth. He was a good and decent man, well bred and cultured. But he made no significant mark on his place and time in history, nor did he have any ambition to do so. Franklin expressed great affection for Rosy, but it was clear that Rosy's path would not be his own.

Rosy's son, James Roosevelt Roosevelt, Jr., or Taddy, provided Franklin with a strikingly different model. Whereas Rosy was the quintessential aristocrat, Taddy rebelled against his upper-class heritage. At Groton, where he and Franklin were enrolled together, Taddy was an outcast, who, to Franklin's embarrasment, was constantly getting into trouble. Later, after dropping out of Harvard, he scandalized the family by marrying a Hungarian-born prostitute whom he had met while making the rounds of the notorious tenderloin district of New York City. In grand eccentric fashion, he refused to live off of his inheritance and went to work as an auto mechanic. When Taddy died he left his $5 million fortune to the Salvation Army.[12]

Rosy and Taddy showed Franklin what he did not want to become in life. But in his fifth cousin, Theodore Roosevelt (TR), Franklin found the model of what he did want to become. Neither self-satisfied like Rosy, nor rebellious like Taddy, TR unquestioningly accepted his superior station in life, but believed that wealth and social standing carry with them certain obligations, most important, the obligation to serve and lead mankind. This he did with energy and flair. His career, which began in the New York State legislature the year Franklin was born, included stints as assistant secretary of the navy and governor of New York and later climaxed in the White House; with it, Theodore Roosevelt made politics a respectable calling for young men from respectable families. Not coincidentally, TR became Franklin's great hero at the same time Franklin's father, in his late sixties and suffering from heart disease, was becoming an invalid. At Groton, Franklin took vicarious pleasure in his cousin's much-publicized exploits during the Spanish-American War, and he cheered when TR was elected governor of New York. One of the few times Franklin ever expressed displeasure with his parents occurred when, for some unexplained reason, they decided that he could not accept an invitation to spend the weekend at TR's home in Oyster Bay, New York. "Please don't make any more arrangements for my future happiness," he wrote his parents.[13] He even began to take on some of his cousin's physical characteristics and mannerisms, and by the time he left Groton he was wearing pince-nez in the Theodore Roosevelt style.

In 1900, Roosevelt left one exclusive school and entered another, Harvard University. During the next four years he took courses from some of America's greatest scholars, including Frederick Jackson Turner and Edward Channing in history and Josiah Royce in philosophy. But none of his teachers made much of an impression on him. Nor, for that matter, with a C to B-minus average, did he make much of an impression on any of them. In truth, Roosevelt's main interests lay outside the classroom.

As at Groton, he sought the goodwill of others at Harvard. His quest met with mixed success. He tried out for the football team and the rowing crew, but in both cases failed to survive the final cut. He did, however, make his way into a half-dozen or so prestigious social clubs. But the most prestigious—and snobbish—club of them all, Porcellian, to which both his father and TR had belonged, turned him down, and those who know him best said that Porcellian's rejection left a permanent scar.[14]

Roosevelt earned at least some campus renown by virtue of his editorship of Harvard's undergraduate newspaper, the *Crimson*. His editorials took the form of earnest homilies extolling the virtues of friendship, civic responsibility, tradition, and school spirit. One editorial, which Roosevelt considered particularly daring, berated the football team for its lackluster performance against the Carlisle Indians. "All that is needed," he wrote, "is a spirit in the team of aggressive, vigorous determination—a spirit that will begin fighting when the game begins and will not vanish before the game ends."[15]

During his senior year Roosevelt became engaged to Eleanor Roosevelt, his fifth cousin once removed and the favorite niece of his hero, Theodore Roosevelt. Although Franklin and Eleanor had much in common, the circumstances of their upbringing had been strikingly different. Eleanor's earliest memories were of a beautiful but insensitive mother who, unable to conceal disappointment over her daughter's plain looks and awkward manner, called Eleanor "Granny," even in the presence of others. She had fonder memories of her father, Elliott, who was Theodore's brother and, oddly enough, Franklin's godfather. Elliott was warm and generous, and Eleanor adored him. But he was also an unstable man who was given to bouts of depression, a habitual philanderer who made life miserable for his wife, and an alcoholic who spent long absences from home drying out in sanatariums. Eleanor's mother died when she was eight, a brother died when she was nine, and her father died when she was ten. Eleanor, meanwhile, was shunted off to the home of a stern and repressive grandmother.

Eleanor's upbringing left her as shy and insecure as Franklin was outgoing and self-confident. She thought of herself as unattractive and unappealing, and at first she may have been surprised, perhaps even suspicious, of Franklin's romantic attentions. In fact, his attentions were not surprising at all. For despite Eleanor's self-image, she was attractive, intelligent, quietly engaging, and unusually mature for her 19 years. Moreover, as the niece of TR, who by this time had become the president of the United States, she was much more prominent than Franklin. When they announced their engagement, newspapers took much notice of Eleanor, almost none of Franklin. Years later, someone asked Roosevelt why, when he met a newly engaged couple, he always made a point of congratulating both the prospective bride and groom. He explained, probably only partly in jest, that when he was engaged, everyone had congratulated him for getting Eleanor but no one had congratulated Eleanor for getting him.[16]

Franklin's mother posed the only obstacle to the impending marriage. When Franklin and Eleanor first told Sara of their intentions, she got them to promise to keep their engagement secret for a year. They were so young, Sara explained, that they needed time to test the depth of their commitment. They were young: he was 21 and she was 19. But Sara almost certainly hoped that the couple's ardor would diminish, and that they would postpone or even call off the marriage. Sara had no specific complaint about Eleanor; if Franklin had to marry, she would be a perfectly suitable life's companion. But for the time being at least, Sara did not want anyone, including Eleanor, to come between her and her beloved son.

Sara's efforts were to no avail, and on 17 March 1905, St. Patrick's Day, Franklin and Eleanor were married in New York City. Franklin's old headmaster at Groton, Endicott Peabody, presided over the service. President Theodore Roosevelt gave the bride away and, as was his habit, became the center of attention. But Franklin seemed not to mind. Not only had he secured Eleanor, he had forged an intimate new relationship with the man he most admired in the world.

During the early years of his marriage, Franklin tried to find a niche for himself in life. His father, who had died during Franklin's freshman year in college, had always wanted him to be a lawyer. Upon graduating from Harvard in 1904, Franklin honored his father's memory by enrolling in the Columbia School of Law. But the intricacies of the law held little interest for him, and he withdrew from school after the first year. He had learned enough, however, to pass the state bar examination and to acquire a position as managing clerk with the prestigious New York City law firm of Carter, Ledyard, and Milburn.

Like his father, Franklin preferred a more active life, and before long he was considering a career in politics. Of course, there had been a time when he thought that the political arena was no place for a gentleman. But TR had changed that. And it was TR who was on his mind one day in 1907, when he and his fellow law clerks were discussing their plans for the future. When it came Roosevelt's time to speak, he explained that he did not intend to make a career of the law. He wanted instead to enter politics and eventually to become president of the United States. Like his illustrious cousin, he would serve first as an assemblyman in the New York legislature, then as assistant secretary of the navy, then as governor of New York. "Anyone who is governor of New York," he said in a matter-of-fact way, "has a good chance to be President with any luck." One of the law clerks later recalled that Roosevelt spoke with such sincerity and conviction that he made the grand scheme seem entirely plausible.[17]

In 1910 a chance encounter opened up for Roosevelt the possibility of a start in politics. Early that year, John E. Mack, the district attorney of Roosevelt's home county and a power in local Democratic politics, visited Roosevelt on a routine legal matter. Their business concluded, Mack asked the young attorney if he would be interested in running for the state legislature. Roosevelt said he would, whereupon Mack and other party leaders arranged for him to receive the Democratic nomination for a seat in the New York State Senate.[18]

At the outset of Roosevelt's campaign, it appeared that his political career would be short-lived. Only once since the Civil War had voters in his solidly Republican district sent a Democrat to the state senate. He even faced an uphill struggle in the working-class pockets of Democratic strength, where his patrician appearance—replete with pince-nez, dandified clothing, and cultivated accent—hardly seemed likely to inspire the confidence of wage-earners. In the beginning, Roosevelt's campaign manager calculated his chances at no better than one in five.

As the campaign progressed, however, it became clear that Roosevelt also had some powerful advantages. One was his magic name, which provided immediate and favorable identification on the part of voters with his famous cousin. A more important advantage was the weakened condition of the opposing Republican party, which by 1910 was hopelessly divided, both in New York and across the nation, between conservative and progressive factions.

It also became clear as the campaign developed that Roosevelt was in his element. Nothing he had previously done in his 28 years, be it at Groton or Harvard or in the practice of law, had so stirred his interest or brought out his best efforts as the race for the state senate. Early on, in order to cover the sprawling district, he abandoned the traditional horse and buggy and rented a shiny red automobile. On the stump, Roosevelt obviously lacked the skills of a polished orator. To Eleanor he appeared "high strung and, at times, nervous," and during some speeches he would pause so long trying to think of what to say next that she feared he would never go on. But what he lacked in poise, he more than made up for by the earnestness of his approach and by his obvious desire to please. Insofar as Roosevelt stressed any issues, they were the all-purpose ones of bossism and corruption in government. He was against both.

On election day the Democrats swept New York State and the nation. Roosevelt won with 52 percent of the vote. He had run a competent campaign, and had obviously ingratiated himself with the voters. But in the final accounting, the decisive factor in his election was the overall strength of the Democratic party. In this, his first political outing, good fortune was on his side.

2

RISE TO POWER, 1910–1928

Roosevelt's career between 1910 and 1928 followed with uncanny precision the course he had earlier described to his fellow law clerks. First, he occupied a seat in the New York legislature; then he served as assistant secretary of the navy; next, in 1920, he gained a position he had not predicted, the Democratic vice presidential nomination; and finally in 1928, he was elected to the governorship of New York, which positioned him for a future run at the presidency.

Yet Roosevelt's rise to power was far from a smooth ascent. Along the way, he experienced two crises, either one of which could have destroyed his career. A love affair with his wife's personal secretary threatened to break into public scandal, and his crippling attack of polio seemed to be an insurmountable obstacle. In the end, however, neither crisis prevented Roosevelt from pursuing the course he had originally set for himself. Indeed, in totally unexpected ways, his bout with polio may even have enhanced his political fortunes.

Roosevelt had the good fortune to enter public life during one of the most politically, socially, and materially productive periods in American history, a period historians later called the Progressive Era. During this era, which spanned roughly the first two decades of the century, the nation grappled, in mostly creative ways, with the problems caused by industrialization, urbanization, and immigration. Progressive reformers demanded, among other things, curbs on corporate power, steps to alleviate the plight of the urban poor, and a more efficient political system free of corruption. Reformers looked to government to help meet these demands, and as a result, government at all levels expanded its power and influence at an unprecedented rate. The United States also began for the first time to play a major role in world affairs. Because Roosevelt entered public life during the Progressive Era, rather than during the quiescent periods before and after it, he came to accept as the norm change and reform and an expansive role for government, both at home and abroad.

During the formative years of his political career, he had the additional good fortune to observe at close range some of the greatest practitioners of the art of politics in American history. The era was unusually rich in leadership. Presidents Theodore Roosevelt and Woodrow Wilson headed the list of luminaries, and together they laid the foundations for the modern presidency. With their competing philosophies of government, they also helped shape the ideological contours of politics in the twentieth century. Under Roosevelt's expansive "New Nationalism," government would regulate, rather than break up, large corporations and also establish a permanent apparatus to ameliorate social and economic problems. Under Wilson's "New Freedom," which envisioned a more limited role for government, the state would seek to restore business competition by intervening periodically in the economy to curb monopolistic practices. In addition to Roosevelt and Wilson, there were secondary figures of great distinction, most notably Robert M. La Follette, William Jennings Bryan, and Eugene V. Debs. All in all, it was an auspicious time for an ambitious young man to launch a career in public service.

No sooner had Roosevelt taken his seat in the state senate than unexpected circumstances thrust him into the political spotlight. When the legislature convened in 1911, its first order of business was to elect a United States senator, for at that time members of the upper house of Congress were still being selected by state legislatures. The selection process appeared at first to be a cut-and-dried matter. The Democratic party controlled the legislature; Tammany Hall, the powerful political machine based in New York City, controlled the Democratic party; and Charles F. Murphy, the machine's leader, controlled Tammany Hall. Presumably, then, Boss Murphy could dictate the choice of senator, and that was precisely what he tried to do. As a reward for past services to Tammany,

Murphy decided to award the senate seat to William F. Sheehan, known to all as "Blue-eyed Billy" Sheehan.[1]

A small group of Democratic legislators denounced Murphy's high-handed tactics and organized to fight Sheehan's election. Roosevelt, who had been nurtured on stories of Tammany's villainy, immediately cast his lot with the insurgents. Because his name ensured them publicity, his wealth shielded him from possible Tammany-inspired financial reprisals, and his spacious rented house near the capitol served as a convenient meeting place for the insurgents, the Hyde Park senator became nominal spokesman for the anti-Sheehan faction.

The fight dragged on for many weeks, during the course of which Roosevelt attracted statewide and even national attention. Before it was over, the insurgents forced Murphy to withdraw the Sheehan nomination. In the end, however, the resourceful Tammany chief maneuvered the insurgents into supporting a candidate who was even more closely identified with the machine than Sheehan. Despite its inglorious ending, the Sheehan affair played an important role in Roosevelt's early career. It allowed him to gain more publicity during his first months in office than most state legislators earn in a lifetime, and for the most part it was the right kind of publicity, for it identified him with the popular cause of reform.

Roosevelt knew a good thing when he saw it, and in the aftermath of the Sheehan fight he continued to denounce the bosses. Boss Murphy and his ilk, he declared, were like noxious weeds that must be "plucked out, root and branch."[2] Ultimately, however, Roosevelt could derive only limited benefits from the single issue of clean government. People wanted honesty and efficiency in government, to be sure; but they wanted a decent standard of living even more. And to the extent that public officials helped them realize that goal, they were willing to tolerate a little corruption on the side. Thus, the "good government" theme was useful as far as it went. But if Roosevelt wanted to advance beyond the narrow confines of the New York State Senate, he clearly had to develop an interest in issues that bore more directly on the lives of ordinary citizens.

Eventually, he did seek to broaden his appeal. He endorsed, although without much feeling, such social welfare measures as workmen's compensation and restrictions on the number of hours of work that employers could extract from women and children. He also supported the conservation of national resources, public control over electric power, and women's suffrage. Despite his later claims to the contrary, however, he played no significant role in any of these social and economic reform efforts.[3]

In 1912 Roosevelt delivered a speech in Troy, New York, that indicated how far he had come and the general direction in which he was moving. The wellspring of modern history, he said, had been the quest for individual liberty, but unfettered individualism had created problems of its own. The time had now come, he argued, to emphasize the blessings of community living and to recognize that community interest transcended individual interests. Thus, the community, acting through government, was justified in regulating individuals, groups, or businesses if their behavior injured the general welfare. As an example, Roosevelt pointed out that in the past landowners had been free to do with their property whatever they wished, even if it meant stripping the land of trees and foliage. But now, he said, "we are beginning to see that it is necessary for our health and happiness . . . that individuals and lumber companies should not go into our wooded areas like the Adirondacks and the Catskills and cut them off root and branch for the benefit of their own pocket."[4] Roosevelt argued that the time had come for the age-old competitive struggle for personal advantage to give way to a spirit of cooperation in pursuit of the general welfare. Cooperation was the key, he said, making obsolete contemporary concerns over such problems as the trusts and the struggle between capital and labor. This speech, with its emphasis on community and national interest and its advocacy of an expanded government, clearly reflected the influence of Theodore Roosevelt. In fact, it was little more than an abbreviated, and much-simplified, version of the widely heralded New Nationalism address that the former president had delivered two years before. The breezy optimism that had the great problems of the day dissolving in the wake of good-hearted cooperation, however, was more Franklin than Theodore.

Roosevelt grew and matured in office, but he nonetheless remained an outsider. He neither sought nor gained entry into the inner circle that governed state affairs. He held most of his colleagues at arm's length, as though he feared contamination. They, in turn, regarded him as an overly educated, overly privileged self-seeker incapable of understanding ordinary people and their problems. "Awfully arrogant fellow, that Roosevelt," remarked one veteran Tammany boss. Another one, practically exhausting his stock of epithets, described Roosevelt as among "the snobs in our party . . . political accidents . . . fops and cads who come as near being political leaders as a green pea does a circus tent."[5] Frances Perkins, a social worker and labor lobbyist, shared the disdain of the bosses for the Hyde Park senator. "I have a vivid picture of him operating on the floor of the Senate," she later recalled. He was "tall and slender, very active and alert, moving around the floor, going in and out of committee rooms, rarely talking with the members, who more or less avoided him, not particularly charming (that came later), artificially serious of face, rarely smiling, with an unfortunate habit—so natural that he was unaware of it—of throwing his head up. This, combined with his pince-nez and great height, gave him the appearance of looking down his nose at most people." Perkins, whose passion for social causes had been stirred by Theodore Roosevelt, believed that Franklin Roosevelt acted the way he did "because he really didn't like people very much and because he had a youthful lack of humility, a streak of self-righteousness, and a deafness to the hopes, fears, and aspirations which are the common lot."[6]

But not everyone held a low opinion of him, for even then he was capable of arousing strikingly different feelings in different people. "Almost at that very first meeting," recalled a middle-aged reporter in reference to an interview he had had with Roosevelt during the Sheehan fight, "I made up my mind that . . . nothing but an accident could keep him from becoming president."[7] The reporter was Louis McHenry Howe, who soon became the most important person in Roosevelt's political life.

Gnomelike and slovenly, Howe defiantly boasted that he was so ugly that little children took one look at him and ran the other way. But he also possessed shrewd political instincts, including an uncanny sense of timing and an imagination rich in ingenious tactical devices. Addicted to politics but barred from playing a starring role because of his appearance and manner, Howe apparently projected his ambitions onto Roosevelt, and almost from their first acquaintance, worked tirelessly on his behalf. It was remarkable enough that Howe should have sensed great possibilities in the young state senator, but it was even more remarkable that Roosevelt should have sensed in the odd little reporter great usefulness to his own career. But Roosevelt had a talent for attracting selfless and capable subordinates and for quickly recognizing those qualities in them.

Howe proved his usefulness in 1912, when Roosevelt ran for reelection. Forced into bed by an attack of typhoid fever, Roosevelt summoned his new friend to run the campaign. Howe promptly took charge, saturating the senatorial district with full-page newspaper advertisements, circulars, and personalized letters, all proclaiming the virtues of the bedridden candidate. Roosevelt won handily.

Despite his victory, Roosevelt faced an uncertain future in New York State. His incessant attacks on the Tammany machine had deeply angered Democratic leaders and given them ample cause for seeking revenge. Although they had failed to deny him reelection to his senate seat, they had another weapon at their disposal: the power to thwart any ambitions he might have for higher office. So while Roosevelt was safe from reprisal as long as he retained his senate seat, his opportunities for advancement appeared to be slim.

A combination of good fortune and careful calculation on Roosevelt's part resolved this dilemma. In 1911, he had endorsed Governor Woodrow Wilson of New Jersey for the Democratic presidential nomination. He had doubtless hoped that if Wilson became president, his early endorsement might earn him a place in the new administration and thereby remove him from the corner into which he had painted himself in New York. Happily for Roosevelt, everything worked according to plan. In 1912, Wilson received the nomination, then went on to defeat his two major opponents for the presidency, Theodore Roosevelt, who headed the third-party Progressive ticket, and William Howard Taft, the hapless incumbent and Republican party standard-bearer. Franklin Roosevelt's reward, in the form of the assistant secretaryship of the navy, Cousin Theodore's old post, was not long in coming. It was ironic that TR's defeat in the election had helped Franklin continue to follow in TR's footsteps.

Just turned 31 and with no previous administrative experience, Roosevelt eagerly assumed his new responsibilities. With the faithful Howe installed as his assistant, he managed the day-to-day affairs of one of the largest and fastest-growing bureaucracies in Washington. In the process he greatly widened his circle of acquaintances. He talked naval strategy with ranking admirals, procurement matters with corporate executives, and labor conditions in the navy's shipyards with union chiefs. He also established useful relationships with newsmen, thus ensuring that his activities received the widest possible publicity. With his love of ships and the sea, Roosevelt carried out the routine ceremonial functions of the office with boyish enthusiasm. He took delight in the 17-gun salutes that greeted his appearance on fleet inspection tours; he even designed a special flag bearing an insignia for the assistant secretary, which he ordered run up the pole whenever he boarded a ship.[8]

To the chagrin of his superiors, Roosevelt also took delight in issuing broad proclamations concerning military and foreign affairs. Clearly taking his cue from Cousin Theodore, a vociferous critic of the Wilson administration, he advocated naval expansion and a larger role for the United States in international affairs. The world was a dangerous place, he said, and the United States must be prepared to protect its interests. In 1914, when political unrest in Mexico threatened the holdings of American businessmen, Roosevelt wanted to send in the marines. "Sooner or later," he told reporters, "the United States must go down there and clean up the Mexican political mess. I believe that the best time is right now." His statement embarrassed him and the administration, for even as he spoke, cooler heads were resolving the crisis through diplomatic channels. With unquestioned faith in the superiority of American ways, Roosevelt supported the march of the flag into foreign lands not only to protect American interests but also to civilize supposedly backward peoples. The natives of Haiti, he once said, had been "little more than primitive savages" before the uplifting experience of armed American intervention.[9]

Roosevelt's bellicose statements frequently set him at odds with other members of the administration, especially his own chief, Secretary of the Navy Josephus Daniels. Roosevelt believed that the homespun, former North Carolina newspaper editor and reformer was a naïve idealist, hopelessly out of his depth as navy secretary. "The funniest looking hillbilly" he had ever seen, Roosevelt said of Daniels, as he entertained friends at social gatherings with mean-spirited imitations of his chief.[10] Roosevelt, who had demonstrated astute good judgment in the case of Louis Howe, badly misjudged Daniels, an intelligent and shrewd politician who often took a broader view of events than his inexperienced deputy. Moreover, Roosevelt seemed oblivious to the political realities inherent in his relationship with the secretary. Daniels wielded much influence in the Democratic party, and a bad word from him could have jeopardized Roosevelt's career. But fortunately for Roosevelt, Daniels had a seemingly inexhaustible supply of patience. He genuinely liked Roosevelt, recognized his talents, and charitably attributed his excesses to the zeal of youth. Although several times Daniels would have been fully justified in firing Roosevelt for disloyalty and insubordination, he did nothing to hurt Roosevelt's career and much to help it.

As his relationship with Daniels demonstrated, Roosevelt still lacked the cautious foresight of a seasoned politician. More dramatic evidence of that deficiency could be seen in his decision in 1914 to run as an avowed anti-Tammany candidate for a seat in the United States

Senate from New York, which by that time had implemented the new system of direct election of senators. Before entering the race, Roosevelt failed to take the elementary precaution of securing a presidential endorsement. Nor did he consult Howe, who, sensing the risks involved, almost certainly would have raised objections. Instead, he plunged headlong into the Democratic primary, only to find the Tammany Tiger with revenge on its mind, ready and waiting to pounce. Tammany's candidate, who emerged only after Roosevelt had already committed himself, was no Blue-eyed Billy Sheehan. Rather, he was James W. Gerard, a man of impeccable credentials whose position as Wilson's ambassador to Germany instantly neutralized any advantage Roosevelt might have derived from his affiliation with the Wilson administration. Gerard humiliated Roosevelt in the primary, winning by close to a three-to-one margin.

Roosevelt learned a lesson from this experience. He now knew that he had no future as a champion of the anti-Tammany cause. Thereafter, he carefully refrained from directly attacking the New York organization. Later, as president, he exercised similar restraint in dealing with big-city machines in other states. Roosevelt learned another lesson as well: he learned to adhere to the old political tradition of letting the office seek the man, and in subsequent elections he played the role of disinterested public servant heeding the call of his party.

Upon reassuming his duties in the Navy Department, Roosevelt brashly injected himself into the public debate over military preparedness, much to the dismay of Secretary Daniels and President Wilson. In August 1914 war broke out in Europe, and Roosevelt argued that the United States should respond by drastically increasing its military might, even to the extent of putting itself on a war-footing. Critics of preparedness feared that a program of the type Roosevelt proposed entailed great risks: it might undercut needed domestic reforms; it might enrich at the taxpayers' expense large corporations, especially munitions makers; and it might involve the United States in a war in which it had no clear interest. Unmoved by such concerns, Roosevelt lashed out at the political leaders and the large segments of the population that failed to share his views. "Most of our citizens don't know what national defense means," he said. "Let us learn to trust the judgment of the real experts, the naval officers. Let us insist that Congress shall carry out their recommendations."[11] Roosevelt went so far as to leak to Republican critics of the administration and to the press confidential information indicating that the United States was unprepared to defend itself in the event of attack. Justifying his actions to Eleanor, he wrote: "The country needs the truth about the Army and Navy instead of the soft mush about everlasting peace which so many statesmen are handing out to a gullible public."[12] Another motive, less noble than the dissemination of truth, may also have inspired Roosevelt's actions. He almost certainly was angling for Daniels's job, and if by chance a series of embarrassing revelations should force the secretary to resign, he, Roosevelt, would presumably assume command.

From the beginning of the European war, Roosevelt hoped that the United States would enter the conflict on the side of the Allied powers, principally Great Britain and France, and against Germany. In April 1917, he got his wish. Like Cousin Theodore at the outbreak of the Spanish-American War, Roosevelt immediately wanted to resign from his post and enlist in the armed services. Although he had frequently been a thorn in the side of their administration, Secretary Daniels and President Wilson turned down his request, telling him that he was needed in Washington. To his everlasting disappointment, when he later toured the battlefields of Europe, it was as an observer and not as a participant.

Roosevelt carried out his wartime responsibilities as though the fate of the world hinged on his performance. He not only helped mobilize the navy for combat, but also took it upon himself to advise military leaders on matters of strategy and tactics. One pet scheme of his, which was eventually implemented, called for a massive antisubmarine-mine barrage of the North Sea. Still, had he not gone on to future greatness his tenure as assistant secretary of the navy would have earned him no more than a brief footnote in the history of the period.

During the war, Roosevelt experienced a crisis that threatened to shatter his family life and destroy his political career. The crisis grew out of his love affair with Lucy Mercer. Almost from the beginning of their marriage, Franklin and Eleanor had been slowly drifting apart. One reason for this distancing was a difference in their personalities. Outgoing, sociable, and self-centered, Franklin loved the world and all its pleasures. First in Albany and then in Washington, he reveled in the social life. In the evenings after work he liked nothing better than to attend festive parties; sometimes, in the company of old college friends, he would stay out until three or four in the morning. On Sundays, when Eleanor thought he should be in church, he preferred to play golf with male cronies. Eleanor, by contrast, was serious and virtuous. "Duty first" was her motto. At the parties Franklin so enjoyed, she felt shy and awkward, and she was further nagged by the feeling that everyone's time could be better spent on more important things. Moreover, with the example of her father and brother, both alcoholics, in mind, she believed that indulgence in life's pleasures too easily led to excess. From the beginning, Eleanor was clearly disappointed in the fun-loving, pleasure-seeking side of her husband's nature. As she later put it in her remarkably candid autobiography, "These first years I was so serious and a certain kind of orthodox goodness was my ideal and ambition. . . . But what a tragedy it was if in any way my husband offended against these ideals of mine— and, amusingly enough, I do not think I ever told him what I expected!"[13]

Problems of a more intimate nature may also have added to domestic tensions. Eleanor later confided to her daughter that she had possessed decidedly Victorian attitudes toward sex. But she performed what she considered to be her wifely duties, and one child followed another until she had given birth to six in all, one of whom died in 1909 at the age of seven months. Of this period, Eleanor later recalled, "I was always just getting over a baby or about to have one."[14] After the sixth child was born in 1916 and for the remainder of their marriage, Eleanor maintained a separate bedroom. Insecure in her new role as wife and mother, Eleanor fell under the domination of her well-meaning but strong-willed mother-in-law. Sara even went so far as to design, build, and decorate a home for Franklin and Eleanor and an adjoining one for herself, all without consulting Eleanor. Overwhelmed by her mother-in-law, unsure of herself, and disappointed in Franklin, Eleanor was unhappy. Through it all, Franklin seemed not to notice.

The demands of public life further strained their relationship. Franklin was so preoccupied with his career that Eleanor had to assume almost total responsibility for managing the household and raising their five children. In addition, she felt uncomfortable in the carefully prescribed role she was expected to play as the wife of a politician. That role required her to attend endless rounds of receptions and teas, to be charming and gracious at all times, to hold no strong opinions of her own, and never to offend anyone or to do anything that might embarrass her husband.

For the most part, Eleanor did what official Washington expected of her. But at least on one occasion she caused her husband acute embarrassment. During the war, when the government was asking citizens to serve and to sacrifice, a reporter from the *New York Times* interviewed Eleanor about the economy measures she had implemented in the large Roosevelt household. Eleanor proudly explained that she and her staff were doing their part. At one point she said, "Making the ten servants help me do my saving has not only been possible but highly profitable." When the article appeared, Franklin was clearly annoyed by his wife's gaffe. "All I can say," he wrote Eleanor, "is that your latest newspaper campaign is a corker and I am proud to be the husband of the Originator, Discoverer and Inventor of the New Household Economy for Millionaires! Please have a photo taken showing the family, the ten cooperating servants, the scraps saved from the table. . . . Honestly you have leaped into public fame, all Washington is talking of the Roosevelt plan."[15]

Lucy Mercer, the other woman in Franklin's life, first entered the scene in 1913, the Roosevelts' first year in Washington, when Eleanor hired her as a social secretary. But it was not until the war years that her relationship with Franklin deepened into love. Descended from a distinguished old Maryland family that had fallen on financial hard times, Lucy was intelligent, charming, and beautiful, the sort of woman, people said, with whom men naturally fell in love. Franklin apparently found in Lucy the kind of uncritical acceptance that Eleanor was unable to provide. Lucy, for her part, thought Franklin to be the most beautiful and charming man she had ever met.

Eleanor suspected the worst as early as the summer of 1917. But her suspicions were not confirmed until a year and a half later, when, in the process of organizing her husband's correspondence, she came across some intimate letters that Lucy had written to Franklin. Eleanor thereupon confronted her husband with the evidence and with an ultimatum: either he would stop seeing Lucy, or he would agree to a divorce, which in those days would have ruined his political career. Accounts vary as to what happened next. According to some family insiders, Franklin's mother raised the stakes by threatening to cut Franklin out of the family inheritance if he abandoned his wife and children. In this version, Franklin, willing to forsake fame and fortune for the woman he loved, agreed to a divorce, only to find that Lucy, a devout Catholic, would not marry a divorced man. According to a more plausible account, Franklin was unwilling to sacrifice either family or career, and he agreed to terminate the affair.[16]

Whatever the truth of the matter, the end result was the same. For the time being at least, Franklin and Lucy broke off their relationship; soon thereafter, Lucy married a much older man; and Franklin and

Eleanor, their old intimacy lost forever, forged in its place a highly effective partnership that served both of them well. Additionally, some family members believed that the crisis toughened and matured Roosevelt, who until this time had had almost everything his way. But it was Eleanor upon whom this painful episode had the much greater impact, at once reinforcing her childhood feelings of inadequacy and, in the long run, strengthening her resolve to be her own person.

In 1920, having survived the first major crisis of his life, Roosevelt became his party's candidate for the vice presidency. Democratic power-brokers selected him for several reasons. He had a famous name; as a New Yorker, he provided regional balance for presidential candidate James M. Cox of Ohio; he had a good record as assistant secretary of the navy; and he was handsome, articulate, and energetic. Ironically, Roosevelt owed his selection in part to Tammany Hall, thus demonstrating the wisdom of the live-and-let-live attitude he had taken toward the machine following his earlier defeat in the senate race.

As a campaigner, Roosevelt still lacked polish. He continued to imitate Theodore Roosevelt, who had died the year before, but the effort did not always work to his advantage. "Franklin is as much like Theodore as a clam is like a bear-cat," observed the Chicago *Tribune*.[17] During a speech in Montana, Roosevelt so overdid the imitation of his cousin's swaggering style that he got himself into trouble. Defending Woodrow Wilson's ill-fated League of Nations, he claimed that the United States would actually have twelve votes in the League instead of one because it would be able to control the votes of supposedly pliant Latin American republics. Not content with this realistic but imprudent assessment, Roosevelt boasted, falsely, "I have something to do with the running of a couple of these little Republics. Until last week I had two of these votes in my pocket. . . . One of them was Haiti, I know, for I wrote Haiti's constitution myself, and if I do say it, I think it was a pretty good constitution." The Republican presidential candidate, Warren G. Harding, promptly denounced Roosevelt's imperialistic-sounding pronouncement as "the most shocking assertion that ever emanated from a responsible member of the government of the United States." In the end, Roosevelt did what politicians usually do in such circumstances. He claimed that he had been misquoted.[18]

Despite his blunder, the campaign counted as a plus for Roosevelt. In the process of visiting 32 states and delivering nearly 1,000 speeches, he made a name for himself, established useful relationships with party leaders throughout the country, and put together a highly efficient and loyal staff, most of whom remained with him after the election. Even though he and Cox went down to defeat, Roosevelt seemed certain to figure prominently in the future of his party.

As he awaited his next political opportunity, he practiced law and business. In the latter capacity, he engaged in a series of speculative, even foolhardy, ventures, including wildcatting for oil, marketing lobsters, and running a dirigible passenger service between New York and Chicago. Most of his schemes lost money; some were of such dubious probity that a prestigious business organization once admonished Roosevelt for lending his name to unsound investments. Some of his public pronouncements during the decade echoed the probusiness sentiments of the conservative Harding and Coolidge administrations of the 1920s. Government regulation of industry, he said, was too unwieldy and too expensive: "The public doesn't want it; the industry doesn't want it."[19]

Roosevelt's career as a businessman demonstrated the ease with which he adapted himself to changing circumstances. During the period of reform, he had been a reformer. Now, during the business-dominated twenties, he became a businessman extolling the virtues of the free-enterprise system. As the decade wore on and as Roosevelt sensed increasing public weariness with the indulgent excesses of the period, he began to talk once again of the need for idealism and reform. Then and later, Roosevelt moved effortlessly from one era to another, sometimes leading and sometimes following, but always in step with the times.

In 1921, Roosevelt experienced a crisis much more severe than the Lucy Mercer affair, a crisis that by almost all odds should have ended his political career. In August of that year, he and his family were vacationing at their summer home on Campobello Island, off the coast of Maine. For Roosevelt a vacation meant strenuous physical activity, for that was how he liked to unwind and relax. An avid outdoorsman, he loved to sail and swim and to play golf and tennis. Usually such activities left him feeling exhilarated. But one afternoon he returned home with the children after a typically rigorous outing feeling chilled and weary. Too tired to dress for dinner, he went to bed early. The next morning as he climbed out of bed, he detected numbness in his left leg. "I tried to persuade myself that this trouble with my leg was muscular, that it would disappear as I used it," he later recalled. "But presently, it refused to work, and then the other."[20] Before long, he was running a high fever and experiencing excruciating pain. He lost the normal functioning of his bowels and bladder and was unable to walk or even stand. Doctors eventually diagnosed the illness as infantile paralysis, the dreaded killer and crippler that usually afflicted children.[21]

Franklin Roosevelt, at the age of 39, was now severely crippled for life. Although his digestive tract, bowels, bladder, and sexual organs eventually returned to normal, the principal muscles below his waist were almost completely paralyzed. Never again would he be able to walk without assistance. From now on, such routine tasks as getting into and out of bed, bathing, going to the bathroom, and dressing all required elaborate effort.

Given the severity of Roosevelt's disability, it would not have been surprising if he had decided to retire to the privacy of Hyde Park. This was precisely what his mother wanted him to do. But Roosevelt would have no part of it, and with the encouragement of Eleanor and Louis Howe, he resolved to make every effort to resume a normal life.

For him, a normal life meant walking again. Refusing to admit to himself or to anyone else that his paralysis could be permanent, he devoted the better part of the next seven years to rebuilding his hopelessly atrophied muscles. During those years, everything in the Roosevelt household was made to revolve around Franklin's single-minded pursuit of rehabilitation. He required everyone to subordinate their needs to his effort to walk again and resume his political career. Nurses and physical therapists were hired. Exercise equipment was installed. At Hyde Park, Sara had ramps built and an old elevator reactivated. To maintain his business and political correspondence, Roosevelt once again sought out Louis Howe, who left his family and moved into the Roosevelt's New York City townhouse, displacing from her room daughter Anna Roosevelt, who resented the intrusion of an outsider into the family's life. For her part, Eleanor, who had gained a measure of independence since the Lucy Mercer affair, now became more closely involved than ever in her husband's life.

In his struggle to walk, Roosevelt tried all the then-known cures and therapies; when one thing failed to work, he tried something else. Finally he placed his hopes for recovery in the buoyant, mineral-rich waters of Warm Springs, Georgia, a dilapidated health spa dating to the antebellum period. Roosevelt eventually invested two-thirds of his personal fortune in Warm Springs, transforming it in the process into a major center for the rehabilitation of polio victims. In the end, however, the miracle he expected never materialized, although he never gave up hoping.

Although Roosevelt never regained full use of his legs, to a remarkable extent he did manage to compensate for his disability. Through strenuous exercise, he was able to lift himself into and out of a wheelchair. With the help of heavy steel leg braces, he managed to stand on his feet for long periods of time. Eventually, with those same leg braces and with a strong arm to lean on, he learned to walk short distances. He even had an automobile fitted with hand controls so that he could drive. Later, as president, he delighted in trying to evade anxious Secret Service agents as he sped across the back roads at Hyde Park and Warm Springs, which he knew like the back of his hand.

One of Roosevelt's greatest achievements was to focus unprecedented public attention on the plight of people with disabilities. For the rest of his life, he served as a source of hope and inspiration to the victims of polio and other crippling diseases, and he provided dramatic proof to the public as a whole that persons with physical disabilities could lead useful and productive lives. Moreover, Roosevelt played a major role in initiating efforts that ultimately led to the virtual eradication of polio in the United States. In addition to founding the Warm Springs Foundation, he helped establish the National Foundation for Infantile Paralysis, one of the first modern disease-fighting private organizations. Although Roosevelt did not live to see it, the National Foundation eventually financed the research that led to a successful vaccination for polio.

Significantly, although everyone knew that Roosevelt was a victim of polio, most people during his lifetime were unaware of the extent of his disability or of the excruciating pain he endured. This was no accident. Perhaps fearing that the public would be reluctant to elect a cripple to high office, he went to great lengths to conceal the severity of his impairment. For one thing, he prohibited newsmen from photographing him in a wheelchair, or in the act of being lifted into or out of an automobile, or being carried up a flight of stairs. One time, while giving a speech, Roosevelt leaned for support against an unsteady rostrum. Suddenly, the rostrum gave way and pitched Roosevelt off the stage. After being helped back to the stage, he resumed his speech as though nothing had happened. "No sob stuff," he had earlier warned the press, and the incident went unreported. Because of Roosevelt's elaborate precautions and because of the willingness of the press to cooperate in what one observer later described as a "conspiracy of silence," most people assumed that Roosevelt's attack of polio had been relatively mild and that he had almost completely recovered from it.[22]

Then and later, there was much speculation about the effects of Roosevelt's struggle against infantile paralysis on his personality and character. In the presence of close friends and family members he occasionally showed signs of discouragement and depression. Most of the time, however, he appeared to maintain his cheery disposition and his optimistic view of life. But some people who knew him believed that the inner man had undergone a transformation. Polio, they said, had strengthened his character, purged him of the last vestiges of superficiality and arrogance, and most important, imbued him with a deep sympathy for the disadvantaged. Polio undoubtedly did toughen and mature Roosevelt, but there is no evidence that it produced any fundamental change in his political sympathies; he remained on the political spectrum where he had always been—a little to the left of center. The major change in Roosevelt that polio brought about was reflected in his temperament and style. He emerged from the crisis less impulsive and more cautious and calculating. No longer was he the self-righteous state senator baiting the Tammany machine, or the insubordinate assistant secretary of the navy challenging his superiors, or the outspoken vice-presidential candidate, barnstorming the country and boasting that he had written the Haitian constitution. Rather, when Roosevelt reentered public life, he was a mature politician whose every word and action seemed calculated for its effect on others.

In ways that no one could possibly have foreseen at the outset, polio turned out to be a great blessing for Roosevelt politically. Indeed, if he had not been stricken, it is entirely possible that he might never have been elected governor of New York or later president of the United States. For one thing, Roosevelt's struggle against infantile paralysis enhanced his personal appeal. Although he still had to convince skeptics that he had the physical stamina to withstand the rigors of public life, his triumph over adversity gave a heroic dimension to his life that had been missing before. In a way, polio did for Franklin Roosevelt what the Spanish-American War had done for Theodore Roosevelt.

More important, polio prevented Roosevelt from seeking public office at a time when such a quest would probably have damaged his career. As it turned out, the period of his convalescence was also a most unpropitious time for aspiring Democratic politicians. Riding the crest of economic prosperity, the Republican party had firmly entrenched itself in power at the national level. The Democratic party, meanwhile, was in disarray. Preoccupied with the explosive issues of race, religion, and prohibition, Democrats were hopelessly divided along urban and rural lines. If Roosevelt had run for office in such circumstances, he probably would have been mortally wounded in the cross-fire between warring factions in his own party. Polio, however, left him no choice but to remain safely behind the front lines. Even after his condition improved, he found that ill-health provided a convenient excuse for avoiding politically risky situations. In the mid-1920s, for example, some of his supporters launched a movement to draft him for a senate race. As the clever Howe put it to Roosevelt, "I hope your spine is still sufficiently strong to assure them that you are still nigh death's door for the next two years. Please try to look pallid, and worn and weary."[23]

Prolonged political inactivity entailed even greater risks. But Roosevelt was not going to remain out of the spotlight for long, lest people forget him. In 1924 he made his first public appearance since he had fallen ill. The occasion was the meeting of the Democratic National Convention, where he was to place in nomination for the presidency the name of New York governor Alfred E. Smith. Assembled politicians did not soon forget the dramatic scene: when the time came for Roosevelt to address the convention, he slowly made his way on crutches to the podium. All eyes were fixed on him; spectators held their breath for fear that he would stumble and fall. When he finally reached the rostrum, he carefully laid aside his crutches, tossed his head back in his characteristic manner, and flashed a triumphant smile. The hall shook with applause. His performance was by all accounts the high point of an otherwise dismal convention.

Following his convention triumph, Roosevelt began corresponding with party leaders throughout the country. He also used his frequent visits to Warm Springs as an excuse to confer with powerful southern Democrats. In these and in other ways he worked himself back into the center of party affairs. Eleanor, too, helped ensure that people did not forget her husband. In New York she ably represented his political interests and also exposed him to a variety of important people and causes that otherwise might have escaped his notice.

In 1928, despite his own and Louis Howe's misgivings, Roosevelt ran for the governorship of New York. To Roosevelt and Howe, the timing seemed all wrong, for 1928 looked like another Republican year. But Al Smith, the incumbent governor and Democratic presidential nominee, pleaded with Roosevelt to make the race. Actually, Smith regarded Roosevelt as a political dilettante, not to be taken entirely seriously. But he believed that Roosevelt would strengthen the Democratic ticket in upstate New York and thereby enhance his own chances of carrying New York in the presidential race. Smith apparently also believed that if Roosevelt did win the governorship, he, Smith, would become the power behind the scenes. Roosevelt declined at first, but Smith persisted, and Roosevelt finally consented to run.

The candidate's health quickly surfaced as a major issue in the campaign. The Republicans, feigning sympathy for Roosevelt, criticized Smith for dragooning a helpless invalid into making the race. In order to lay the issue to rest, Roosevelt conducted a strenuous campaign, exhausting his staff and the press in the process. Recounting the details of his hectic schedule to one audience, Roosevelt quipped, "Too bad about this unfortunate sick man, isn't it?"[24]

Roosevelt's estimation of Democratic prospects in the November elections was at least partially borne out. In the presidential contest Al Smith suffered a crushing defeat at the hands of Herbert Hoover. Roosevelt, however, won a narrow victory.

"Anyone who is governor of New York has a good chance to be President with any luck," Roosevelt had told his fellow law clerks many years earlier. Yet from the perspective of 1928, it appeared that the newly elected governor would need more than a little luck, for formidable obstacles remained between him and the White House. One of those obstacles was the thorny underbrush of New York politics through which he would have to pass. Another was the demoralized and divided state of the Democratic party. But the most imposing obstacle of all was the opposition party. With the highly competent and popular Herbert Hoover about to assume the presidency, it appeared that nothing short of disaster could interrupt Republican rule.

3

GOVERNOR AND PRESIDENTIAL
CANDIDATE, 1929–1933

Between 1929 and 1932, Roosevelt experienced one triumph after another. He compiled a good record as governor of New York, bested several rivals for the 1932 Democratic presidential nomination, and in the
midst of the most severe economic crisis in the nation's history, defeated
Herbert Hoover for the presidency. Despite his successive triumphs,
however, Roosevelt failed to dispel lingering doubts about his character
and intellect. Many observers, with no particular axes to grind, viewed
him as a superficial charmer, blessed with a golden boy personality and
exceptionally good luck. These observers underestimated Roosevelt.
There was more substance to his leadership than they gave him credit
for. But they also had a point. Even at his best, he gave no one any
particular reason to think that he was destined for great distinction.

A tendency to underestimate Roosevelt surfaced at the very beginning of his governorship. Because Al Smith had personally selected Roosevelt as his successor, Smith and his followers expected Roosevelt to
serve as a figurehead while the former governor wielded the real power
behind the scenes. Following the election, Smith, who believed that
Roosevelt was so sick that he would die within a year, reserved a suite
at the DeWitt Clinton Hotel in Albany to help manage state affairs.[1]

But the former governor misjudged his successor, who knew instinctively that to establish himself as a serious presidential contender, he

needed to emerge from Smith's shadow and avoid being too closely identified with Smith's urban anti-Prohibition wing of the party. Roosevelt owed much to his fellow New Yorker, to be sure; but like most successful leaders, he was not about to allow gratitude to jeopardize his political survival, and upon assuming office in 1929, he moved quickly to establish himself in his own right. Although he retained many of Smith's appointees, the new governor installed persons loyal to himself in the key positions. He pointedly ignored his predecessor's repeated offers to confer on matters of policy, prompting Smith to complain, "Do you know, by God, that he has never consulted me about a damn thing since he has been Governor? He has ignored me."[2] By easing Smith from center stage, Roosevelt took a small but necessary step in his pursuit of the presidency. Most contemporary political observers, however, failed to grasp the significance of Roosevelt's efforts to distance himself from his predecessor. Journalist Walter Lippmann, for one, believed that Roosevelt needed all the help he could get and that he was foolish to shun Smith's offer of assistance.

Having met the Smith challenge Roosevelt engaged in a similar test of will with the Republican-dominated legislature. Two years earlier, New York voters had approved a constitutional amendment transferring broad budgetary responsibilities from the legislative to the executive branch of government. When Roosevelt submitted his first budget, the legislature attempted to regain control of the purse strings. The ensuing controversy, involving complex legal and constitutional issues, finally ended up in the courts, where Roosevelt prevailed and thus strengthened his grip on the reins of power.

Roosevelt became a forthright spokesman for liberal reform. During his first term he supported, though he did not initiate, proposals for farm relief, old age insurance, development of water power, regulation of utilities, conservation of natural resources, more humane treatment of prisoners, including abolition of the death penalty, and increased spending for education and for the physically and mentally handicapped. In the end, however, he proved to be better at articulating the issues than at steering his proposals through the Republican legislature. Part of the difficulty he experienced as a legislative leader stemmed from the fact that during his own stint in the senate, he had played the role of outsider and therefore had not mastered the inner workings of the legislature. Then, too, he never quite overcame the habit of looking upon lawmakers, even the best of them, as potential Tammany spoilsmen. On the administrative side, Roosevelt appointed honest and competent persons to public office, and he established ties with the intellectual community by consulting with university professors on many issues. Roosevelt's tenure in Albany by no means earned him a place among the great governors in American history, such as Robert La Follette or even Al Smith, whose legacies included pioneering political and social reforms. But he was one of the ablest state executives of his own time.

Roosevelt made his most original contribution to public life in the area of public relations, where he mastered traditional techniques of communication and helped develop new ones. His twice-daily press conferences and his informal "give-and-take" relationship with reporters brought him maximum publicity. To reach outlying areas of the state, beyond the range of major publications, he created a news bureau in Albany, which distributed free information concerning state affairs. As one reporter noted, the bureau's reports, "newsy rather than political, but never failing to mention 'Governor Franklin D. Roosevelt,' were soon sifting into the most stalwart Republican weeklies."[3] His widely publicized inspection tours, which often took him into remote parts of the state, brought him into contact with persons who probably had never before seen a governor.

Roosevelt also used radio effectively, and in a series of informal addresses he sought to mobilize support for his legislative program. He was not the first politician to realize the potential inherent in this newest instrument of mass communications. Calvin Coolidge, who believed that radio might render the old-fashioned "rear platform" speech obsolete, had made numerous radio broadcasts from the White House. As governor and as presidential candidate, Al Smith had also spoken frequently over the radio. In fact, Smith's final broadcast of the campaign, in which he talked directly to the radio audience, may have served as a model for Roosevelt's own addresses.[4] Roosevelt, however, was blessed with a better radio voice than most politicians, and he knew instinctively how to project his personality across the airwaves.

The stock market crash of 1929 and the ensuing depression presented Roosevelt with his greatest challenge as governor. The crisis caught him, as it did most Americans, with his guard down. His first reaction to "the recent little Flurry down town," as he referred to the crash, was to express to Louis Howe the hope that he might be able to purchase at bargain prices some items he wanted to buy at a local estate sale.[5] As conditions worsened, Roosevelt still failed to appreciate sufficiently the seriousness of the situation, and he bore some personal responsibility for the banking crisis that gripped the state in 1930. Early that year, he scoffed at demands for reform of the Empire State's banking system, even though a fact-finding committee, which he himself had appointed, uncovered indisputable evidence of unsound financial practices. In December those same practices led to the collapse of one of the largest banks in the nation, the Bank of the United States in New York City, which defaulted on the savings of some 400,000 depositors, many of them persons of modest income.

Demonstrating a remarkable ability to regain his balance, Roosevelt shifted blame from himself, where it belonged, at least in part, to the Republican legislature; not only this, he also identified himself with a reform that he had earlier opposed. "The responsibility for strengthening the banking laws," he indignantly told the legislature, "rests with you. The time to act is now. Any further delay is inexcusable."[6]

By 1931 Roosevelt could no longer ignore deteriorating economic conditions. In New York City alone, according to one estimate, 800,000 persons found themselves out of work. Beggars began appearing on Manhattan street corners, while on those same corners jobless men and women tried to sell everything from pencils and cheap neckties to apples. In 1931 the four largest hospitals in the city recorded 95 cases of starvation. At night homeless men and women picked through the garbage cans left outside of restaurants, searching for scraps of food.

New York's public welfare agencies and private charities, which were among the best organized and best financed in the nation, tried valiantly to meet the needs of the unemployed. These organizations set up 82 breadlines and served 85,000 meals a day to people who might otherwise have starved. Eventually, however, the financial resources for such activities gave out, and social workers, wealthy philanthropists, and political activists demanded state intervention.

Although Roosevelt did not initiate the movement for unemployment relief, he quickly made its cause his own. In 1931, at his urging, the legislature created the Temporary Emergency Relief Administration (TERA), the first state agency of its kind in the nation. Under the able direction of Harry Hopkins, a social worker, TERA attempted to create jobs for the unemployed and if necessary, to provide them with food, shelter, and clothing.

Roosevelt performed his most important service to the cause of unemployment relief by articulating its public justification. Then and later, some critics accused him of lacking any clear and coherent political philosophy. Journalist Elmer Davis, for instance, expressed the widely held view when he said, "You could not quarrel with a single one of his generalities. But what they mean (if anything) is known only to Franklin D. Roosevelt and his God."[7] Critics such as Davis had a point: Roosevelt did not display a particularly speculative cast of mind, examine ideas for their own sake, or read deeply on any subject. But some of Roosevelt's defenders made a virtue out of his philosophical innocence, arguing that it allowed him to adapt more readily to changing circumstances. Yet the debate over the merits of Roosevelt's nonideological approach obscured the extent to which he did articulate a coherent public philosophy. With remarkable regularity and disarming simplicity of language, he discussed such subjects as the nature of society and the proper role of government.

In defense of unemployment relief, for example, Roosevelt argued that such aid conformed to the fundamental purposes of government. After all, he said, because government is simply the machinery by which citizens provide for their own mutual protection and well-being, they have every right to expect from their government protection against joblessness and want, just as they expect protection from other hazardous circumstances beyond their control. As for those who had escaped the hardships of the depression, Roosevelt argued, they had an obligation, as part of the social compact, to assist those in need. In justifying an increase in income taxes to pay for unemployment relief, he said: "It is clear to me that it is the duty of those who have benefitted by our industrial and economic system to come to the front in such a grave emergency and assist in relieving those who, under the same industrial and economic order, are the losers and sufferers. I believe their contribution should be in proportion to the benefits they receive and the prosperity they enjoy."[8] Roosevelt also argued from the point of view of enlightened self-interest. Because of the organic nature of modern society, he believed, all individuals and groups, regardless of class, occupation, or region, depend upon one another for their very survival. As he stated it, "The 'self-supporting' man or woman has become as extinct as the man of the stone age. Without the help of thousands of others, any one of us would die, naked and starved." Because citizens depend upon one another for their survival, they have a direct stake in each other's well-being; mutual self-interest, therefore, necessitates public assistance to distressed individuals and groups, such as farmers, the elderly, and the jobless. "In the final analysis," he said, "the progress of our civilization will be retarded if any large body of citizens falls behind."[9]

Roosevelt's arguments in support of unemployment relief and other forms of government aid signified an important new emphasis on the part of American liberals. He maintained that government, in addition to fulfilling its traditional obligations, such as national defense, must now seek to reduce life's physical risks. At the outset of the depression, Roosevelt argued that modern government must protect its citizens "from disease, from ignorance, from physical injury, and from old-age want." Following the crash, he added joblessness and economic insecurity to the list.[10] Roosevelt's emphasis on physical security contrasted sharply with the emphasis of a previous generation of progressive reformers, who had subordinated material concerns, at least rhetorically, to abstract moral goals.

An abiding faith in progress, which meshed nicely with his own temperament, constituted another key component of Roosevelt's public philosophy. Few American political leaders have ever been as comfortable in their time and place in history as Roosevelt. Although he conceded that setbacks and even reverses had occasionally slowed the forward march of history, he seemed to believe that the world had evolved in such a way that he lived in the best of all possible worlds and that the future would be even better. Then and now, most politicians locate the "good society" in some real or imagined past, even as they plunge into the future. Roosevelt, by contrast, displayed a strikingly unsentimental view of history. Old ways, he believed, are not necessarily good ways. "Progress means change," he said. "A perfect system of 1918 may be out worn ten years later."[11] Roosevelt also maintained that social consciousness had kept pace with material development. He liked to point out, for example, that previous generations often had treated their poor, their elderly, and their physically and mentally handicapped in ways that would strike modern men and women as barbaric. Roosevelt coupled this unsentimental view of history with a similarly unsentimental view of another icon of American life, local government, which many people nostalgically associated with better times. When the need arose, he could denounce the evils of federal bureaucracy with the best of them; more often, however, he emphasized the limitations of local government. He once described county and municipal governments in New York State as "archaic in design, unsuited for the purpose for which they are established, unsatisfactory in their functioning, and profligate in the spending of the taxpayers' contributions."[12]

A conspicuous exception to Roosevelt's belief in progress involved his distaste for urban life. He believed that cities had become too congested and that people could find greater happiness in the more whole-some environment of the countryside, where, as he put it, "there is contact with earth and with nature and the restful privilege of getting away from pavements and from noise."[13] Yet Roosevelt by no means un-critically accepted all the values of rural America. He claimed, for ex-ample, that bigotry and intolerance flourish more readily in the isolation of the countryside than in the city.[14] Nor did he support a "back to the land" movement, whereby "city slickers," taking up hoe and rake, would suddenly transform themselves into yeoman farmers. He envisioned in-stead a decentralized America in which the population achieved better distribution and in which aggregations of farms and factories dotted the landscape.

Roosevelt's celebration of progress and change contrasted sharply with some of his personal habits. Owing to his disability, but also to his temperament, he practiced the same routine day after day. He sur-rounded himself with so many personal reminders of the past that his desk often resembled the display table of a pawn shop. Superstitious by nature, he refused to travel on the thirteenth day of the month or to light three cigarettes off the same match; later, during each of his polit-ical campaigns, he insisted upon wearing the same worn fedora for luck. Finally, no matter how hectic his schedule might be, he could not stay away for very long from the unchanging environment of his ancestral home at Hyde Park. During the 1930s, when surviving members of the old Hudson River families began to die or to sell their mansions to real estate developers, Roosevelt devised a plan to convert the area into a national historic site, thereby preserving for all time the Hyde Park of his childhood and youth.[15]

In 1930 Roosevelt's reelection by an impressive margin established him as the leading contender for the Democratic presidential nomination two years hence. As the lengthy nominating process got under way, how-ever, opposition to his candidacy threatened to deprive him of the prize he had sought for so many years. Given prevailing political realities, some opposition was inevitable and therefore beyond his power to pre-vent. As economic conditions worsened and as President Hoover's pop-ularity continued to decline, it seemed almost certain that in 1932 the Democrats would be nominating the next president. This likelihood of victory naturally encouraged several prominent Democrats, whose am-bitions had been stifled by 12 years of Republican rule, to challenge Roosevelt for the nomination. The challengers included Al Smith and William Gibbs McAdoo, both of whom believed, justifiably, that their experience and service to the party gave them as much claim to the nomination as Roosevelt.

Roosevelt also encountered opposition of an ideological nature. Since 1928, conservatives, led by party chairman John Jacob Raskob, had occupied the leadership positions in the Democratic party. Formerly a Republican industrialist associated with the DuPont and General Motors corporations, Raskob stood for states' rights, balanced budgets, and a free hand for business. Raskob had given an indication of his economic views as well as his bad sense of timing when, on the eve of the stock market crash, he had declared that anyone with a few sound investments "not only can be rich but ought to be rich."[16] During the depression, Raskob identified the repeal of Prohibition as the nation's most urgent priority. Economic considerations, rather than the desire for a good time, probably lay at the heart of his position, for he hoped that resumption of the manufacture and sale of alcoholic beverages would allow the federal government to reap additional revenues from the alcohol tax, thereby reducing its need to rely on personal and corporate taxes. As the election year neared, party chairman Raskob searched for a candidate compatible with his own views. Although some reformers questioned the authenticity of Roosevelt's liberal credentials, Raskob considered him to be an out-and-out radical, and in order to block his nomination he encouraged other Democrats, including Al Smith and Newton D. Baker, to enter the field.[17]

In April 1932, Roosevelt delivered a much-publicized radio address that intensified opposition to his candidacy among conservatives. The speech, written by Raymond Moley, a Columbia University professor and a member of Roosevelt's newly formed Brain Trust, accused the Hoover administration of failing to mobilize in the war against the depression the entire nation, especially "the forgotten man at the bottom of the economic pyramid." In the highly charged atmosphere of the depression, many conservatives interpreted Roosevelt's reference to "the forgotten man" as an incitement to class conflict. Al Smith, who some said had traded in his brown derby for a top hat, declared, "I will take off my coat and vest and fight to the end against any candidate who persists in any demagogic appeal to the masses of the working people of this country to destroy themselves by setting class against class and rich against poor."[18]

Miscalculations by Roosevelt and the co-managers of his campaign, Louis Howe and James A. Farley, also strengthened the hand of his opponents. These miscalculations stemmed in part from overconfidence. Following Roosevelt's reelection victory in 1930, the trio issued over

Farley's signature an adolescentlike dare, saying, "I do not see how Mr. Roosevelt can escape becoming the next presidential nominee of his party, even if no one should raise a finger to bring it about."[19] Overconfidence probably also inspired Roosevelt's ill-fated decision in April to enter the Massachusetts primary, in which Smith dealt him an embarrassing defeat.

Ultimately, however, fresh doubts about Roosevelt's personal fitness for the presidency posed the most serious threat to his nomination. Despite a solid record of achievement as governor, undeniable popularity with the voters, and a coherent philosophy, Roosevelt discovered that once again many influential persons, whose good opinion he had sought, believed that he lacked substance. These persons included elder statesmen in the Democratic party, such as Bernard Baruch, and thoughtful journalist-intellectuals, such as Walter Lippmann and Edmund Wilson. Lippmann gave the skeptical view of Roosevelt its classic expression: "Franklin Roosevelt is no crusader. He is no tribune of the people. He is no enemy of entrenched privilege." Then Lippmann delivered his devastating punchline: "He is a pleasant man who, without any important qualifications for the office, would like very much to be President."[20]

This view of Roosevelt derived from three principal sources: his response to Tammany corruption, his shifting positions on international issues, and most important, certain personality traits. During his second term, irrefutable evidence surfaced of wrongdoing on the part of state officials affiliated with his old nemesis, Tammany Hall. In one case, a county sheriff amassed a fortune of several hundred thousand dollars in excess of his salary. When asked to account for the money, he said that he had found it in "a wonderful [tin] box."[21] James J. Walker, the flamboyant mayor of New York City, also had difficulty accounting for irregularities in his financial affairs. The corruption issue posed a dilemma for the governor. If he waged too vigorous an investigation into corruption charges, he would risk incurring the wrath of Tammany and other big city machines. On the other hand, if he ignored evidence of corruption, he would damage his standing among Southerners and Westerners, for whom Tammany Hall epitomized the evils of the big city, and among many liberals in all sections of the country, who even in the midst of the depression, felt as strongly about the corruption issue as they did about economic recovery. In the end, the man who had launched his career as the foe of Tammany Hall satisfied practically no one; he did just enough to anger Tammany loyalists but not enough to quiet the reformers.

At the same time, he came under attack from William Randolph Hearst, the powerful newspaper mogul, who assailed him for supporting American membership in the League of Nations. To appease Hearst, Roosevelt announced that he no longer favored League membership. His statement, coupled with his handling of the Tammany scandals, helped fix in the minds of many persons an image of irresoluteness and opportunism.

Certain personality traits, especially an ebullient optimism, mightily reinforced this image. Writer Milton MacKaye found in Roosevelt "all light and no darkness; all faith and no skepticism; all bright hope and no black despair. One expects shadow and depth in a great man." In the midst of the most severe economic crisis in the nation's history, Roosevelt's "slightly unnatural sunniness," in Edmund Wilson's words, suggested to some that he either had lost touch with reality or lacked the normal range of human emotions.[22] Clearly, at this stage in Roosevelt's career, his most pronounced personal characteristic, his optimism, undermined confidence in his leadership.

Roosevelt had always possessed a cheery disposition, but that attribute had become more pronounced as a result of his attempt to conceal from the public the extent of his disability. Ironically, if he had revealed to the public the details of his bout with polio, he probably could have convinced some of his critics that he possessed the "shadow and depth" they seemed to be looking for. Yet the risks of any such disclosure probably outweighed the benefits, for even with Roosevelt's efforts at concealment, rumors of his physical and mental incompetence dogged him continually. Some of the rumors took particularly ugly forms, such as the one that had him suffering not from polio but from syphilis. Even after Roosevelt received a clean bill of health from a committee of eminent physicians, the whispering campaign continued. Yet as bad as some of the rumors were, they probably would have been worse and more widespread had he not engaged in his elaborate deception.

When the Democratic convention opened in Chicago in late June 1932, Roosevelt had pledges of support from a majority of the delegates. But that still left him 100 votes shy of the two-thirds margin then needed for the nomination itself. On the first three ballots, Roosevelt made only minuscule gains. Then, on the fourth ballot, probably his last chance to win before the convention began to search in earnest for a compromise candidate, he went over the top.

Most accounts of the convention attributed Roosevelt's victory to last-minute maneuvers, such as his selection of John Nance Garner of Texas as his running mate, but his nomination owed more to long-standing and broadly based developments. He benefited particularly from the continuing division of Democrats, especially along urban and rural lines. If Al Smith and William Gibbs McAdoo, the leaders of the two major factions within the party, neither of whom favored Roosevelt, had been able to agree on an alternative candidate, they would have prevented Roosevelt's nomination. In the end, however, they proved unable to reach such an agreement, at which time McAdoo, unwilling to deadlock the convention or risk the nomination of a Smith candidate, went over to Roosevelt's side. Roosevelt, for his part, had carefully positioned himself to take advantage of rifts within the Democratic party.

Already a master of the dramatic gesture, Roosevelt remained in Albany during the balloting, but then broke precedent by flying to Chicago to accept the nomination in person. The acceptance speech itself contained a rousing call to action. Fusing biblical and martial imagery in a style reminiscent of Theodore Roosevelt's famous "We Stand at Armageddon" speech during the 1912 presidential campaign, the Democratic nominee urged his followers to abandon false prophets and to "constitute ourselves prophets of a new order of competence and of courage." "This is more than a political campaign," he said. "It is a call to arms. Give me your help, not to win votes alone, but to win in this crusade to restore America to its own people." Roosevelt also unexpectedly supplied his campaign with a memorable slogan, saying, "I pledge you, I pledge myself, to a new deal for the American people." At the time, neither the candidate nor his advisers attached any particular significance to the phrase, but the words "new deal," like "the forgotten man" several months earlier, caught the fancy of cartoonists and newspapermen, who thereafter affixed the phrase to Roosevelt's program.[23]

Roosevelt's address momentarily stirred the convention delegates, but it failed to erase their lingering doubts about his fitness for the presidency. The convention, one reporter wrote, had selected "the man who would probably make the weakest President of the dozen aspirants"; another reporter quipped, "The Democrats have nominated nobody quite like him since Franklin Pierce." Some observers had a higher regard for Roosevelt's running mate, John Nance Garner, who was speaker of the United States House of Representatives. "It's a kangaroo ticket," complained one of the Texan's admirers, "stronger in the hindquarter than in front." Echoing that view, the *Washington Post* editorialized, "It is an odd and embarrassing situation in which the tail of the kite becomes more important and influential than its head."[24]

In advising Roosevelt to stay close to home before the election, Democratic party professionals themselves may have betrayed a lack of confidence in their man. Campaigns do not win elections, they said, reminding Roosevelt that while he and James Cox had barnstormed the country in 1920, the eventual winners had stayed at home. This advice reflected the conventional wisdom, but it probably also concealed fears that Roosevelt lacked the intellectual capacity and physical endurance to withstand the rigors of a national campaign. To prove the skeptics wrong, as well as for the sheer joy of it, Roosevelt decided to wage a vigorous campaign.

Meanwhile, at a gathering some observers compared to a funeral, the Republicans had renominated Herbert Hoover. Although the events of 1932 arrayed them on different sides, the Iowa-born and Stanford-educated incumbent and his challenger had emerged from similar political backgrounds. Both had entered public service during the Progressive Era, in Hoover's case, following a spectacular career as a businessman and international mining engineer. Both had admired Theodore Roosevelt, served under Woodrow Wilson, and identified with the wing of the progressive movement that emphasized honesty and efficiency in government. In 1920, Roosevelt, then assistant secretary of the navy, had expressed to a friend his admiration for Hoover: "He is certainly a wonder, and I wish we could make him President. There couldn't be a better one."[25] According to an associate, long before Roosevelt joined James Cox on the Democratic ticket in 1920, he had hoped for a Hoover-Roosevelt slate. Hoover, however, joined the Republican party and went on to serve with distinction as secretary of commerce in the Harding and Coolidge administrations.

In nominating Hoover for the first time in 1928, the GOP had put forth one of the best-qualified persons ever to seek the presidency. Ironically, if voters had been able to foresee the coming of the depression, they would have had all the more reason to cast their ballots for Hoover, for from his management of Belgian relief during the war to his efforts to aid the victims of the Mississippi River flood in 1927, he had devoted much of his life to the relief of human suffering.

Few presidents upon taking office have offered as much promise of success as Hoover; by the same token, few presidents have fallen from public favor as quickly or as completely as he. By 1932, his very name had become synonymous with inept leadership and callous indifference to human suffering. On the outskirts of cities and towns across the country, little shantytowns appeared, offering shelter to homeless victims of the depression. The residents scornfully referred to their ramshackle communities as Hoovervilles.

Hoover did not deserve all the criticism he received. Contrary to his Nero-like image, he rejected the hands-off approach that most of his predecessors had taken during periods of economic distress. Following the stock market crash, in rapid order, he extracted from the nation's financial and industrial leaders pledges to maintain current production and employment levels; he increased spending for public works; and he eased credit and monetary strictures—all in an attempt to stimulate the economy. At the same time, however, he imposed definite limits on government intervention. Believing that federal relief to the unemployed would destroy the character and initiative of the recipients, he argued that the primary responsibility for meeting the needs of the jobless resided at the state and local level. With an optimistic view of human nature, confirmed by his experience as director of the Belgian relief organization, he maintained that in times of trouble, citizens and groups, acting voluntarily, would assist persons in distress. Hoover possessed a noble but unrealistic vision, for the magnitude of the depression eventually exceeded the ability of voluntary efforts to cope. By 1932, according to one estimate, only one person in four who needed relief actually received it.

In opposing federal relief to the unemployed, Hoover found himself in good company, for most political leaders, including Roosevelt, shared his belief about the debilitating effects of the "dole," as they derisively called it. Roosevelt, who supported a state system of unemployment compensation, also agreed with the president that responsibility for meeting the needs of the jobless rested primarily at the state and local levels. As a practical matter, however, the public heard Roosevelt, as governor, explaining why government should aid the jobless, and Hoover, as president, explaining why it should not.

During the 1932 campaign, Hoover proved to be his own worst enemy. His speeches, delivered in a flat, metallic tone, contained lengthy, fact-filled defenses of his administration. As if to impress audiences with his learning, he used words such as *sisyphean, vacuous, supervened,* and *attenuated.* A British journalist, trying to explain why an audience responded so unenthusiastically to a particular performance of the president, concluded that it was because of "the dispiriting influence of Mr. Hoover's personality, his unprepossessing exterior, his sour, puck-ered face of a bilious baby, his dreary, nasal monotone reading interminably, and for the most part inaudibly, from a typescript without a single inflection of a voice or gesture to relieve the tedium." Gutzon Borglum, the sculptor, fastened on Hoover an unforgettable image when he said, "If you put a rose in Hoover's hand, it would wilt."[26]

The president frequently seemed insensitive to the effect his remarks had upon others. In his home state of Iowa, for instance, where hard times were forcing many farmers to abandon the land, he told an audience that conditions "could be so much worse that these days now . . . would look like veritable prosperity."[27] By July 1932, when army troops routed the so-called Bonus Army of World War I veterans in Washington, D.C., Hoover had become an object of ridicule, scorn, and even hatred. Crowds booed him in Detroit, and they pelted his car with rotten eggs in Nevada. As the president's train passed through southern Wisconsin, authorities arrested a man who was trying to pull up the railroad spikes.

Roosevelt, for his part, waged a cautious campaign. With almost all political experts predicting victory for him, he clearly wanted to avoid saying or doing anything that would alienate any important bloc of voters. One adviser captured the essence of Roosevelt's strategy when he urged the candidate to be discreet when discussing agricultural matters in public, but to assure key farm leaders in private that as president he would "do more than you propose in the platform and your speeches," but that "you cannot say in your speeches all that you will do." Accordingly, Roosevelt spoke in code words and catch phrases, each intended to appeal to one group or another but each falling short of committing himself to a specific course of action. One time, when one set of advisers urged him to come out for high tariffs and another set of advisers for low tariffs, he casually told aides to weave the two seemingly irreconcilable positions together.[28]

On one issue, however, the issue of government spending, he did not equivocate. Accusing Hoover of having engaged in an orgy of spending, Roosevelt promised to reduce federal expenditures by 25 percent. Although some critics later cited his pledge to cut spending as evidence of his insincerity, Roosevelt was merely reflecting the conventional wisdom of the period to which even liberals subscribed: budgets should be balanced.

Despite his frequent equivocations, the Democratic candidate probably managed to convince victims of the depression that he cared more about their suffering than the president did. While Hoover was telling Iowa farmers that things could be worse, Roosevelt was telling Kansas farmers that they lived in the "shadow of peasantry." Upon his return from one campaign trip, Roosevelt told a friend, "I have looked into the faces of thousands of Americans. They have the frightened look of lost children. . . . They are saying: 'we're caught in something we don't understand; perhaps this fellow can help us out.'"[29]

As expected, Roosevelt swept to victory on Election Day. He received 57 percent of the popular vote to 40 percent for Hoover, and he carried 42 states to only 6 for Hoover. "This is the greatest night in my life," the victor declared when he learned the results. Yet the outcome of the election represented only a qualified triumph for Roosevelt. As the editors of *The New Republic* noted, "All informed observers agree that the country did not vote for Roosevelt; it voted against Hoover."[30]

The period between Roosevelt's election in November and his inauguration in March marked the nadir of the depression. After a brief upturn in the summer, the economy plunged to new lows. As winter set in, one out of every four workers desperately searched for employment. Roosevelt had failed to arouse much enthusiasm during the campaign, and little that he did during the interregnum dispelled the prevailing mood of gloom.

Shortly after the election, he rebuffed Hoover's efforts to enlist his cooperation in formulating a joint approach to international monetary and debt problems, both of which had reached the crisis stage. Roosevelt met with the president, but because he disagreed with Hoover's approach to the problem, and because he did not want the president's unpopularity to rub off on him, he refused to be drawn into an agreement. In the eyes of Hoover and his partisans, Roosevelt's refusal to cooperate displayed either profound ignorance of economic realities or a cold-blooded willingness to allow the economy to hit rock bottom rather than to share with the incumbent any credit for recovery.

Nor did Roosevelt's other activities inspire much confidence in his leadership. In February 1933, a month before the inauguration and even as the nation's banking system verged on collapse, the president-elect boarded a luxurious yacht, the *Nourmahal*, for an 11-day Atlantic cruise. As Roosevelt, in the company of Vincent Astor and other wealthy friends, sailed to the Bahamas and Nassau, one columnist quipped that the voyagers had obviously "dismissed from mind . . . the well-known

Forgotten Man!"[31] Roosevelt, it seemed, had not yet fully grasped the importance of appearances in public life.

In this case appearances were deceiving, for behind the scenes he had been busily preparing to assume the presidency. For one thing, he had been discussing possible policies and appointments with a wide variety of persons, including the members of his so-called Brain Trust, the group of university professors and other experts whom he had assembled to advise him during the campaign. Although Roosevelt's association with academicians attracted much attention, he was not the first politician to enter into such an arrangement. At the turn of the century Governor Robert La Follette of Wisconsin had linked the state university with the state government, and at one time or another presidents from Theodore Roosevelt to Herbert Hoover had utilized the services of college professors. Roosevelt's Brain Trust thus marked the culmination, and more systematic use, of a long-standing trend.

One product of the president-elect's deliberations with his advisers stirred little public enthusiasm: the new Cabinet. In making his selections, Roosevelt, like most presidents, sought political, geographic, and religious balance. He did break tradition by appointing as secretary of labor Frances Perkins, the first woman to be nominated for a cabinet position, although the fact that she had no union affiliation caused concern in labor circles. And Roosevelt did appoint other persons of ability and promise, such as Harold L. Ickes for interior; Henry A. Wallace for agriculture; and Cordell Hull for state. Yet with the possible exception of Hull, none of Roosevelt's appointees had a national reputation, and the cabinet as a whole offered little promise of a new deal. By passing over prominent Democrats such as Al Smith and Newton Baker, Roosevelt appeared to have used the selection process to settle old scores and to ensure that he did nothing to boost the careers of potential rivals.

As the inauguration neared, a dramatic incident suddenly caused many people to view Roosevelt in a different light. On the evening of his return from the *Nourmahal* cruise, he appeared in Bay Front Park in Miami and delivered a brief speech. At the end of his remarks, Roosevelt sat in the back seat of his open touring car and chatted briefly with Anton J. Cermak, the mayor of Chicago, who also happened to be visiting the resort city. Suddenly, a short, curly-haired man jumped out of the crowd and, from a distance of no more than 35 feet, fired a pistol at Roosevelt. The assailant missed his target but hit five other persons, including Mayor Cermak. Secret Service agents, fearing the presence of other gunmen, immediately ordered Roosevelt's car to leave the park. As the car sped away, Roosevelt caught a glimpse of the fallen Cermak, and he ordered his driver to return to the scene of the shooting so that he might assist the victims. Roosevelt's car then carried the Chicago mayor to the hospital, while the president-elect cradled the mortally wounded Cermak in his arms. Through it all, Roosevelt remained completely in command of the situation. Later that evening, after all the reporters had left, his aides expected him to betray some sign of the ordeal he had been through. As one of them recalled, however, "There was nothing—not so much as the twitching of a muscle, the mopping of a brow, or even the hint of a false gaiety—to indicate it was any other evening in any other place. Roosevelt was simply himself—easy, confident, poised, to all appearances unmoved." When Roosevelt went to bed, his aides, still reeling from the incident, stayed up for hours talking about what had happened. In the morning, they asked the Secret Service agent who had been stationed outside of Roosevelt's room if the president-elect had been able to sleep. "I was curious myself," the agent replied, "so I stole in several times. Each time Mr. Roosevelt was fast asleep." "I have never seen anything more magnificent," Raymond Moley wrote years later, "than Roosevelt's calm that night."[32]

In a life-and-death situation, Roosevelt had demonstrated remarkable composure and courage. After the incident, some people, perhaps including Roosevelt himself, attached almost religious significance to his brush with death, believing that he must have been spared for a purpose. At the very least, many Americans sensed for the first time that they had elected a better man than they had thought.

4

RISE OF THE NEW DEAL, 1933–1936

During his first term, Franklin Roosevelt, playing a kind of Wizard of Oz role, presided over one of the most creative and constructive periods in the history of American government. "Come at once to Washington," a legislator wired a friend. "Great things are under way."[1] Under the auspices of the New Deal, the national government, while failing to bring full economic recovery, provided needed assistance to the unemployed and other disadvantaged groups and repaired some of the economic structural damage that had helped cause the depression. Furthermore, although democracy was in retreat throughout much of the world, the New Deal reinvigorated the American democratic system, spurring in the process the growth of a voting coalition that would shape national politics for decades to come. Two forces—intertwined but separately important—relentlessly surged through those exciting years: these were the unfolding New Deal measures, and the Roosevelt presence.

Like Abraham Lincoln, Roosevelt assumed office at a time of great national peril. In 1861, Lincoln had faced the prospect of war and disunion; on a cold, drizzling inauguration day in March 1933, Roosevelt confronted the imminent economic collapse of a nation. Worse still, Americans sharply disagreed among themselves over the causes of, and the proposed cures for, the depression. Even the experts seemed hopelessly divided. Some people compared the depression to a natural disaster, such as a hurricane or earthquake, over which society had no control; in their view, government intervention in the economy, except for a little fiscal belt-tightening here and there, would only prolong hard times. Marxists, on the other hand, argued that capitalism had reached the end of its life cycle and that only government ownership of the means of production and strong centralized economic planning would end the nation's misery. Between these two extremes, neither of which commanded much public support, ranged a plethora of views. Many farmers and their spokesmen in Congress, like the Populists of the 1890s, singled out restrictive monetary policies as a major cause of the nation's distress, and they argued that an expansion of the money supply would increase farm prices and farm incomes and ultimately stimulate industrial production. Other persons advocated a fiscal approach, calling upon the government to adopt a combination of spending and taxation policies in an attempt to restore mass purchasing power. They, in turn, were eventually divided into those who would match government outlays by levying taxes, especially on the rich, and those who, influenced by British economist John Maynard Keynes, would deliberately accumulate deficits. Still other persons, drawing upon the experience of the United States during the war, favored a partnership between business and government. Thus, the problem Roosevelt faced at the outset was not a lack of proposed solutions to the depression but an abundance of possible remedies, many of which seemed entirely plausible, given the existing state of economic knowledge. Moreover, because no industrial nation had ever successfully combated so severe and prolonged a depression, historical experience offered almost no help in evaluating the merits of competing proposals for recovery.[2]

Roosevelt had only a vague idea of what he would do, but he nevertheless exuded the confidence of a man who believed that a solution to the depression could be found and that he was the one to find it. Initially, he and his advisers identified agriculture as the key to recovery. Raise farm prices and farm incomes, they believed, and economic revitalization would ultimately follow. With their enhanced purchasing power, farmers, who constituted one-fourth of the population, would buy more goods and services, thereby stimulating business and industry and creating jobs. Meanwhile, before this agriculture-induced recovery had time to take effect, the government had an obligation to provide some relief to the unemployed, preferably in the form of public works, and to maintain the fiscal integrity of the government by curtailing spending.

Roosevelt further believed that to achieve and then sustain recovery, the government needed to encourage city-dwellers to move to less-congested areas of the country so as to provide a better balance between rural and urban populations. Finally, Roosevelt maintained that the depression stemmed in part from a crisis of the spirit and that recovery would require Americans to recommit themselves to moral and religious values. "You know," Roosevelt told James Farley on the eve of the inauguration, "I think a thought to God is the right way to start off my administration. A proper attitude toward religion, and belief in God, will in the end be the salvation of all peoples."[3]

In this spirit, Roosevelt delivered his inaugural address, which, with its memorable assurance that "the only thing we have to fear is fear itself," its excoriation of the "money changers," and its promise of "action and action now," gave the nation a sudden, unexpected boost of confidence. The most striking passages, reflecting Roosevelt's view of the president as moral leader of the nation, called upon people to renounce exclusively material values: "This is a day of national consecration. . . . Happiness lies not in the mere possession of money; it lies in the joy of achievement, in the thrill of creative effort. The joy and moral stimulation of work no longer must be forgotten in the mad chase of evanescent profits. . . . Our true destiny is not to be ministered unto but to minister to ourselves and to our fellow men." The new president received his greatest applause when he said that if Congress did not enact his program or a program of its own, he would "ask Congress for the one remaining instrument to meet the emergency—broad Executive power to wage a war against the emergency, as great as the power that would be given to me if we were in fact invaded by a foreign foe."[4] Millions of Americans heard the address over the radio, and during the ensuing weeks many of them wrote the White House to praise Roosevelt and pledge their support. For a nation rendered numb by the depression, Roosevelt's inaugural provided a huge shot of adrenaline.

Immediately upon taking office, Roosevelt summoned Congress into special session. There ensued the famous Hundred Days, from 9 March to 16 June, during which legislators passed and the president signed some fifteen major recovery and relief measures. This unprecedented productivity seemed to provide something for everyone: the Agricultural Adjustment Act (AAA) offered farmers the promise of higher prices; the National Industrial Recovery Act (NIRA) authorized industries to organize in an effort to eliminate inefficiency and wasteful competition; that same measure recognized the right of labor to organize and engage in collective bargaining; the Federal Emergency Relief Administration (FERA) furnished the unemployed with funds for food, shelter, and clothing; the Public Works Administration (PWA) and the Civilian Conservation Corps (CCC) promised to put the jobless back to work; other measures protected homeowners, bank customers, and stock market investors.[5]

This flurry of legislation, combined with the president's dynamic presence, prompted an immediate and dramatic reassessment of Roosevelt. Early in the first term, two persons who had served with him in the Wilson administration chanced to meet outside the White House. One of them, expressing a nearly unanimous sentiment, said to the other, "That fellow in there is not the fellow we used to know. There's been a miracle here."[6] To a veteran reporter, it seemed as though the oath of office had somehow "transfigured" Roosevelt "from a man of mere charm and buoyancy to one of dynamic aggressiveness."[7] The new president unquestionably deserved praise; and yet many of his new admirers, as if to compensate for having previously underestimated him, now tended to exaggerate his personal accomplishments. At the very least, their view of Roosevelt as mastermind of the entire New Deal—"the boss, the dynamo, the works," as one reporter put it—overlooked the contributions of other key participants in the legislative assault on the depression, especially members of Congress, whom he followed more often than he led.[8] This view also obscured Roosevelt's own stated preference for moral and inspirational leadership and public education, as opposed to legislative craftsmanship.

Although Roosevelt dominated the public spotlight during the Hundred Days, only two of the 15 measures enacted, the Economy Act and a bill creating the Civilian Conservation Corps, actually originated with him. The Economy Act, which cut the pensions of veterans and the salaries of federal employees and thereby further eroded mass purchasing power, not only partially fulfilled Roosevelt's campaign pledge to reduce government spending but also reflected his own conventional views on fiscal matters. The president's other major handiwork, the CCC, which employed 500,000 young men, most of them city dwellers, on conservation projects, reflected Roosevelt's long-standing interest in preserving natural resources and in achieving a better balance between urban and rural populations. Other New Deal measures, however, far from being the brainchild of one person, evolved from a richly collaborative process involving not only the president but also members of Congress, representatives of well-organized interest groups, presidential aides, and government bureaucrats. Of these participants in the New Deal, Congress played the most important role in shaping the legislation of the Hundred Days.

At least since Reconstruction, Congress had been a perennial target of public ridicule and scorn and a favorite subject for American humorists. Thus Mark Twain had written: "It could probably be shown by facts and figures that there is no distinctly native American criminal class except Congress." Some 40 years later, Will Rogers quipped that Americans had "come to feel the same when Congress is in session as we do when the baby gets hold of a hammer. It's just a question of how much damage he can do with it before we can take it away from him."[9]

Such unflattering characterizations certainly did not apply to the Seventy-third Congress, which convened in March 1933, or to its successors during the Roosevelt administration. In terms of their accomplishments and the overall quality of their members, these Congresses probably equaled, if they did not surpass, the record of any previous Congress in American history. Charles A. Beard, the most prominent historian of the time, compared one of the New Deal Congresses with Congress during the early days of the Republic and concluded that "for disinterestedness, absence of corruption, and concern with the public good, the present body is of a higher order." Beard also found that congressional floor debates during the New Deal produced speeches that "for breadth of knowledge, technical skill, analytical acumen, close reasoning and dignified presentation, compare favorably with similar utterances made in the preceding century by the so-called great orators."[10]

To be sure, no legislators of the stature and influence of Daniel Webster, Henry Clay, or John C. Calhoun sat in Congress during the New Deal. But its members did include persons of uncommon intelligence, high-mindedness, and creativity, such as Sens. Hugo Black, Robert M. La Follette, Jr., George W. Norris, and Robert F. Wagner, and Reps. Fiorello La Guardia, David J. Lewis, Maury Maverick, and Sam Rayburn. The Democrats commanded majorities in both houses of Congress. In the Senate, leadership fell to the quick-tempered but able Joseph T. Robinson of Arkansas, and in the House, to a devoted follower of William Jennings Bryan, Speaker Henry T. Rainey of Illinois. In both houses, southern Democrats controlled most of the key committee chairmanships, and as long as the race issue did not arise, they supported the New Deal. The minority party, for its part, proved unusually cooperative, especially in the Senate, where Republican leader Charles L. McNary, a veteran of the farm relief battles of the 1920s, maintained a moderate course and where progressive Republicans such as La Follette, Norris, and Bronson Cutting played key roles in the formulation of New Deal legislation.[11]

During the Hundred Days, Congress, nearly half of whose members had been elected to office after the beginning of the depression, accepted Roosevelt's inaugural challenge to formulate a recovery program. Consequently, most of the legislation originated in, or took shape in response to, the national legislature. The Federal Emergency Relief Act, which appropriated $500 million for relief to the jobless and probably touched more lives than almost any other early New Deal program, was a major case in point. The struggle for federal assistance to the unemployed had begun in the fall of 1931, when Hoover was president. Then, several prominent social workers had gone from door to door on Capitol Hill pleading with legislators to sponsor relief legislation. Three lawmakers responded: Robert M. La Follette, Jr., heir to Wisconsin's famous political dynasty and, at 36, the youngest member of the Senate; Edward P. Costigan, a quietly effective Democratic senator from Colorado; and Rep. David J. Lewis of Maryland, a genuine self-made man, who, at age nine, had gone to work in a Pennsylvania coal mine and at age 16 had taught himself to read and write not only in English but also in French and German. The La Follette-Costigan-Lewis bill had assumed various forms and passed through several stages of consideration, gathering more and more supporters at each stage. Finally, in the summer of 1932, during the waning months of the Hoover administration, Congress had passed, and Hoover had signed, a scaled-down compromise, the Emergency Relief and Construction Act, which authorized loans to the states for relief purposes. Passage of the measure represented the crossing of an ideological Rubicon; for the first time, the federal government had formally, if grudgingly, accepted responsibility for the plight of the unemployed. Thus, by the time Roosevelt entered the White House, the passage of additional federal relief bills had become a certainty, and the measure that finally did pass conformed closely to the original La Follette-Costigan-Lewis proposal.[12]

In addition to relief legislation, Congress created two key New Deal institutions that became identified in the public mind with the president: the Federal Deposit Insurance Corporation (FDIC) and the Tennessee Valley Authority (TVA). In the case of the FDIC, the brainchild of Sen. Arthur Vandenberg of Michigan, Rep. Henry Steagall of Alabama, and others, Roosevelt originally frowned on the idea of federal insurance for bank deposits, saying that such a practice would protect bad banks as well as good ones. He reversed himself when it became clear that Congress would pass the measure with or without his approval. On the other hand, in the case of the TVA, for which Sen. George Norris of Nebraska and the progressive bloc in Congress had been fighting for many years, Roosevelt not only enthusiastically supported its creation but broadened its scope to include regional planning and development.[13]

Several times, congressional initiatives prodded the administration into action. Thus, for example, Roosevelt put forth the national industrial recovery bill in part to head off a movement led by Sen. Hugo Black of Alabama to create new jobs by limiting the hours of work in factories to 30 per week. The president also required prodding to support public works. During his first months in office, he blew hot and cold on the idea of large-scale government construction projects to stimulate the economy. One day, for example, he told several legislators that he not only favored public works, but he wanted them to draft the appropriate legislation; two days later, he told reporters that he doubted that public works would do much to stimulate the economy. The legislators, puzzled by Roosevelt's apparent reversal, decided to force his hand, and in May Sens. La Follette, Costigan, and Bronson Cutting introduced a $6 billion public works bill, the largest single proposed expenditure for public works up to that time. In response to these and other demands for public employment, the president incorporated into his national industrial recovery measure an appropriation of $3.3 billion for federal works projects.

Still another feature of the early New Deal, monetary policy, also bore the indelible stamp of congressional initiative. During the Hundred Days, inflationary pressures intensified in Congress. Representatives from farming and silver-mining states, who hoped to stimulate economic recovery by increasing the money supply, advocated measures ranging from the issuance of greenbacks, to the reduction of the gold content of the dollar, to government purchases of large quantities of silver. Roosevelt, who feared an epidemic of uncontrolled inflation, eventually utilized a variety of devices to ward off more drastic action by Congress.[14]

For the most part, the relationship between Roosevelt and Congress functioned smoothly. With no detailed recovery plan of his own, Roosevelt, unlike Hoover, frequently encouraged the legislative branch to assume the initiative. To the extent that he involved himself in the details of legislative matters, he served as a moderating force, as he did in the case of monetary policy.

Although Congress played the leading role, representatives from well-organized interest groups and members of the Roosevelt administration also helped shape the legislation of the Hundred Days. In the case of the Agricultural Adjustment Act, the cornerstone of the administration's farm policy, Secretary of Agriculture Henry A. Wallace summoned to Washington representatives of the nation's most powerful farm organizations, including the American Farm Bureau Federation. They proceeded to hammer out an agreement acceptable to most farm interests. Similarly, in writing the National Industrial Recovery Act, the centerpiece of the New Deal's recovery program, administration officials worked closely with spokesmen for big business. In fact, although that recovery measure had diverse origins, in its final form it closely resembled a plan for government-industry cooperation emanating from the nation's leading business organization, the United States Chamber of Commerce.[15]

Just as the formulation of New Deal legislation involved a collaborative effort, so, too, did its execution. Many measures that Congress enacted invested the executive branch of government with broad, probably unprecedented, powers to implement the law. The Agricultural Adjustment Act, for example, allowed the president to choose from among a half dozen or so different approaches to aiding farmers. Roosevelt, in turn, delegated a good deal of authority over the day-to-day operations of government to trusted cabinet members and other subordinates, such as Hugh S. Johnson, the gruff, outspoken head of the National Recovery Administration (NRA); Jesse Jones, director of the Reconstruction Finance Corporation (RFC) and perhaps the most underrated member of the administration; Harold Ickes, the combative but highly competent secretary of the interior and director of the Public Works Administration (PWA); and Henry Wallace, the secretary of agriculture, whom one reporter later described as "a man immensely knowledgeable about farm problems but a mystic and an unreliable oddity when too far from the furrow and the manure pile."[16] Later, after Roosevelt's first treasury secretary, William Woodin, resigned due to ill health, Henry Morgenthau, Jr., Roosevelt's close friend and Dutchess County neighbor, played an important role in monetary and taxation matters.

In time, the most influential member of the administration was Harry L. Hopkins, who at age 43 headed the Federal Emergency Relief Administration (FERA), the first of many posts he occupied during the Roosevelt years. The son of an Iowa harness maker, Hopkins combined a cynical view of politics and politicians with a social worker's concern for the poor. A brilliant administrator, with a knack for cutting through red tape, he disbursed more than $5 million in relief to the unemployed during his first two hours on the job. Hopkins could be studiously irrev-erent, tactless, and abrasive, and he took particular delight in deflating the pretensions of the self-satisfied. But these very qualities, along with his intelligence, his basic decency, and above all his ability to get things done without fuss, made him a presidential favorite. Reporter Raymond Clapper captured the essence of the Roosevelt-Hopkins relationship. "Many New Dealers have bored Roosevelt with their solemn earnest-ness," Clapper recorded. "Hopkins never does. He knows instinctively when to ask, when to keep still, when to press, when to hold back; when to approach Roosevelt direct, when to go at him roundabout." On the negative side, Hopkins, who probably aspired to succeed Roosevelt in the White House, displayed a weakness for palace intrigue. He was, in the words of one White House insider, "an Iowan combination of Mach-iavelli, Svengali, and Rasputin."[17] Hopkins also acquired a habit of tell-ing Roosevelt what the president wanted to hear and not always what he needed to hear.

In terms of competence, integrity, dedication, and diversity of back-ground, members of the Roosevelt administration set a high standard, especially below the cabinet level and through the middle ranks of the burgeoning bureaucracy. To be sure, time-servers and opportunists also found their way into the New Deal conglomerate, but they came in fewer numbers than usual. Noting the type of people that flocked to Washing-ton to work in the New Deal, literary critic Edmund Wilson wrote, "Everywhere in the streets and offices you run into old acquaintances: the editors and writers of the liberal press, the 'progressive' young instruc-tors from the colleges, the intelligent foundation workers, the practical idealists of settlement houses." Wilson added that "the bright boys of the Eastern universities, instead of being obliged to choose, as they were twenty years ago, between business, the bond-selling game and the field of foreign missions, can come on and get jobs in Washington." Wilson might also have added that the New Deal attracted bright young women, who, inspired in part by the activities of Eleanor Roosevelt and Frances Perkins, found in the Roosevelt administration unprecedented opportu-nities for service.[18]

The strength of Roosevelt's supporting cast, both in Congress and in the executive branch, enabled him to concentrate on the functions he believed lay at the heart of the presidency: moral leadership and pub-lic education. "I want to be a preaching president—like my cousin," he said. The presidency, he explained another time, "is not merely an administrative office. That's the least of it. It is more than an engineering job, efficient or inefficient. It is predominantly a place of moral leadership." He added, "Isn't that what the office is—a superb opportunity for reapplying, applying in new conditions, the simple rules of human conduct we always go back to?"[19]

In his capacity as moral leader, Roosevelt delivered essentially the same message he had been delivering since his days as editor of the *Harvard Crimson.* People must demonstrate care and compassion for one another and subordinate self-interest to the general interest. Thus, he pleaded with businessmen to have "the vision to lay aside special and selfish interests," and he told clergymen that economic recovery depended upon "a willingness to sacrifice individual gains, to work together for the public welfare." Roosevelt also encouraged a revival of religious sentiment. "I doubt," he once said, "if there is any problem—social, political or economic—that would not melt away before the fire of such a spiritual awakening."[20] In promoting religion, Roosevelt intended not to dampen but to deepen concern for worldly matters, for he took as his inspiration the New Testament's emphasis on social responsibility, and he expected others to do the same.

Behind Roosevelt's preachments lay a vision of an ideal society toward which he wanted the United States to move. In this society, a kind of Christian commonwealth, the golden rule would govern human conduct, and people would live in harmony among themselves and with nature. The physical setting of Roosevelt's earthly paradise combined the advantages of both urban and rural life. It would afford its citizens plenty of elbow room but also convenient access to work and to the modern conveniences of life. Citizens would enjoy as their right a decent standard of living and, insofar as possible, protection from the physical hazards of life. Yet Roosevelt did not envisage an egalitarian society. Distinctions based on birth, wealth, talent, and race would persist in his well-ordered world, but they would run in tandem with—and be moderated by—a sense of interdependence and mutual respect.

In addition to moral leadership, Roosevelt viewed public education as an essential function of the presidency, and as he had done as governor, he regularly furnished the public with explanations of, and rationales for, the actions of his administration. "The whole fate of what the Government is trying to do," he said, depended "on an understanding of the program by the mass of the people." His "fireside chats," press conferences, speeches, and messages to Congress contained explanations of government actions so straightforward and logical that they made sense out of a bewildering multitude of events. Thus, for example, he described the goals of his administration as relief, recovery, and reform; although these goals were no different from Hoover's, Roosevelt's alliterative phrasing provided a compelling way of looking at the New Deal and suggested a clear sense of order and direction. Roosevelt, said historian Charles A. Beard, "has discussed in his messages and addresses more fundamental problems of American life and society than all the other Presidents combined."[21] Roosevelt also had an aptitude for choosing vivid metaphors and similes, and when he compared himself to a quarterback whose play calling depended on the outcome of the previous play, he perfectly captured the experimental nature of the New Deal. Roosevelt's addresses dispelled the mystery surrounding government affairs and gave the public an insider's sense of participation; but they also implied that the New Deal had a degree of conscious planning and direction that it actually did not possess, and they exaggerated the importance of the president in shaping events.

During the Hundred Days, as Congress hammered out the details of New Deal legislation, Roosevelt devoted nearly as much attention to foreign affairs as to domestic matters, although his debut as a world strategist met with much less success than his debut as national leader. Upon assuming office, Roosevelt raised the hopes of internationalists whom he had disappointed by abandoning the League of Nations during the campaign. In a series of meetings at the White House, he conferred with representatives from Great Britain, France, Canada, China, Japan, and a half-dozen Latin American countries. In these meetings Roosevelt discussed the possibilities of collective efforts to combat the worldwide depression, reduce armaments, and deter aggression. He also displayed for the first time his personalized style of diplomacy: he met alone with most of the foreign dignitaries, and he made no effort to keep records of the proceedings. Secretary of State Hull eventually learned the details of the meetings not from Roosevelt but from his contacts in foreign embassies. "I fear we are doomed to many improvisations from this regime," J. Pierrepont Moffat, an assistant secretary of state, noted in his diary. "But," Moffat added, "the country is thriving on them."[22]

Nothing came of Roosevelt's early forays into international relations, for even as he was meeting with foreign leaders, he was endorsing monetary, debt, and other domestic policies that were incompatible with any long-term international agreements. Roosevelt made his commitment to nationalism official in June 1933, when he scuttled the World Economic Conference, which he himself had done much to tout. His blistering "bombshell" message repudiated monetary stabilization, the formulation of a fixed ratio between the American dollar and foreign currencies. This not only broke up the conference but earned for Roosevelt a reputation for unreliability in foreign diplomatic circles. In truth, the conference was probably doomed before it began. None of the major participants, least of all the United States, was willing to reach an agreement except on its own terms, and those respective terms were largely incompatible. But Roosevelt, with his indefatigable optimism, had raised hopes in the United States and in Europe that the conference might somehow perform miracles. Then he dashed those hopes with his bombshell message.

Roosevelt demonstrated before and during the conference that he did not fully understand the issues at stake, for some of his statements contained inaccuracies and contradictions. This lack of understanding was no crime in itself, for the complexities of international finance defied easy comprehension. But his apparent belief that he had mastered the intricate details of the subject, coupled with his ability to convince others that he knew more about certain subjects than he actually did, contributed to the false expectations and ultimately to the bitter disillusionment that accompanied the World Economic Conference. All in all, Roosevelt's debut on the world scene was not an auspicious one.[23]

When the Hundred Days ended in June, Roosevelt believed that he and the Congress had put together a program that, with a little tinkering here and there, would lift the country out of the depression. Hence, when Congress reconvened in 1934, the president did not seem as receptive to major legislative initiatives as he had been at the outset of his administration. He did support important measures that created the Securities and Exchange Commission (SEC) to regulate the stock market, insured home loans by private lenders, devalued the dollar in hopes of raising prices, and empowered the president to negotiate reciprocal trade agreements with foreign nations. Beyond these, however, he refused to go, as he demonstrated during the debate over public works. In November 1933, Harry Hopkins had complained to Roosevelt that the Public Works Administration, under the direction of Harold Ickes, had been much too slow to set up works projects. After five months in operation, Hopkins pointed out, the PWA had employed fewer than 1 million out of some 10 to 12 million jobless. In fact, Roosevelt, who had little faith in public works as an economic stimulus, had put Ickes in charge of the PWA precisely because he knew that "Honest Harold" would move cautiously in initiating construction projects and thereby would avoid even the hint of scandal that might accompany the expenditure of such large amounts of money. In any event, Hopkins argued that with winter coming on, something had to be done to help the jobless, and he persuaded the president to divert money from the PWA to a new agency under his control, the Civil Works Administration (CWA). In contrast to Ickes, Hopkins acted with lightning speed, putting 4 million people to work building or improving highways, schools, airports, parks, and other public facilities. The imaginative Hopkins also utilized the specialized skills of out-of-work teachers, artists, and writers. The most successful work relief program of the entire New Deal, the CWA pumped nearly $1 billion into the economy, augmenting, directly or indirectly, the buying power of at least 12 million persons and stimulating industrial production.

The very success of the CWA probably led to its undoing, for it directly challenged the belief that work done by private enterprise was by nature more useful and efficient than work done by government. Conservative critics generalized from a few isolated instances of corruption and inefficiency in CWA ranks and condemned the entire program. In response, Roosevelt decided to phase out the CWA as soon as possible. The cost of the program bothered Roosevelt, but so too did the prospect of creating a permanent class of persons dependent for their livelihood on the federal government. In words that would have gratified Herbert Hoover, Roosevelt told advisers that if the CWA continued much longer, it would "become a habit with the country. . . . We must not take the position that we are going to have permanent depression in this country, and it is very important that we have somebody to say that quite forcefully to these people." When Roosevelt announced his intention to scuttle the CWA, supporters of public works in Congress fought to save the agency, but to no avail. At the president's direction, Hopkins dismantled the CWA as quickly as he had set it up, and by April 1934, the 4 million men and women who had worked on agency projects found themselves out of work and back on the relief rolls.[24]

Roosevelt's decision to scuttle the CWA demonstrates the near impossibility of characterizing his approach to the depression. During the 1932 campaign he had called for experimentation. He would try one thing, he said, and if that didn't work, he would try something else. Commentators called this approach pragmatism, by which they meant

59

practicality. By any objective standard, the CWA experiment worked. It provided relief, and it stimulated the economy. Yet at the peak of its success, Roosevelt chose to abandon it. At the same time, he chose to continue programs whose results were much less positive, such as the National Industrial Recovery Act.

In addition to the proposal to extend the CWA, two important measures designed exclusively to boost the well-being of the wage-earning segment of the work force languished on Capitol Hill for want of presidential support. In each case, Roosevelt found himself at odds with a fellow New Yorker, Sen. Robert F. Wagner. Born in Germany and raised in a working-class neighborhood in New York City's Upper East Side, Wagner had ascended through the ranks of Tammany, serving first in the state legislature, then on the state supreme court, and finally in the United States Senate, where, as the author of a half-dozen or so enduring pieces of legislation, he achieved great distinction. Years before, during their joint service in the state senate, the two New Yorkers had frequently crossed swords, and, although they had long since become political allies, they remained slightly wary of each other.[25]

The first of Wagner's legislative initiatives in 1934 sought to address an increasingly urgent labor problem. Following the passage of the NIRA in 1933, organized labor had made some impressive advances, even managing to gain a foothold in such bastions of anti-unionism as the automobile and steel industries. By 1934, however, many industries had launched all-out efforts to block any further labor gains. Some industries established employer-dominated unions—"kiss-me clubs," workers scornfully called them. Other industries were less discreet; they resorted to brute force, employing such practices as industrial espionage, the stockpiling of munitions, and strikebreaking in an attempt to block the growth of organized labor. Consequently, labor-management disputes increasingly flared into violence, and in 1934 alone, 46 workers died as a result of clashes with local authorities and company guards. From Philadelphia to California's Salinas Valley and from Milwaukee to Trion, Georgia, labor turbulence shook whole communities. In May 1934, striking workers at Toledo's Auto-Light factory fought pitched battles with bayonet-bearing national guardsmen. In July, when San Francisco police killed two strikers, workers brought the Bay City to a standstill. Also that month clashes between workers and authorities in Minneapolis produced sickening scenes of violence. An eyewitness told of seeing one man "stepping on his own intestines, bright and bursting in the street, and another holding his severed arm in his right hand."[26]

As industrial warfare intensified, it became abundantly clear that the prolabor provisions of the NIRA offered inadequate protection to workers who wanted to organize. Wagner introduced a labor relations bill not only in an attempt to bring harmony to the workplace but also to boost the economy, for he believed that unionization would lead to higher wages and thereby increase mass purchasing power. Roosevelt remained unmoved by Wagner's arguments. Viewing the bill as class legislation and preferring moral suasion to coercion, the president persuaded the disappointed New York senator to defer action until a future session of Congress.

Roosevelt similarly rebuffed legislative efforts to create a federal-state system of unemployment compensation. Proponents argued that just as people needed health insurance as a hedge against illness, so, too, they needed unemployment insurance as a hedge against another of modern life's uncertainties. Congress had been debating the issue since the Hoover administration, and by 1934, a majority of its members favored unemployment compensation in some form or other. Although proponents disagreed among themselves over funding mechanisms, they united in support of a bill introduced by Wagner and Rep. David Lewis of Maryland that would encourage the states to experiment with compensation systems of their own. Wagner and Lewis had every reason to believe that the president's endorsement would be forthcoming, for he had supported the principle of unemployment insurance since his governorship, and had already approved an earlier version of the bill. As time went on, however, Roosevelt had second thoughts, and in the summer he withdrew his support from the bill, saying that the entire issue needed further study. Even though he promised to support an even more comprehensive measure the following year, proponents of unemployment compensation threw up their hands in frustration. "One cannot be too optimistic about the future promises of persons who are instrumental in blocking present progress," complained one of the framers of the Wagner-Lewis bill.[27]

Still a third measure, the Costigan-Wagner anti-lynching bill, died due to lack of presidential support. Although the lynching of blacks by white mobs, mostly in the South, had long been a national scandal, the depression seemed to exacerbate racial tensions. In 1933 alone, 28 such incidents occurred. For decades, the National Association for the Advancement of Colored People (NAACP) had been seeking legislation to make lynching a federal offense, and in 1934 the organization's leaders decided to try again. They knew, however, that without strong presidential backing, antilynching legislation would fall victim to a filibuster by southern Democrats in the Senate. They had reason to believe that Roosevelt would be sympathetic, for he had condemned lynching in his State of the Union address and in other public pronouncements. Yet despite intense lobbying by congressional sponsors of the bill, NAACP director Walter White, and Eleanor Roosevelt, the president refused to throw himself into the fight and thereby doomed the bill to defeat. Even if Roosevelt had intervened, he probably would not have been able to achieve a favorable outcome; moreover, as he feared, he almost certainly would have alienated southern congressmen whose support he needed for other legislation. Nevertheless, his decision to remain aloof from the battle not only disappointed many of his liberal supporters but also demonstrated the self-imposed limitations of his moral leadership.

In fairness to Roosevelt, his refusal to involve himself in the anti-lynching fight did not reflect the entire record of his administration on race relations. Although some New Deal programs, such as the National Industrial Recovery and the Agricultural Adjustment acts, imposed hardships on blacks, other programs, especially in the areas of relief and public works, provided them with needed assistance. Moreover, some members of the administration, most notably, Interior Secretary Harold Ickes and Eleanor Roosevelt, warmly embraced the crusade for civil rights. The record of the Roosevelt administration in regard to minorities seemed exceedingly modest by later standards, but by 1934, the New Deal had done enough that many blacks were beginning to reexamine their traditional affiliation with the party of Lincoln.[28]

By the time Congress adjourned in the summer of 1934, the nation was experiencing unusual political turbulence. Sen. Huey P. Long, of Louisiana had founded the "Share Our Wealth" movement and was alarming liberals and conservatives alike by attracting millions of supporters, especially in the South. A 67-year-old California doctor, Francis Townsend, was organizing millions of elderly citizens in a crusade for old-age pensions; every week 40 million listeners, located mostly in northeastern and midwestern industrial centers, were tuning in to hear radio priest Father Charles Coughlin castigate the money power; on the West Coast, novelist Upton Sinclair was attracting a large following with his End Poverty in California movement and his "production-for-use" platform. Third-party movements in the Midwest—Floyd Olson's Farmer-Laborites in Minnesota and Robert and Philip La Follette's Progressives in Wisconsin—seemed to portend further challenges to the two-party system. Although the leaders of all of these movements offered far-reaching proposals, such as Huey Long's plan to confiscate great wealth, the movements themselves did not fit neatly into established ideological categories. Many observers at the time and some historians later viewed these insurgent movements as evidence of radical fervor among the masses. To a great extent, however, a vision of a simpler society, one untouched by the depersonalizing effects of big cities, big business, and big government, lay at the heart of these protests. As such, they represented reactions to modernization as much as, or more than, a fundamental dissatisfaction with capitalism. But whatever their ideological moorings, Long, Coughlin, Townsend, and the others drew to their banners millions of persons, who, in this, the fifth year of the depression, were searching desperately for a solution to their plight.[29]

During 1934, vocal segments of the business community also began to express strong dissatisfaction with the course of events. Although Roosevelt retained many friends in industrial and financial circles, most businessmen, if they thought very long about it, could find something in the New Deal to which they strenuously objected. Some railed at the president for failing to fulfill his campaign pledge to balance the budget. They rallied behind Lewis Douglas, the conservative director of the budget, who, believing that continued deficits threatened the fate of Western civilization, resigned from the government out of frustration with Roosevelt's fiscal policies. Businessmen also complained about the president's abandonment of the gold standard and his subsequent currency manipulations, his supposed coddling of organized labor, and New Deal regulatory agencies such as the Securities and Exchange Commission.

Criticism from business and conservative quarters became increasingly strident in tone. It disturbed and baffled Roosevelt, for he believed that business had fared well under the New Deal. After all, corporate profits had increased since 1933, the government had levied no new taxes on corporate wealth, and one of the New Deal's major programs, the NIRA, had given to businesses exactly what they had been clamoring for, the freedom to regulate themselves. Moreover, the administration, through Jesse Jones's Reconstruction Finance Corporation, had spent as much money on direct subsidies to failing banks and businesses as it had on assistance to the unemployed in the form of relief and public works.

In the face of growing unrest on all sides, Roosevelt seemed to falter. When Congress convened in 1935, he had all he could do to prevent a full-scale rebellion against his leadership in the national legislature. Although lawmakers approved his request for $5 billion for public works, which led to the creation of the famous Works Progress Administration

(WPA), congressional insurgents almost succeeded in attaching to the measure a provision that would have required the administration to pay workers on federal projects the prevailing wage in various sections of the country, thus placing the government in direct competition with private industry for labor services. Only an all-out effort by Roosevelt's allies prevented the provision from becoming law. The administration failed to head off a movement to restore the cuts in veterans' pensions that he had made two years earlier; Congress passed the measure over Roosevelt's veto. Finally, the Senate dealt the president the single biggest defeat of his first term when it refused his request for American membership in the World Court, an adjunct of the League of Nations.

Although Roosevelt remained personally popular with most Americans, some Washington observers began to wonder if their earlier unfavorable assessments of the president had not been right all along. In March 1935, Walter Lippmann said, "We have come to a period of discouragement after a few months of buoyant hope. Pollyanna is silenced and Cassandra is doing all the talking. . . . Within the Administration itself there is a notable loss of self-confidence which is reflected in leadership that is hesitant and confused."[30] Lippmann might have been expected to find fault with the president, if only to save face after his now-famous "pleasant man" column. But many of Roosevelt's friends were saying the same thing, and some of them feared that if he did not take the initiative, he would have difficulty getting reelected in 1936.

Finally, during the summer of 1935, a combination of factors forced Roosevelt's hand. Criticism of the president from conservative quarters was growing increasingly strident; Huey Long, Father Coughlin, and Dr. Townsend continued to talk about the possibility of a third party in the 1936 elections; and the Supreme Court overturned the NIRA. Through all of these tribulations, Roosevelt's supporters pleaded with him to seize control of events while he still could. In June, just as legislators were preparing to leave the capital for the summer, Roosevelt suddenly insisted that they postpone adjournment until they had passed four key measures: a bill curbing the spread of holding companies, a banking-reform measure, the Wagner labor proposal, and a social-security bill. A week later, he added tax reform to his "must" list. There ensued a period of legislative activity comparable to that of the first Hundred Days.

Although Roosevelt provided this impetus to their final passage, most of the enactments of the second Hundred Days developed independently of the president, as had those of the first Hundred Days. For example, the National Labor Relations Act, or Wagner Act, which guaranteed to labor the right to organize and engage in collective bargaining, was the very same measure that Roosevelt had persuaded Senator Wagner to shelve a year before. In 1935, the New York senator reintroduced the bill, and Roosevelt eventually put it on his "must" list, but only after the Senate had already acted favorably upon the measure and the House seemed certain to do the same. The president, Labor Secretary Frances Perkins later recalled, "never lifted a finger" for the measure. "All the credit for it belongs to Wagner." Similarly, after calling for reform of the nation's banking system, Roosevelt showed little interest in the details of what became a major reform of the Federal Reserve system as it made its way through Congress.[31]

The most controversial item on Roosevelt's "must" list, tax reform, underscored his personal preference for moral preachment to legislative craftsmanship. In June, sounding like Huey Long, the president told Congress that vast accumulations of personal wealth, especially in the form of inherited wealth, threatened democratic values. The people had every right to rectify this situation, Roosevelt said, for they had been silent partners in the creation of great American fortunes. To strike at the concentration of wealth, Roosevelt urged Congress to increase taxes along progressive lines. Roosevelt's message heartened liberals, including Long, and angered conservatives, who dubbed his proposals a "soak the successful" scheme. But then, during the ensuing commotion, Roosevelt performed one of those maneuvers that over the years exasperated his supporters, kept his opponents off balance, and earned him a reputation for inscrutability. Although he had submitted to Congress a detailed list of proposals, he had not specified any timetable for congressional consideration of them. When administration floor leaders and reporters sought him out for clarification, he made himself conspicuously unavailable for comment, leading to speculation that he would not press for tax reform during the current session of Congress. Only an ingenious series of moves by a small band of Senate progressives, led by Wisconsin's La Follette, salvaged the president's proposals before adjournment. On the face of it, the resulting Wealth Tax Act of 1935 hardly seemed worth all the fuss. It did increase gift and estate taxes, impose the highest and most progressive income surtax rates in history, and levy a variety of corporate taxes. But it contained no inheritance tax, and considered in conjunction with other New Deal tax laws, it had a negligible impact on the distribution of the nation's wealth.[32]

The new law fell far short of Roosevelt's own announced goals, but all along he had seemed more interested in its political and symbolic impact than in any leveling effects it might have had. According to several of his aides, he hoped that his proposals would undercut support for Huey Long—"stealing Huey's thunder," as he put it. Roosevelt also reputedly told friends that to preserve capitalism and to combat the "crackpot ideas" of Long and others, "it may be necessary to throw to the wolves the forty-six men who are reported to have incomes in excess of one million dollars a year."[33] More important, Roosevelt almost certainly intended tax reform—much as Theodore Roosevelt had intended his infrequent, but much publicized, attempts at trust-busting—to assert the primacy of the national interest over private interests and to warn of what might be in store for those who persisted in their selfish and socially irresponsible ways. In Franklin Roosevelt's case, the warning had little effect, for the Wealth Tax Act, despite its modest impact, only solidified opposition to the New Deal from entrenched wealth.

In the case of the Social Security Act, which established systems for old-age and survivors' insurance and unemployment compensation, Roosevelt simultaneously encouraged the formulation of a program and limited the scope of the final product. By the mid-1930s, 125 foreign countries and 18 states provided some form of assistance to the elderly. By that time, too, legislators had introduced into Congress bills to establish systems for old-age insurance and unemployment compensation. To coordinate these ongoing legislative activities, Roosevelt created a cabinet-level committee to develop an economic security program, and in 1935 he urged Congress to enact the committee's recommendations.

Roosevelt was no latecomer to the cause of social security. For many years, he had been arguing, often eloquently, that society had an obligation to protect its citizens from the vicissitudes of modern life, and in doing so he had helped create public support for a government-sponsored social security system. Privately, he told aides that he favored a comprehensive cradle-to-grave program, presumably including national health insurance. Given Roosevelt's enthusiastic support for the cause, some proponents of social security expressed surprise and deep disappointment when, in the final accounting, he helped limit the scope of the program. For one thing, fearful that too broad a program would lessen the likelihood of its passage, he successfully opposed inclusion in the bill of a national health insurance provision. He also insisted that a special tax on the earnings of currently employed workers, rather than income taxes, should provide the principal source of funding for the old-age insurance system established by the new law. Critics of the president's funding plan argued that a payroll tax was unfair because it would impose the heaviest burden on those persons least able to afford it; critics also argued that a payroll tax would remove billions of dollars of purchasing power from the masses and retard economic recovery. Roosevelt held firm, however, arguing that his plan would protect the Social Security system from future political assault. "We put those payroll contributions there so as to give the contributors a legal, moral, and political right to collect their pensions and their unemployment benefits," he explained, adding, "with those taxes in there, no damn politician can ever scrap my social security program."[34]

Despite its limitations, the Social Security system ranks among the most important and enduring achievements of the New Deal. Although modest in its original form, it provided a base upon which future generations constructed a modern welfare state. Moreover, Roosevelt's controversial financing scheme probably did help shield the system from conservative assault.

Then and later, many observers thought that they detected a significant shift in emphasis from the first to the second Hundred Days, although the precise nature of that shift remained in dispute. Some believed that during the latter period, Roosevelt moved to the left of the political spectrum. Whereas once he had sought to appeal to all of the people, including the rich and well born, now he directed his attention to the disadvantaged classes. Other observers, however, argued that the administration moved in a conservative direction, conservative in the sense that it abandoned central economic planning, as embodied in the NIRA, in favor of a regulated yet competitive marketplace. Ideological considerations unquestionably did occupy the attention of many of Roosevelt's advisers and cohorts in Congress. Yet the president remained largely removed from these debates, and while in 1935 he added a little fire and brimstone to his sermons, his central message remained the same.

In August 1935, Roosevelt's call for a "breathing spell" from any new initiatives signified the end of one of the most productive periods in American legislative history. Although Congress and the administration would add important details during succeeding years, by 1935, they had completed the basic structure of the New Deal. The critics were right, of course: the New Deal did display conspicuous flaws. No consistent economic or fiscal philosophy lay behind it, and as a result some of its programs worked at cross-purposes. Other programs, such as the NIRA, which Roosevelt described as the cornerstone of the New Deal, fell far short of their objectives. Indeed, in 1935, when the Supreme Court overturned the NIRA, its decision was more in the nature of a mercy killing than a mortal blow to a vital government agency. Then, too, for all the talk of social and economic justice, critics were right in saying that persons of property and substance often received a disproportionate share of New Deal benefits. Indeed, for every dollar the government spent on unemployment relief and public works, it spent another dollar subsidizing banks and businesses. In the case of the Agricultural Adjustment Act, large landowners and commercial farmers in the South reaped the lion's share of government payments, while the poorest of the poor—sharecroppers and tenant farmers—sometimes found themselves in worse shape than before. Above all, recovery seemed as elusive a goal for the New Dealers as it had been for the Hoover administration. Although conditions had improved since Roosevelt took office, unemployment remained appallingly high. On any given day during 1935, one out of five Americans could not find work; during the entire year, many more than that found themselves jobless at one time or another.

Yet despite its shortcomings, the New Deal engaged in an astonishing range of activities and had an enduring impact on American life. The Federal Emergency Relief Administration, under the bold direction of Harry Hopkins, kept the wolf away from many doors, even if its system of direct relief to the unemployed sometimes did carry with it the humiliating stigma of charity. Home- and farm-mortgage refinancing rescued millions of American families from foreclosure. The Public Works Administration and the Works Progress Administration not only created millions of jobs but also built highways, schools, hospitals, and recreational facilities and performed an astonishing variety of other useful services. PWA workers built the Triborough Bridge and the Lincoln Tunnel in New York, and the port of Brownsville in Texas. Throughout the country, WPA workers served hot lunches to schoolchildren, taught illiterate adults to read and write, and brought medical and dental services to the poor. WPA artists painted murals on post office walls, while WPA actors performed Shakespeare in Harlem.

Other New Deal programs addressed some of the structural weaknesses that had contributed to the economic collapse. The Federal Deposit Insurance Corporation helped restore confidence in the nation's banking system, as did the separation of commercial and investment banking and the large bank stock purchases by the Reconstruction Finance Corporation. The Agricultural Adjustment Administration, by purchasing crop surpluses and by paying farmers to restrict production, increased farm prices and farm incomes. The New Deal, as its radical critics claimed, doubtless did strengthen capitalism. Paradoxically, however, individual capitalists did not always emerge from the New Deal with their power intact. Businessmen still maintained a commanding position in the direction of economic affairs, but to a greater extent than ever before, they now had to share power with previously excluded groups, such as organized labor. They also had to account for their actions before such public regulatory agencies as the Securities and Exchange Commission. In time, most businessmen found that they could live with and even prosper under New Deal reforms. During the 1930s, however, all they knew was that they had had to yield to others a measure of control, however small, over their own affairs.[35]

If Roosevelt had not restrained some congressional initiatives, the New Deal might have had an even greater impact on American life than it did. Left to its own devices, Congress might, for example, have created a program for national health insurance, and it almost certainly would have adopted more inflationary measures than it did. Yet even if it had had a free hand, Congress probably would not have spent enough to bring the country out of the depression. Even the leading proponents of spending in Congress, such as La Follette, Long, and Wagner, who wanted to spend a good deal more than Roosevelt, refused to sanction deficits on the scale that later experience demonstrated would have been necessary to end the depression. Nor did the public support greater federal expenditures. In 1935, according to a Gallup poll, 60 percent of the public believed that the government was spending too much on relief and recovery measures.[36]

Of all the changes the New Deal wrought, none surpassed in importance the transformation of public attitudes toward the federal government. Diplomat George F. Kennan, who grew up in the Midwest, once recalled that before the depression, "when times were hard, as they often were, groans and lamentations went up to God, but never to Washington."[37] After 1933 as never before, people directed their pleas to Washington, and within Washington to the president, who was rapidly eclipsing in public esteem Congress and all other participants in the New Deal.

5

THE ROOSEVELT PRESENCE, 1933–1936

Even before the end of his first term, Roosevelt's presidency had already assumed mythical proportions, as friends and foes alike credited him with almost superhuman feats. Some ardent admirers even attached religious significance to his presidency, viewing him as a recipient of divine guidance; ardent critics, on the other hand, depicted him as an unmitigated evildoer, a destroyer of the American way. Roosevelt's larger-than-life image was rooted in large part in his knack for identifying himself in the public mind with the New Deal, including those measures to which he had initially been opposed or indifferent; in his matchless skills as a communicator; and most important, in his ability to create an illusion of intimacy between himself and the public that somehow made him seem personally involved in the everyday lives of American citizens. Indeed, this illusion of intimacy transformed public perceptions of, and expectations from, the presidency and constitutes one of Roosevelt's most enduring, though troublesome, legacies. In 1936, Roosevelt's overwhelming reelection triumph, coupled with the emergence of a new and enduring political coalition, added an aura of invincibility to an already luminous image.

From the beginning of his presidency, many people viewed Roosevelt as a combination friend and savior. A government field investigator,

Martha Gellhorn, while touring North Carolina, found Roosevelt's portrait, usually clipped from a local newspaper, in every home. He was, she observed, "at once God and their intimate friend; he knows them all by name, knows their little town and mill, their little lives and problems. . . . He is there, and will not let them down." Another field investigator, Lorena Hickok, reported from New Orleans, "People down here all seem to think they know the President personally!"[1] In unprecedented numbers, people wrote personal letters to their friend in the White House, frequently enclosing songs or poems of tribute that they had composed in his honor. The songs alone, most of them written by nonprofessionals, eventually numbered in the thousands and filled in excess of 50 storage boxes at the White House. People also sent him personal gifts, ranging from homemade pies and cakes to elaborate handicrafts. One man spent over two years crocheting a bedspread for the president. Between 5,000 and 8,000 people wrote to Roosevelt every day, and most of them seemed convinced that he would personally read their letters. One man, for example, invited him to visit on his next trip to Dallas. "I will fix you a real dinner of hot biscuits, fried potatoes, chicken, chicken gravy and butterscotch pie," the man promised, adding, "we have a comfortable home, something that a working man could not have prior to your Presidency." Some people viewed Roosevelt as their last hope, and they wrote him heart-wrenching pleas for help. An 18-year-old woman from Detroit begged the president for $25 so that she could buy a coat. "If I wont get any help from you Dear Mr. President than I will take my life away," she wrote. "I can't stand it no longer. We were thrown out on the street a few times. I hate to live the way I'm living now."[2] More sophisticated writers, realizing the unlikelihood of the president actually reading their letters, wrote to Eleanor instead.

Roosevelt deliberately encouraged people to believe that he personally read and answered the mail by authorizing aides to compose letters and sign his name to them. Although most elected officials undoubtedly adopt this practice from time to time, probably no public official before Roosevelt had employed it on so large a scale or with such sophistication. As early as 1912, when illness confined Roosevelt to bed during his campaign for reelection to the state senate, Louis Howe mailed thousands of "personalized letters" bearing facsimiles of the candidate's signature. During the years leading up to Roosevelt's campaign for the presidency, Howe raised letter-writing, in Raymond Moley's words, "to mass production levels," at one stage employing three skilled imitators of Roosevelt's signature. Lorena Hickok attested to the effectiveness of the personalized letter technique. "Another funny thing," she wrote Harry Hopkins, "is the number of letters you see around over the President's and Mrs. Roosevelt's signatures. They are seldom anything more than the briefest and most formal acknowledgment of a letter—usually a letter of complaint or an appeal for help. But I doubt if any other President—or his wife— has ever been so punctilious about acknowledging letters. And these people take them all very seriously, as establishing a personal relation."[3] As a variation on the personalized letter, White House staff members did sign their own names to many letters but explained that the president had asked them to write on his behalf. The sense of intimacy instilled by these practices was not, of course, totally illusory. Roosevelt's aides did refer constituent problems to the appropriate government agency for action. Moreover, they reported to the president trends in the opinions of letter-writers, and they occasionally sent him particularly striking letters. The fact remained, however, that Roosevelt neither wrote nor signed most of the letters that bore his signature.

The famous fireside chats powerfully reinforced the bonds of intimacy between Roosevelt and the public. Happily for Roosevelt, his early tenure coincided with the ascendency of radio as a major form of communication. At the beginning of the 1930s, radio reached fewer than half of all American households; by the end of the decade, it reached the vast majority of households. Social workers reported that destitute families would sometimes relinquish furniture or bedding before they would give up their radios.[4] Well above average as a platform speaker, Roosevelt had few, if any, equals among public officials as a radio performer. His pleasant baritone voice, his crisp and clear enunciation, his distinctive patrician accent, and his simple and direct manner made him seem, in the words of one of his advisers, like "a friend or relative, who had figured out a way to prevent foreclosure of the mortgage." Roosevelt delivered his radio addresses, not from an easy chair in front of a fireplace as many people may have imagined, but from behind a bank of microphones and in front of an audience of 20 or 30 friends and advisers. Yet once he went on the air, he seemed to forget his surroundings, visualizing instead individual families, gathered with their neighbors around the radio. "His head would nod and his hands would move in simple, natural, comfortable gestures," said Frances Perkins. "His face would smile and light up as though he were actually sitting on the front porch or in the parlor with them." His listeners responded enthusiastically. An unemployed southern millworker told a WPA interviewer that Roosevelt "can speak his thoughts the plainest of any man I ever heard speak. He's spoke very few words over the radio that I haven't listened to."[5] Although Roosevelt conveyed an impression of spontaneity, he and his aides left little to chance, painstakingly preparing each of the 27 radio addresses he delivered during his presidency and scheduling the broadcasts during peak listening hours, usually sometime between nine and eleven on Sunday evenings.

Not only the fireside chats, but all of Roosevelt's public addresses underwent elaborate preparation and involved the labors of many persons. Like every other aspect of his career, speechwriting was a collaborative effort. It was not unusual for a dozen or more persons to take part in the preparation process. In fact, over the years, Roosevelt's advisers supplied him with many of his most memorable lines and phrases, such as the "forgotten man," the "new deal," the "good neighbor," and "the only thing we have to fear is fear itself." Yet by all accounts, Roosevelt had an unerring ear for the sound of good writing, and he placed his own distinctive stamp on his speeches. "I was never present when a big speech was born," wrote speechwriter Charles Michelson, "that the President did not take the political viands offered and cook them in his individual way. . . . Roosevelt is a better phrase maker than anybody he ever had around him."[6]

Roosevelt's deft handling of the news media further strengthened the personal ties between him and the public.[7] Two of his presidential forebears laid the foundations upon which Roosevelt built his relationship with the press: Theodore Roosevelt's colorful exploits had provided reporters with a bountiful source of news copy, and Woodrow Wilson had held the first modern news conferences. After the Wilson administration, relations between the president and the press had deteriorated. Harding was too uninformed to serve as a reliable news source; Coolidge required reporters to submit their questions in writing before press conferences, then simply shuffled to the bottom of the pile questions he did not choose to answer; and Hoover, as the depression worsened, scrupulously avoided almost all contact with reporters. But Roosevelt revived and expanded upon the practices of Theodore Roosevelt and Woodrow Wilson, and hardly a day went by that people did not see his name or photograph on the front pages of their newspapers.

Not only did Roosevelt institutionalize the presidential press conference, but he transformed it into an art form. Twice weekly, usually on Tuesday or Wednesday morning and on Friday afternoon, between 100 and 200 reporters would crowd into his office. There, from behind a desk cluttered with memorabilia and with his cigarette holder tilted at the characteristic angle, the president held forth. Writer John Gunther recalled that during one 20-minute news conference, the president's expressive face recorded, by turns, "amazement, curiosity, mock alarm, genuine interest, worry, rhetorical playing for suspense, sympathy, decision, playfulness, dignity, and surpassing charm." From the beginning, Roosevelt earned exceedingly high marks from White House correspondents, who appreciated his friendly and hospitable manner, his responsiveness to questions, his unfailing news sense, and his impressive command of information. One newsman described him as "the best newspaperman who has ever been President of the United States," while another said that he was so persuasive that he "could recite the Polish alphabet and it would be accepted as an eloquent plea for disarmament."[8]

Beneath Roosevelt's jaunty manner and the easy give-and-take of the news conference lay, as with the fireside chats, cool calculation. Roosevelt rarely made unplanned disclosures of information, and when circumstances required, he could be as uncommunicative as Calvin Coolidge. Marveling at the president's ability to deflect, divert, and dilute questions, John Gunther concluded that he had "never met anyone who showed greater capacity for avoiding a direct answer while giving the questioner a feeling he *had* been answered."[9] Roosevelt barred completely from discussion one sensitive subject, his disability. By gentlemen's agreement, most photographers refrained from taking pictures that would call attention to the president's paralysis, most reporters declined to mention the subject in their dispatches, and all editorial cartoonists depicted him as an able-bodied man with full use of his legs. In 1936, during an appearance at the Democratic National Convention in Philadelphia's Franklin Field, Roosevelt fell flat on his face as he made his way to the speaker's podium. Despite the presence of photographers and correspondents, the incident went unreported. On those rare occasions when publications did break the code of silence, such as the time *Life* magazine printed a photograph of Roosevelt in a wheelchair, White House officials only redoubled their efforts at concealment.

To ensure that photographs and newsreels of the president not only concealed his infirmity but portrayed him in a flattering manner, Roosevelt's image-conscious press secretary, Stephen Early (who previously had worked for the Paramount Newsreel Company) formulated an elaborate set of rules to govern the activities of cameramen. Among other things, he required photographers to stand at least 12 feet away from the president, to request permission before taking candid shots, and to use only certain specified kinds of photographic equipment. In 1935, after the publication of a picture of the president rubbing his eyes, Early told cameramen that thereafter they could shoot only when he gave them a cue.[10]

Although reporters grumbled from time to time, they complied with the restrictions on their activities because they liked and respected Roosevelt, generally sympathized with his policies, and did not want to jeopardize their access to the best news source in Washington. They also believed that by supplying the public with vital information, they were playing a key role in the democratic process. Moreover, although the rigorousness of Roosevelt's press conferences never approached that of the question period in the British Parliament, they did require him to regularly account for his actions in a way that no president had ever had to do before.

White House letter-writing, the fireside chats, and press coverage all combined to create a sense of intimacy between Roosevelt and the public. Yet this sense of intimacy contained a striking element of paradox. Although the people felt closer to Roosevelt than they had to any previous president, in a practical sense they probably had never been farther removed from the presidency. In an earlier age, presidents had made themselves more accessible to the public. Thomas Jefferson, proclaiming "pell mell is our law," received visitors on a first come, first served basis. Andrew Jackson, at whose legendary inaugural celebration thousands of well-wishers had crowded into the executive mansion, overturning furniture and shattering punch bowls, entertained many ordinary citizens in the course of his official duties. Abraham Lincoln set aside several hours of each day to greet visitors; according to his private secretary, he spent three-fourths of his time meeting people. As one of his biographers described it, "Lincoln would throw his door open at ten and let in a river of raucous humanity—interviewers, politicians, office seekers, businessmen, sobbing mothers who wanted their sons released from the army, and pretty young wives who flirted with him to promote their military husbands."[11] By Roosevelt's time, security considerations alone had so restricted access to the White House that the chances of an ordinary citizen meeting the president were virtually nonexistent. Yet, many people seemed to believe—perhaps even needed to believe—that they could communicate with Roosevelt, if not in person, then at least by letter, and that the president watched out in a personal way for their welfare.

In addition to his image as a friend and protector, Roosevelt projected another powerful image with strong religious overtones. Many Americans either read the Bible or were thoroughly familiar with its stories, and for them the depression appears to have triggered conscious or unconscious associations with events in Scripture. Thus, for example, the depression seemed like some Old Testament plague, coinciding as it did over much of the country with droughts, dust storms, and locust and boll-weevil infestations. From the Puritan vision of a "city upon the hill" through Woodrow Wilson's crusade to make the world safe for democracy, Americans had a habit of viewing themselves as a chosen people who enjoyed providential guidance, and this too reinforced the tendency to interpret the depression in biblical terms. Roosevelt, for his part, consistently employed biblical imagery as a rhetorical device. Thoroughly familiar with the words and phrases of the King James version of the Bible from his Episcopalian upbringing, he apparently first employed biblical imagery during his gubernatorial campaign in 1928. Before one appearance, he was reading over the draft of a speech on hydroelectric power that had been written by a speechwriter when he decided to dictate a new opening: "This is a history and a sermon on the subject of water power, and I preach from the Old Testament. The text is 'Thou shalt not steal.'"[12] Thereafter, as befit a man who wanted to be a preaching president, Roosevelt employed biblical allusions, as well as biblical cadences and diction. In his inaugural address, for example, he began by saying, "This is a day of national consecration"; he talked of driving the money changers from the temple; and he ended with a plea for divine guidance.[13]

Viewing the depression in biblical terms ultimately led many people to view Roosevelt as an agent of God. "When he spoke, it seems as though some Moses had come to alleviated us of our sufferings," a Kansas man wrote to Eleanor Roosevelt. "He is the Moses who is leading us out of the wilderness," a Texas congressman said during the first Hundred Days. "I honestly believe," a New Hampshire man wrote the president, "that our God made you, Sir, much differently than all other men, and he let us have you—when we needed you the most." Early in the first term, Roosevelt's rival for the 1932 Democratic nomination, Newton D. Baker, described him as "a providential person at a providential moment," while William Cardinal O'Connell called him "a God-sent man." The tendency to identify Roosevelt as an agent of God not only helped account for the intensity of emotions he aroused but also attested to the existence of a spiritual dimension in American public life that scholars later termed, after Rousseau, civil religion.[14]

Just as Roosevelt aroused in his supporters a quasi-religious fervor, so he stirred in his opponents fear and hatred. "No other word than hatred will do," wrote journalist Marquis Childs, describing an attitude that he found especially pervasive among members of America's upper class. "It is a passion, a fury, that is wholly unreasoning. . . . It is a consuming personal hatred of President Roosevelt and, to an almost equal degree, of Mrs. Roosevelt."[15] Roosevelt-haters depicted him as a dangerous radical out to destroy the American way. Criticism of the president assumed more bizarre forms as well. According to one rumor that regularly made the rounds of the nation's boardrooms and country clubs, Roosevelt suffered from insanity, probably brought on by syphilis. In the usual telling, someone would claim to have a friend or a friend of a friend, wholly reliable in any case, who had actually visited the White House and had heard hysterical laughter emanating from the president's office. A variation of this story had Sen. William E. Borah entering the White House study only to find the president cutting out paper dolls. No tale, it seemed, was too far-fetched for confirmed Roosevelt-haters. Thus, some of them believed that he had feigned his attack of polio in a cynical attempt to elicit public sympathy; that he had been involved in the kidnapping of the Lindbergh baby and had ordered the assassination of Huey Long; and that during the wedding of his son Franklin, Jr. and Ethel Du Pont, he had slipped away from the crowd, sneaked into the Du Pont library, and stolen some valuable stamps from the Du Pont collection.[16]

Even Roosevelt's personal habits, from the tilt of his cigarette holder to the "My Friends" salutation of his fireside chats, annoyed his extreme critics. Some persons hated Roosevelt so much that they could not bring themselves to pronounce his name, and before long, the phrase *that man,* usually uttered in a sputtering rage, brought instant recognition. J. P. Morgan's family habitually warned visitors to avoid mentioning the president's name in the aging financier's presence for fear of giving him apoplexy; once, when someone slipped and mentioned Theodore Roosevelt, Morgan reputedly said, "God damn all Roosevelts."[17] Cartoonist Dorothy McKay captured the anti-Roosevelt mood by depicting a schoolboy scrawling Roosevelt's name on the sidewalk and a little girl running up to the front door of her house and saying, "Mother, Wilfred wrote a bad word!"[18]

In response to attacks from the rich and well born, Roosevelt offered a parable of his own. "In the summer of 1933," he said, "a nice old gentleman wearing a silk hat fell off the end of a pier. He was unable to swim. A friend ran down the pier, dived overboard and pulled him out;

but the silk hat floated off with the tide. After the old gentleman had been revived, he was effusive in his thanks. He praised his friend for saving his life. Today, three years later, the old gentleman is berating his friend because the silk hat was lost."[19] Roosevelt's story reflected his quite plausible belief that, despite the wailings of capitalists, he and the New Dealers had saved capitalism.

There seemed no better indication of the personal nature of Roosevelt's presidency than the amount of attention the press and public lavished on his private life and personality. Americans had always been interested in the personal lives of their presidents, of course, but in Roosevelt's case they displayed an almost insatiable appetite for even the mundane details of his unofficial activities and personal habits. People knew, for example, what brand of cigarette he smoked (Camels), the identity of his favorite song (supposedly "Home on the Range"), the name of his dog (Fala), and the current marital status of his four sons and one daughter.[20] If they read their newspapers and magazines carefully, they also knew what time he got up in the morning, what time he went to bed at night, and that he liked to read mysteries before turning out the lights.[21] Eleanor Roosevelt, who became the most politically active first lady in American history, received only slightly less attention than the president himself.

One question about Roosevelt above all the others seemed to preoccupy people: What was he really like? They may have come to different conclusions, but on one trait, his contagious zest for life, everyone agreed. Whether in public or in private, he displayed a buoyancy of spirit that suggested that he lived in the best of all possible times and was enjoying every minute of it. Before he became president, this exuberant spirit had struck some sensitive observers as oddly out of place in a world mired in depression. Now, however, it struck many of those same observers as Roosevelt's and the nation's most valuable resource. Serenity was another indisputable characteristic of his. One journalist described him as "apparently the least worried man in the country." More than anyone he had ever met, the president's doctor said, Roosevelt "had equanimity, poise and a serenity of temper that kept him on the most even of keels." His physical appearance mirrored his apparent inner peace. Except for having put on a few extra pounds and his hair being a shade grayer, he looked healthier at the end of his first term than he had at the beginning. "On none of his predecessors has the office left so few marks as on Mr. Roosevelt," observed columnist Anne O'Hare McCormick.[22]

As for the sources of his serenity, some looked to the nurturing family environment of his childhood and youth. Others emphasized the influence of religious faith. A good Episcopalian, Roosevelt did not wear his religion on his sleeve. An irregular churchgoer who shunned overt displays of piety, he once told Frances Perkins that he could do almost anything in the "goldfish bowl" of the presidency except say his prayers. Nor did he express any interest in theological issues. "I think it is just as well not to think about things like that too much," he said to Eleanor.[23]

Still, those persons closest to him, including family and friends, believed that religious faith lay at or near the core of his personality. They further believed that he viewed himself in much the same way as many Americans did—as a providential figure. "Religion," his son James wrote, "was a real and personal thing from which he drew much strength and comfort." Speechwriter Robert E. Sherwood described Roosevelt's religious faith as "the strongest and most mysterious force that was in him."[24] And although he disliked conspicuous displays of religiosity, he not only studded his speeches with biblical metaphors but probably invoked God's name and encouraged religious belief more often than any previous president. "No greater thing would come to our land today," he told the National Council of Churches in 1934, "than a revival of the spirit of religion—a revival that would sweep through the homes of the nation and set the hearts of men and women of all faiths to a reassertion of their belief in God and their dedication to His will for themselves and for their world." He added: "I doubt if there is any problem—social, political or economic—that would not melt away before the fire of such a spiritual awakening."[25]

Despite his religious orientation, Roosevelt displayed some conspicuously impious habits, the most pronounced of which was deceitfulness. Truthfulness in all situations may not be the most desirable trait in politicians or presidents, but in Roosevelt's case, the lack of truthfulness frequently exceeded the needs of political advantage or concealment of his infirmity. Even as president, for example, he fabricated, or at least greatly embellished, stories about his childhood and youth. In one story he claimed that as a student at Groton, he and two classmates had hatched an elaborate plot to run away from school and fight in the Spanish-American War. At the last moment, however, a serious attack of illness had foiled the plan. As one historian later demonstrated, this story could not have been true, but Roosevelt told it often, perhaps because it helped compensate for his lack of a military record and enhanced his identification with Theodore Roosevelt. He may have been saying, in effect, that if it had not been for circumstances beyond his control, he, like his famous cousin, would have seen action. Roosevelt also exaggerated his athletic accomplishments, falsely claiming to a reporter on one occasion that he had been a good boxer in school and to Henry Morgenthau on another occasion that he had twice broken his nose playing football.[26] Then, too, he tended to exaggerate the closeness of his relationship with Woodrow Wilson by frequently quoting sage bits of wisdom and advice that the former president had supposedly given him. Wilson may have said the things Roosevelt claimed he did, but it was extremely doubtful that Wilson had had either the time or the inclination to ruminate in the presence of the assistant secretary of the navy about such things as the cyclical nature of American politics.[27] Another series of deceptions concerned Lucy Mercer. Not only did Roosevelt originally conceal from Eleanor the nature of his relationship with Mercer, but late in his presidency, after apparently having promised Eleanor never to see Mercer again, he resumed the relationship.[28]

Roosevelt by no means confined his deceptions to his private life. On at least one occasion, a keen interest in his historical reputation apparently inspired him to attempt to mislead future historians. Although Raymond Moley wrote the original draft of his first inaugural address, Roosevelt later destroyed Moley's draft and placed in his files a manuscript in his own handwriting. Roosevelt attached to the manuscript a note claiming that it was the original version of the inaugural address and that he was the sole author.[29]

Examined separately, Roosevelt's deceptions often seem harmless, nothing more, perhaps, than the embellishments of a good storyteller. Certainly there was no evidence that he ever used his powers of deception to conceal from the public criminal activity or other serious misdeeds within his administration. Yet his lies are all the more puzzling because they seem to have been so unnecessary. What did a powerful and popular president have to gain, for example, by convincing his friend Henry Morgenthau, that he had twice broken his nose playing football at Groton? Perhaps at an earlier stage in his life these stories had served a useful purpose, such as enhancing his image, and perhaps he had told them so often that he came to believe they were true. Or perhaps these stories represented what he wished had happened, in which case they may have suggested feelings of inadequacy on the part of a man who seemed so supremely self-confident. Whatever its psychological dimensions, Roosevelt's habit of deception disappointed even his staunchest supporters. One time a Democratic congressman told Harold Ickes that Roosevelt would have difficulty refuting Huey Long's charge that he, Roosevelt, was a liar. "It is pretty tough," the interior secretary confided to his diary, "when things like this can be said about the President of the United States and when members of his own official family and of his own party in Congress feel that his word cannot be relied upon. It hurts me to set down such a fact, but it is the fact, as I have had occasion to know more than once."[30]

Roosevelt's deceptiveness reinforced the widespread, but almost certainly misleading, impression that he possessed an extraordinarily complex personality. Before he became president, of course, most observers had seen him as a rather simple man. But now they viewed him in just the opposite light. Frances Perkins described him as the most complicated person she had ever known, and Henry Morgenthau said he was "a man of bewildering complexity of moods and motives." According to Undersecretary of State William Phillips, Roosevelt displayed not one personality but three or four of them, which he could turn on and off with "such speed that you often never knew where you were or to which personality you were talking."[31] A famous anecdote involving a chance encounter on Campobello Island between a reporter and Roosevelt enhanced the image of an enigmatic and complex president. The reporter and a friend, it seemed, were strolling through the woods when suddenly, through a thin fog, they saw Roosevelt, seated on the trunk of a tree, his legs crossed in front of him, his hands covering his face. Before they could move, the president lowered his hands to reveal "a kind of drawn grimace over his mouth and over his forehead like a man trying to see something in his mind and suffering." When Roosevelt became aware of the visitors, "it was like a shutter clicking down on a camera the way the smile came back over the look in his eyes and he called out: 'Hello there, Billy. Picking flowers?'" The reporter and his friend, having glimpsed the interior of the man, quickly left the scene, as Roosevelt's laughter echoed in the background.[32] This often-told story, with its hint of the agony at Gethsemane, perhaps also reinforced the tendency to view Roosevelt in religious terms.

The belief that behind Roosevelt's wall of reserve there lay vast complexities accorded him certain political benefits. It enhanced the impression that the New Deal, despite its internal contradictions, conformed to some master plan known only to the president. That belief also encouraged people to search for the hidden meaning behind practically everything Roosevelt said and did, with the result that they often found what they wanted to find. No wonder, then, that the president not only relished his sphinxlike image but did much to foster the impression that he held the answer to the riddle. "Never let your left hand know what your right is doing," he once said to Morgenthau. "Which hand am I, Mr. President?" Morgenthau asked. "My right hand, but I keep my left under the table," Roosevelt answered. Another time, aide Thomas Corcoran told Roosevelt that he never faked like his cousin Theodore. "Oh, but Tommy, at times I do, I do!"[33]

During the first term, Eleanor Roosevelt emerged as a major public personality in her own right. She had long since ceased being the shy and awkward woman Franklin had married 30 years before. Following the Lucy Mercer crisis, she had struck out on her own, involving herself in a variety of political and civic activities. She entered the White House with trepidation, however, fearful that, as during her first, unhappy stay in Washington, public expectations would require her to play the role of politician's wife: to be a gracious hostess; a supporter of good, but noncontroversial, causes; basically an appendage to her husband. She need not have worried. A whirlwind of activity, Eleanor assumed more public responsibilities than any first lady in American history. She wrote books and articles, held press conferences, gave speeches, traveled extensively, and championed many causes. According to one story, doubtless apocryphal, Franklin once asked the White House usher to send Eleanor to him, only to be told that she had been out of town for three days. A famous cartoon showed two coal miners looking up and saying, "Good gosh, here comes Mrs. Roosevelt." Before long, she actually did visit a coal mine.[34]

On some sensitive social issues, Eleanor stood to the left of her husband. An outspoken supporter of civil rights for blacks, she tried unsuccessfully to persuade Franklin to make antilynching legislation a top priority. Later, during the second term, she stirred controversy by defying a segregation ordinance in Birmingham, Alabama, and by resigning in protest from the Daughters of the American Revolution when that organization prohibited Marian Anderson, the famous black contralto, from performing at Constitution Hall. Eleanor also tirelessly campaigned for women's rights, and the unprecedented number of women who held important positions during the Roosevelt administration attested to her influence. Some members of Roosevelt's inner circle grumbled, especially about Eleanor's support for civil rights, because they feared that it would jeopardize her husband's standing among white southerners. But although the president did not share Eleanor's passion for the cause of racial justice, he made no effort to silence her, explaining, "I can always say, 'Well, that's my wife; I can't do anything about her.'"[35]

Concerning things personal, Eleanor obviously respected and admired her husband. But those who knew her best said that the memories of Franklin's affair with Lucy Mercer still hurt deeply. As reporter and Roosevelt kinsman Joseph Alsop once suggested, Eleanor's hurt may have found expression in her attempt to discipline what she considered to be Franklin's inordinate appetite for worldly pleasures, including eating. At her direction, the White House kitchen served up an unending diet of bland food, much to Franklin's disgust. But as Alsop wryly observed, "if her husband did not like eating badly, why, there were passages in their joint past she had not liked either." Another sore spot between them involved Eleanor's efforts to bring to Franklin's attention important issues that might otherwise have escaped his attention. In 1934, for example, during the congressional debate over antilynching legislation, she arranged a meeting between her husband and Walter White, executive secretary of the NAACP. Frequently, too, she invited spokesmen of other worthy but neglected causes to dinner in the Roosevelts' private quarters at the White House.

Franklin did not always welcome these intrusions into his private life, and one time, when Eleanor insisted upon inviting someone to the White House that the president did not want to see, he snapped, "Just remember, I want dinner to be a relaxation, not an excuse for doing business!"[36] In contrast to Eleanor, Franklin clearly preferred less demanding forms of relaxation. He liked to go deep-sea fishing with old friends such as Vincent Astor and to play poker with political associates such as Edwin "Pa" Watson, William O. Douglas, Stephen Early, Henry Morgenthau, and Harold Ickes, all of whom agreed not to bring up the subject of politics. Later, of course, he once again sought out the company of Lucy Mercer. But whatever the nature of their personal relationship, the Roosevelts formed a highly effective political partnership. And if Franklin cast a long shadow, so, too, did Eleanor.

"There's one issue in this campaign," Roosevelt told Raymond Moley at the outset of the 1936 presidential contest. "It's myself, and people must be either for me or against me." To no one's surprise, the Democrats nominated Roosevelt and Garner for a second term. The Republicans, meanwhile, in a rebuff to the Hoover wing of the party, chose as their standard-bearer the able governor of Kansas, Alfred M. Landon. No standpatter, Landon had bolted his party in 1912 to support Theodore Roosevelt and again in 1924 to support "Fighting Bob" La Follette. He had compiled an excellent record on civil liberties, had courageously fought the Ku Klux Klan in Kansas, and had supported numerous New Deal programs. The Kansas governor, who looked like a small-town banker, clearly lacked Roosevelt's skill as a public performer; given to uttering banalities, he once said to an audience, "Wherever I have gone in this country, I have found Americans."[37] Yet some of his supporters believed that his homespun manner offered a refreshing contrast to Roosevelt's highly cultivated style. Initially, Landon attracted support from some important progressive Republicans of the Theodore Roosevelt ilk, such as William Allen White and Amos and Gifford Pinchot. He also gathered endorsements from some not so progressive Democrats, including Al Smith, who by this time had become an object of scorn .within his own party.

At the outset of the campaign, Landon rejected the advice of his conservative backers to wage an all out assault on the New Deal. If elected, he said, he would pick and choose among government programs, preserving some, reforming others, eliminating waste and inefficiency wherever possible. But in one of his first formal campaign appearances, Roosevelt brilliantly undercut his opponent's moderate approach. With mock sincerity, the president mimicked Landon: "Of course we believe all these things," he said. "We believe in social security; we believe in work for the unemployed; we believe in saving homes. Cross our hearts and hope to die, we believe in all these things; but we do not like the way the present Administration is doing them. Just turn them over to us. We will do all of them—we will do more of them—we will do them better; and, most important of all, the doing of them will not cost anybody anything."[38] Thereafter, Landon abandoned moderation, shrilly denouncing the New Deal and accusing Roosevelt of leading the nation down the road to socialism.

Roosevelt, for his part, adopted a threefold strategy. The first and most innovative component of this strategy involved mobilizing groups that both major parties had previously excluded from presidential politics. These groups included women, blacks, and organized labor. Led by John L. Lewis and his insurgent Committee for Industrial Organization (CIO), labor played an especially important role, contributing nearly

$800,000 to Roosevelt's reelection effort and imparting to the campaign the flavor of a social democratic movement.[39] To the dismay of Democratic chieftains like James Farley, the mobilization of labor and other groups often proceeded outside regular party channels and thus reduced the control of party managers over the campaign organization. Roosevelt further added to their discomfiture by minimizing the importance of party affiliation. During the entire campaign, he rarely mentioned the Democratic party by name, and in a few states he supported liberal Republicans or independents against their Democratic opponents.

The second component of Roosevelt's reelection strategy was defensive in nature. It consisted of emphasizing the economic improvements that had taken place during his administration. He repeatedly urged voters to ask themselves the question, "Am I better off now than I was four years ago?" Although by almost any measurement most people were better off, Roosevelt took no chances on a negative reply. Early in 1936, he told Agriculture Secretary Wallace, "Henry, through July, August, September, October and up to the fifth of November, I want cotton to sell at 12 cents. I do not care how you do it. That is your problem. It can't go below 12 cents. Is that clear?" About the same time, the National Emergency Council (NEC) submitted to the president a detailed report indicating that economic recovery had begun in 1932, before Roosevelt became president. Stephen Early, the White House press secretary, returned the report to the NEC for revision, saying, "The President is insistent that the low point in the depression be fixed as March 1933, or early in the year 1933—this for obvious reasons."[40] Roosevelt need not have juggled figures to ensure a favorable outcome, for the enthusiasm that greeted his campaign appearances indicated that people not only believed that they were better off now than before but that they credited the president personally with the improvement. Wherever he went he heard cries of "Thank you, Mr. President!" and "You gave me a job!" and "You saved my home!"[41]

As the campaign progressed and as Republican criticisms of the president became increasingly harsh in tone, Roosevelt went on the attack. He directed his fire not at Landon by name but at the forces of selfishness and greed that he claimed stood behind the Republican candidate. The politics of attack reached its climax at the end of October at Madison Square Garden, where Roosevelt addressed the most wildly enthusiastic crowd of his career. "We have not come this far without a struggle and I assure you that we cannot go further without a struggle," he said. "We had to struggle with the old enemies of peace—business and financial monopoly, speculation, reckless banking, class antagonism, sectionalism, war profiteering. They had begun to consider the Government of the United States as a mere appendage to their own affairs." Then, his voice taking on an uncharacteristically hard edge, he said, "Never before in all our history have these forces been so united against one candidate as they stand today. They are unanimous in their hate for me—and I welcome their hatred." After the ensuing roar of approval subsided, Roosevelt added, "I should like to have it said of my first Administration that in it the forces of selfishness and of lust for power met their match. . . . I should like to have it said of my second Administration that in it these forces met their master." Not everyone greeted the president's address with approval. Aide Raymond Moley, who was then in the process of a painful separation from Roosevelt over personal and political differences, believed that the speech represented a demagogic incitement of class conflict.[42]

Roosevelt's Madison Square Garden address imbued his campaign with the spirit of a crusade. Yet as the election neared, the goal of that crusade remained unclear, for the candidate had been remarkably tight-lipped about his plans for the future. Before the convention, Roosevelt had directed his aides to make the party's platform inspiring, but short, and with as few specific proposals as possible.[43] To the very end, he resisted Landon's efforts to pin him down to a specific course of action, and he provided as little indication of future intentions as he had during his first campaign for the presidency.

The voters seemed not to mind, however, and on Election Day they gave Roosevelt one of the greatest victories in American electoral history. He swept every state except for Maine and Vermont, receiving nearly 61 percent of the popular vote to 36 percent for Landon. Democrats added to their already top-heavy majorities in both houses of Congress.

The 1936 election signified the emergence of a new Democratic coalition that would shape national politics for decades to come. The Democratic party achieved enduring majority status by expanding its traditional base among white southerners to include large numbers of low-income urban dwellers, most of them of recent immigrant stock. The typical recruit to the party of Roosevelt was a blue-collar worker, of southern or eastern European ancestry, Catholic or Jewish by religious affiliation, living in one of the big cities of the Northeast or the Great Lakes region, and probably voting for the first time. Blacks, where they were not prohibited from voting, and reform-minded academics and intellectuals also joined the new coalition. Despite its heavy representation in the working class, the new Democratic party retained substantial, though not majority, support among businessmen, some of whom probably viewed the New Deal as a bulwark against radicalism or as a check against the old elite that had restricted access to business and financial circles before the depression. Some enlightened businessmen may also have supported Roosevelt out of a sense of social responsibility and because they realized that the New Deal was helping to save, not to destroy, capitalism. "Why shouldn't the American people take half my money from me?" asked Boston millionaire and Democrat Edward Filene. "I took all of it from them."[44]

The New Deal coalition was impressive not only for its vote-getting potential but also for its ability to combine seemingly incompatible elements—southern whites and northern blacks, labor leaders and business executives, urban political bosses and western progressives. The faint outlines of this coalition had already begun to appear late in the 1920s, before Roosevelt's presidency. Yet if he did not create the coalition, his multifaceted image did help to keep its divergent components together.

6

TIME OF TROUBLES, 1937–1938

In the immediate aftermath of the 1936 election, Roosevelt seemed invincible. With the greatest reelection victory in American history to his credit and his party firmly in control of both houses of Congress, there seemed almost no limit to what he might accomplish. With the odds in his favor, Roosevelt boldly struck out on his own. During his first term, as often as not, he had yielded the legislative initiative to Congress. As his second term began, however, he prepared an ambitious agenda of his own, which included enlargement of the Supreme Court and reorganization of the executive branch of government. Later, in an attempt to make the Democratic party more responsive to his leadership, he added to his agenda the purge of errant party members. Roosevelt's initiatives were as potentially far-reaching as anything that had yet come out of the New Deal. If he succeeded, he would greatly augment the powers of the presidency. But he did not succeed. Indeed, by 1938, he had sustained a series of wounds, most of them self-inflicted, that crippled his presidency. By that year, too, he seemed destined to leave the White House not in triumph but in defeat.

Roosevelt's second inaugural address, delivered against a cold, steady rain on 20 January 1937, contained less than the usual amount of verbal back-patting and focused instead on the tasks ahead. Tens of millions of Americans, he said, lacked the basic necessities of life. Day in and day out, the threat of imminent economic disaster hung like a pall over their homes. Millions more lacked the resources for education, recreation, or the makings of a better life for themselves and their families. "I see one-third of a nation ill-housed, ill-clad, ill-nourished," he said to the rain-soaked crowd, adding, "It is not in despair that I paint you that picture. I paint it for you in hope—because the nation, seeing and understanding the injustice of it, proposes to paint it out."[1] No president had ever spoken more movingly about the plight of the poor.

Before the nation could take up the challenge of the inaugural, Roosevelt believed, it had first to deal with an obstructionist Supreme Court.[2] From the beginning of his presidency, he had kept a wary eye on the Court, and for good reason. For a half-century or more, the judiciary had come down on the side of the privileged classes more often than not. Out of the due process clause of the Fourteenth Amendment, it had erected a fortress to safeguard property rights from state and federal regulation. The composition of the Supreme Court at the outset of the New Deal offered further cause for concern. Three justices—Louis D. Brandeis, Benjamin N. Cardozo, and Harlan Fiske Stone—seemed to welcome government action to combat the depression. Four justices—James C. McReynolds, George Sutherland, Willis Van Devanter, and Pierce Butler—who had earned from their detractors the title "The Four Horsemen of Reaction," seemed just as likely to oppose any expansion of federal authority. That presumably left the fate of New Deal legislation to the court's remaining two members, Owen J. Roberts and Chief Justice Charles Evans Hughes, whose ideological predispositions were less clearly defined.

The first important decisions went in favor of the administration, with Roberts and Hughes voting with the liberals to uphold New Deal legislation. But then in 1935, and continuing into 1936, the ax fell again and again. Before the High Court finished its work, it had struck down, in several instances by unanimous decision, the National Industrial Recovery Act, the Agricultural Adjustment Act, and other key federal and state measures. It had also created, in Roosevelt's words, a "no man's land" where neither federal nor state governments had jurisdiction to act. If the Court maintained its present course, as then seemed likely, the legislation of the second Hundred Days, including the Social Security and National Labor Relations acts, would be next to fall.

New Dealers denounced the Court for its adverse decisions, accusing the justices of living in the past and of reading their own conservative political biases into the Constitution. The Court, said Roosevelt, had sought to turn back the clock to the days of the horse and buggy. How much longer, New Dealers asked, would the American people continue to have faith in a system that allowed an unelected judiciary to obstruct the efforts of an elected Congress and an elected president to combat the depression? In response to these criticisms, defenders of the Supreme Court contended that the Founding Fathers had designed the Constitution, with its checks and balances and separation of powers, for just such occasions, when the passions of the moment threatened to undermine the rule of law. As for the issue of political bias, judicial defenders pointed out that even liberal justices Brandeis, Cardozo, and Stone, whom most observers also believed to be the Court's most formidable intellects, had found some New Deal measures objectionable.

That Roosevelt addressed the Court crisis came as no surprise. Given the seriousness of the situation, he would have been irresponsible not to have done so. Yet his plan for resolving the crisis, which critics quickly dubbed court-packing, and the way in which he presented it to the public surprised and shocked much of the nation.

Contrary to the general impression at the time, Roosevelt decided upon court-packing not in haste but after lengthy deliberations, during which he considered various solutions to the Court problem. When he assumed office, he believed that the branches of government should cooperate to fight the depression, just as the diverse elements in American society, such as capital and labor, should subordinate their differences and work together in common cause, too. In this spirit, and rather naïvely, he suggested to Chief Justice Hughes that the two of them meet regularly for the purpose of allowing Hughes to preview legislation and comment on the Court's probable disposition toward it. The chief justice, doubtless eager to preserve the independence of the judiciary and perhaps sensing an attempt to co-opt the Court, flatly refused to participate in such an arrangement. Rebuffed by Hughes, Roosevelt turned from cooperation to confrontation. In the spirit of Andrew Jackson who, in the face of an adverse Court decision had reputedly said, "John Marshall has made his decision, now let him enforce it," Roosevelt considered disobeying the Supreme Court. In 1934, in anticipation of a decision nullifying his abandonment of the gold standard, he prepared a radio address, to be delivered in the event of a negative verdict, saying that in the interests of national security he would not comply with the Court's decision. Whether he actually would have defied a judicial ruling remains unknown, for in the gold cases, the Court unexpectedly decided in the administration's favor. Yet the fact that he even considered taking such an extraordinary step demonstrated the depths of his hostility toward the judiciary. Later, when the Court began in earnest to overturn New Deal legislation, many of Roosevelt's supporters urged him to consider a variety of constitutional amendments, one of which would have allowed Congress to override Supreme Court decisions in much the same way that it overrode presidential vetoes. Roosevelt rejected the amendment process as being too time-consuming and too susceptible to the machinations of well-financed interest groups. During the 1936 presidential campaign, friends and foes alike tried to draw him out on the subject, but with the exception of a vague reference in the party platform to a "clarifying amendment," Roosevelt remained conspicuously silent.

Following the election, he redoubled his efforts to meet the Court challenge. Working almost exclusively with Attorney General Homer Cummings, Roosevelt eventually settled upon a plan whereby, for every federal judge who declined to retire at the age of 70, the president could appoint one additional judge to the court. According to the plan, the president could appoint as many as six new justices to the Supreme Court and 44 new judges to lower federal courts. Court-packing appealed to Roosevelt for obvious reasons. By expanding the High Court from nine to 15 members, he could practically guarantee favorable rulings on future New Deal legislation. Court-packing had the advantage over a constitutional amendment of speed and ease of enactment, for in order to become law, it would require only a majority vote in each house of the heavily Democratic Congress. The Constitution presented no barriers to the plan; indeed, Congress had every right to alter the number of justices on the Supreme Court, and it had done so many times in the past, although admittedly never for the purposes Roosevelt had in mind. Not the least of the attractions of court-packing was the fact that Woodrow Wilson's attorney general had once proposed a somewhat similar approach to judicial reform. Wilson's attorney general had been none other than James McReynolds, who in 1937 was one of the Supreme Court's Four Horsemen. In the privacy of the oval office, Roosevelt may also have convinced himself that because court-packing was less drastic than other plans that he had considered and rejected, it would also be less controversial. But he misread the situation.

In fighting for court reform, Roosevelt faced a stiff test of his legislative leadership. An enduring symbol of national unity, the Supreme Court enjoyed the status of a sacred cow in the American political system, and any attempt to curb its power was bound to encounter powerful resistance. Moreover, because court reform, unlike most of the legislation of Roosevelt's first term, originated in the White House rather than in the Congress, the president found himself in the unaccustomed position of directing the legislative effort. But Roosevelt also brought to the fight some powerful advantages. They included his great reelection victory, his undeniable popularity with the American public, and those swollen Democratic majorities in both houses of Congress.

From the very outset, Roosevelt squandered much of his advantage by making critical mistakes. When he unveiled his plan in February 1937, he disingenuously presented court-packing, not as a means of securing a liberal majority on the court, but as an efficiency measure designed to improve the performance of the entire federal judiciary. The justices, he said condescendingly, especially the older ones among them, simply could not keep up with their work. Nor did they have the physical or mental vigor to deal with the complexities of modern life. The Court, like every organization, periodically needed an infusion of new blood, and to meet this need the president would appoint new jurists to the bench. This pretense fooled no one, and Roosevelt soon abandoned it. But the damage had been done. The president appeared not only devious but also so unsure of the merits of his own plan that he had had to resort to a ruse. A normally pro-Roosevelt editorialist summed up the public reaction to Roosevelt's court-packing announcement: "Too clever—too damned clever."[3]

If Roosevelt had consulted more people before unveiling his plan, he almost certainly would have avoided presenting court-packing as an efficiency measure. Therein lay another critical mistake: He sprang the plan on Congress and the public with no advance notice and without having consulted a single legislator, including his floor leaders, who would have to muster the votes for passage. The legislators felt hurt and angry. Despite the many contributions they had made to the New Deal, Roosevelt apparently did not value their advice enough to seek it on the most important initiative of his presidency. Speaker of the House William Bankhead spoke for many Roosevelt loyalists when he said to a friend, "Wouldn't you have thought that the President would have told his own party leaders what he was going to do? He didn't because he knew that hell would break loose."[4] Curiously, by failing to consult with Congress, Roosevelt repeated Woodrow Wilson's fatal mistake during the debate over the League of Nations.

A storm of protest, unexpected in its intensity, greeted the president's proposal. Some of the opposition came from entirely predictable sources. Judges, state bar associations, professors at elite law schools, conservative foes of the New Deal—all shrilly denounced the president as a would-be dictator bent on undermining the Constitution. Roosevelt expected, perhaps even welcomed, opposition of this sort, and because much of it seemed so transparently self-serving, it probably did little harm to his cause. Such was not the case, however, with the unexpected opposition of many Democrats and liberals. In the Senate, where court-packing would receive its first test, administration stalwarts, such as Tom Connally, Joseph C. O'Mahoney, and Burton K. Wheeler, came out against the president's proposal, while Robert F. Wagner, whose name was synonymous with the New Deal, conspicuously absented himself from the battle. Wheeler's opposition was particularly damaging to the president's cause, for he had been the first United States senator to endorse Roosevelt for the presidency, and he had impeccable liberal credentials. No one, therefore, could accuse him of personal or ideological animus. Nor could Roosevelt credibly claim that his opponents were simply reactionary foes of the New Deal.

Critics such as Wheeler raised numerous objections to court-packing. Most believed that it set a bad precedent. If a liberal president could pack the Court with liberal justices, in the future, a conservative president could just as easily pack the Court with conservative justices. Some critics argued that Roosevelt's proposal did not go to the heart of the problem. After all, increasing the number of justices would not alter the fact that the Supreme Court, even though unelected and therefore unaccountable for its actions, had the power to thwart the public will. For these critics only a constitutional amendment empowering Congress to override Court decisions would protect the people from judicial usurpations of power. Civil libertarians raised objections of a different sort. Oswald Garrison Villard, the grandson of fiery abolitionist William Lloyd Garrison, feared that court-packing would make the highest judicial body in the land too susceptible to the passions and prejudices of the majority and therefore reluctant to protect the rights of blacks and other minorities. As the Court fight took on the characteristics of a family feud, congressional conservatives wisely remained on the sidelines and allowed Democrats and liberals to fight it out among themselves.

Despite the breadth and intensity of the opposition, Roosevelt seemed slow to react. For nearly a month following the announcement of his plan, while public and congressional opinion was taking shape, Roosevelt declined to speak out in his own defense, either out of overconfidence or in the belief that if he gave his opponents enough rope they would hang themselves. Nor during that time did he organize his congressional supporters. To worried advisers who urged him to take the offensive, Roosevelt would say only, "The people are with me. I know it."[5] Finally, in early March, he ended his silence, first with a rousing speech to party faithful in Washington, D.C., then with a fireside chat to the nation.

Once he was in the fray, Roosevelt failed to make much headway on Capitol Hill, where some legislators complained of the administration's clumsy and heavy-handed efforts to win their support. Legislators singled out for censure Thomas G. Corcoran, whom Roosevelt had dispatched to Capitol Hill to mobilize support for court reform. During the first term, the brilliant and versatile Corcoran had helped write some of the president's best speeches ("a rendezvous with destiny" was his phrase), had participated in the drafting of major legislation, and had played a key role in several legislative battles. Yet, for one entrusted with the delicate task of handling the court-packing issue, "Tommy the Cork," as Roosevelt called him, possessed severe handicaps. Chief among them was, in the words of two reporters, his "faint contempt for the legislative process, which he regarded as a messy business, to be got over as quickly as possible, like an attack of the mumps."[6] Working from the premise that every legislator had a price, Corcoran offered patronage, federal projects, and threats of political reprisal to induce congressmen to support court-packing. When he promised Burton Wheeler a role in the selection of Supreme Court justices in exchange for his vote, the Montana senator redoubled his efforts to defeat the president's proposal. Nor did postmaster general and patronage dispenser James Farley help the president's cause. In an off-the-record conversation with reporters that quickly found its way into print, Farley predicted that two key Democratic senators, who had expressed philosophical reservations about court-packing, would end up supporting the president's bill rather than forgo administration support for things they might want in the future.[7] Farley's remark made it impossible for the two senators to return to the administration's fold, even if they had been inclined to do so; moreover, it elevated opposition to Roosevelt's proposal to the high plane of principle. Most legislators did not object to the administration's use of rewards and punishments, for that was a normal part of the political process. But they did object to the administration's operating assumption, as expressed by Corcoran and Farley and sanctioned by Roosevelt, that legislators could be bought and sold and that when they expressed philosophical or moral objections to Roosevelt's plan, they were merely posing for political effect.

In the final accounting, the fatal blows to court-packing came not from a mistake-prone president but from the target of Roosevelt's attack, the Supreme Court, and from its chief justice, Charles Evans Hughes, who orchestrated the Court's deadly counterassault. Tall and stately, with a neatly trimmed white beard, Hughes reminded one journalist of "a whole series of Renaissance portrayals of the senior member of the Trinity."[8] But despite a God-like image, Hughes was a shrewd and resourceful politician whose distinguished career had included stints as governor of New York, Republican presidential candidate, and secretary of state. Chief justices normally stayed out of public debates, allowing their judicial opinions to speak for themselves. Hughes therefore created a sensation when, at a crucial juncture in the Court debate, he broke his official silence and issued a public statement, replete with facts and figures, refuting Roosevelt's claim that the Court had fallen behind in its work. To increase the number of judges, he added, would actually delay the operations of the Court, for it would mean "more judges to hear, more judges to confer, more judges to discuss, more judges to be convinced and to decide."[9] By the time the public had absorbed the full impact of the Hughes statement, Roosevelt probably wished that he had never raised the essentially bogus efficiency issue.

Even more damaging to the president's initiative, however, was the Supreme Court's dramatic change in direction, which the chief justice also helped engineer. When the Court convened in the spring of 1937, it surprised everyone by upholding a series of New Deal measures, including the National Labor Relations Act and the Social Security Act. It also validated a state minimum-wage law that was almost identical to one it had previously declared unconstitutional. These favorable decisions came about because Justices Hughes and Roberts, whose earlier alignment with the conservative justices had helped precipitate the Court crisis, now sided with their liberal colleagues. These two justices, fearing that permanent harm would befall the Court if it fell too far out of public favor, apparently had decided to reverse course even before Roosevelt unveiled his judicial reform plan. The Supreme Court's final contribution to the demise of court-packing came in May, when Justice Van Devanter, one of the Four Horsemen of Reaction, announced his retirement and thus cleared the way for Roosevelt to appoint a justice of his own choosing.

Van Devanter's resignation, in combination with Hughes's public statement and the series of favorable Court decisions, diminished the sense of urgency that had been Roosevelt's trump card and virtually eliminated any possibility that Congress would pass his proposal in its original form. All was not yet lost, however, for if he had been willing to compromise, Roosevelt almost certainly could have had some of what he wanted. Sen. Wheeler and other court-packing foes, perhaps not fully realizing the strength of their position, appeared ready to make concessions, and Senate Majority Leader Robinson believed that he could get the president "a couple of extra justices tomorrow" if the president would agree to it. Roosevelt would have none of it. Confident that he would yet prevail, he rejected talk of compromise and contemptuously dismissed as defeatists those who would settle for anything less than total victory.[10]

Some of Roosevelt's intimates attributed his apparent unwillingness to face reality and his other miscalculations during the Court fight to the loss of Louis Howe, who had died the year before. Almost alone among Roosevelt's advisers, Howe had been able to keep the president's feet on the ground and to bring him the bad news as well as the good. He had stood with Roosevelt from the early, sometimes awkward, performances in the state senate, through the polio crisis, and to the final triumph in the White House; only he could, and literally did, tell the president to "go to hell" when he thought he was wrong. Eleanor Roosevelt believed that after Howe's death her husband never had another adviser who, while remaining totally loyal, would expose him to all possible objections to an intended course of action. "Consequently," Eleanor said, with court-packing doubtless uppermost in her mind, "after Louis' death, Franklin frequently made his decisions without canvassing all sides of a question."[11]

Yet those who believed that Howe would have made a difference in the Court fight overlooked two facts. First, even before the final illness that led to Howe's death, Roosevelt had begun to distance himself from his once-intimate adviser, who had served his great purpose by helping to make Roosevelt president. Second, Roosevelt's behavior during the Court fight, far from being an aberration, was consistent with his behavior during earlier stages of his life. Indeed, in refusing to concede defeat, he displayed the same buoyant optimism that had sustained him during the polio crisis and that had helped dispel the prevailing national mood of defeatism and despair during his first term. But in the case of court-packing, Roosevelt's habit of expecting the best possible outcome in any situation had served only to isolate him from political reality.

In mid-June the Senate Judiciary Committee delivered another heavy blow to the president's initiative. In a carefully prepared report to the full Senate, committee members described his bill as "a needless, futile and utterly dangerous abandonment of constitutional principle," the ultimate effect of which would be "to make this government one of men rather than of law." Demonstrating the breach that had developed between Roosevelt and many members of Congress, the report concluded that court-packing "should be so emphatically rejected that its parallel will never again be presented to the free representatives of the free people of America."[12]

Soon after the committee filed its report, an angry and unrepentant Roosevelt authorized Senator Robinson to salvage what he could out of the original bill. But even the fates seemed to have conspired against court-packing. Before Robinson could negotiate a settlement, he collapsed and died of a heart attack. His death not only destroyed whatever hope remained for compromise, but also exacerbated hard feelings between the president and many of Robinson's colleagues, who believed that the strain of the Court fight had contributed to the majority leader's demise. Some legislators also resented Roosevelt's failure to attend Robinson's funeral in Arkansas and, additionally, what they considered to be his unseemly intervention in the contest to select a new majority leader. Following Robinson's death, Roosevelt made one final attempt to revive court-packing, which prompted an exasperated Democratic senator to say, "Mr. President, it's the hardest thing in the world to tell you something you don't want to hear. It's the hardest thing in the world to give you bad news."[13] The bad news, of course, was that the Court fight was over, but to the very end Roosevelt was unwilling to accept it.

The immediate aftermath of the Court fight yielded one further embarrassment for the president. In August, he had the opportunity to nominate someone to fill the vacancy on the Supreme Court that had been created by Van Devanter's retirement. Oddly enough, in view of all that had happened, Roosevelt's selection process bore a striking resemblance to the process that had produced the court-packing plan. He consulted Attorney General Cummings and no one else, then sprang the nomination on the Senate with no advance notice. If Roosevelt had consulted more widely, he might have learned what many people already knew—that his nominee, Sen. Hugo L. Black of Alabama, had once belonged to the Ku Klux Klan. Following his Senate confirmation, evidence of Black's affiliation with the Klan surfaced in the press, and Roosevelt had to withstand a drumbeat of criticism for having conducted a shoddy investigation into the Alabamian's past. Black himself came to the president's rescue. In a national radio broadcast, he admitted that he had once been a member of the Klan, but he said that he had long since repudiated its philosophy. As if to prove the point, Justice Black went on to compile a distinguished record in the area of civil rights and civil liberties.

Roosevelt later boasted that he had lost the Court battle but won the war. His boast had some basis in fact. After all, by rendering decisions favorable to the New Deal in 1937, the Supreme Court had removed itself as an obstacle to governmental efforts to combat the depression and regulate the economy. Then, too, because of deaths and retirements among incumbent justices, Roosevelt eventually had a chance to appoint an unprecedented eight members to the High Court and to raise a ninth member to the chief justiceship. The fact that a president had tried to pack the Court in the first place and the possibility that, if he had gone about it more skillfully, he might have succeeded, may have deterred future Courts from falling too far out of step with the other branches of government. But if the president ultimately realized his goal of taming the judiciary, he did so at great cost. The Court fight injured his political reputation, emboldened his foes, destroyed Democratic unity, stalled his ambitious legislative program, and spurred the growth of a conservative congressional coalition of southern Democrats and Republicans that, though small in number, blocked many New Deal initiatives. The Court fight also hardened the politician within Roosevelt, instilling in him a determination to punish those who had brought him down and making him less scrupulous about the methods he used to combat his opponents.

A second measure in which Roosevelt had a large personal stake, executive reorganization, fared little better than court-packing.[14] During the first term, the proliferation of alphabet agencies, combined with the already-existing government departments, created a cumbersome federal apparatus in which bureaus exhibited different, even contradictory, administrative philosophies. In 1936, to bring order to, and establish control over, this jerry-built system, Roosevelt created a panel of distinguished political scientists and public administration experts. In 1937, drawing upon the panel's recommendations, the president proposed restructuring the executive branch in such a way as to modernize its procedures; centralize its operations; increase the president's control over budgetary, personnel, and administrative matters; and give the federal government a greater role in national economic planning and in the allocation and use of natural resources.

Roosevelt's campaign to modernize the executive branch highlighted a persistent but little-noticed trait in his intellectual makeup. Whether as a young state senator pledging to cut waste in government, an assistant secretary of the navy calling for a complete overhaul of the federal bureaucracy, a vice-presidential candidate promising to help introduce businesslike practices into government, a polio victim sketching muscle charts and formulating rehabilitation programs for fellow victims, or a country gentleman drawing architectural plans for an addition to his Hyde Park home, Roosevelt had displayed an intellectual affinity for order, efficiency, and planning.

This engineerlike cast of mind went largely unnoticed for the very good reason that Roosevelt's administrative practices and personal work habits seemed disorderly and inefficient. As an administrator, he received uniformly bad grades from his contemporaries, who cited his many breaches of orthodox management practice. He had a habit of assigning the same task to different agencies and individuals, for example, and thereby producing overlapping jurisdictions, duplication of effort, and constant feuding among his subordinates. He also liked to bypass the chain of command by going over the heads of cabinet members and agency heads to deal directly with their subordinates. This practice rankled high-ranking officials in the administration, who worried that Roosevelt did not have complete confidence in them, that he was constantly checking up on them, and that things were going on within their departments without their knowledge.

Close advisers, such as Thomas Corcoran, Benjamin Cohen, and Henry Morgenthau, complained privately that the president mismanaged his own schedule and that he frittered much of his time away on trivial matters.[15] Everyone had a favorite story in this regard. Morgenthau's concerned the day that Roosevelt took time out of a busy schedule to make an inspection tour of the State Department. Someone in the department had been complaining about a shortage of office space, so Roosevelt decided to evaluate the situation for himself. Late one summer afternoon, he had himself and Morgenthau driven to the State Department, where, in the presence of Secretary Hull, Undersecretary Sumner Welles, and other officials, the president spent two hours going into and out of offices to see how crowded they were. In some offices he had himself wheeled alongside filing cabinets, whereupon he opened the drawers and leafed through files. When he came upon inactive files, he sternly lectured his red-faced entourage on the importance of putting the space to better use. The president, Morgenthau observed in his diary, got a "great kick" out of the experience.[16]

Roosevelt's attention to seemingly trivial matters proved especially frustrating to Budget Director Harold D. Smith. During one budget briefing, involving millions of dollars, Roosevelt devoted what Smith considered to be an inordinate amount of time to a minor item in the State Department budget. The department planned to send an employee of the Library of Congress to Latin America to help countries establish national libraries of their own. What attracted Roosevelt's attention were the projected living expenses for the employee, which he judged to be much too high. The president then proceeded, at great length and in much detail, to calculate an alternative budget, which included daily allotments for food, shelter, and clothing.[17]

Roosevelt's office routine confirmed the impression many people had of administrative disorder and inefficiency. Once again, everyone had a favorite story. That of Marriner S. Eccles, Chairman of the Federal Reserve Board, concerned the time he was scheduled to discuss pressing economic problems at a luncheon meeting with the president. Eccles arrived at the White House on time, but he had to wait because, as usual, Roosevelt was running behind in his schedule. When Eccles finally got in to see the president, Roosevelt was still engaged in conversation with the previous visitor, Sen. William Gibbs McAdoo of California. Roosevelt invited Eccles to sit down and told McAdoo that they were about to have lunch. Failing to take the hint, the Californian said, "Oh, that's all right, you two boys go right ahead—I'll talk while you eat." McAdoo finally left, and Eccles began to talk. But just then Fala, the president's little Scottie dog, ran into the room. Roosevelt took a ball from his desk drawer and began tossing it around the room for Fala to retrieve. This went on for a few minutes before Roosevelt said to Fala, "That's enough now. I've got to get back to work." Eccles resumed talking, but after a few minutes he noticed that he had lost the attention of the president who was looking around the room for his dog. Suddenly Roosevelt interrupted Eccles. "Well, I'll be God-damned! Marriner, do you see what I see?" Over in the corner, Fala was committing an indiscretion on the rug. By the time Roosevelt had gotten someone to take out the dog and clean up the mess, Eccles's time had expired. The Federal Reserve Board chairman left the White House in a rage.[18]

Some sympathetic observers claimed to detect a method to Roosevelt's apparent administrative madness. To the extent that he departed from orthodox administrative practice, they argued, he did so because the times demanded an approach that would move the cumbersome federal bureaucracy to action and release the creative energies of public servants. Thus, for example, his habit of assigning the same task to different agencies and individuals blurred lines of responsibility, but it also generated healthy competition among his subordinates. As Roosevelt himself once observed, "A little rivalry is stimulating, you know. It keeps everybody going to prove that he is a better fellow than the next man." Rivalry also kept people honest, Roosevelt believed. "An awful lot of money is being handled. The fact that there is somebody else in the field who knows what you are doing is a strong incentive to strict honesty." His defenders further argued that although his practice of dealing directly with lower-ranking members of the bureaucracy undoubtedly did upset the chain of command and did create some morale problems, it was more than offset by the fact that it gave him direct access to some of the best minds in the administration. Even his tendency to involve himself in seemingly unimportant matters may have served useful purposes, or so the argument went. In fact, Roosevelt's attention to detail contained a large element of illusion. Just as he had given Congress wide latitude in determining legislative priorities during the first term, so, too, he gave trusted subordinates, such as Hopkins, Ickes, and Jesse Jones, much discretion in implementing his policies. "He would give you a job to do," said one aide, "and leave you free to do it by yourself. He never told you how to do it."[19] But every so often, Roosevelt, with much fanfare, would involve himself in some small matter and thereby keep his subordinates on their toes. Following his inspection tour of the State Department, the only such visit he made during his presidency, he asked his staff, "Don't you think that my popping over there served a useful purpose? By nine o'clock tomorrow morning every man in Washington will think that I may come rolling in at any moment."[20] As for the circuslike atmosphere that Eccles had observed in the White House, sympathetic commentators pointed out that Roosevelt sometimes contrived distractions to avoid discussing unpleasant subjects or prematurely committing himself to a position. Above all, his defenders argued, Roosevelt's performance as an administrator should be judged not by the degree to which it conformed to orthodox administrative practices but by the results it produced. By that standard, they concluded, Roosevelt deserves high marks, for, despite the fact that the federal government grew rapidly during the 1930s and assumed unprecedented responsibilities, it conducted national affairs efficiently and without major scandal.

Still, Roosevelt's defenders probably exaggerated the benefits of his approach. More often than not, the government performed well in spite of, not because of, the president's management practices. His competitive approach to administration, for example, went well beyond what was necessary to sharpen the performance of his subordinates. Indeed, at times he seemed to take puckish delight in pitting members of his administration against one another. Then, after he had had his fun, he would bring the warring parties together and, like a patient father dealing with quarrelsome children, try to smooth over the differences. This process, repeated often during the Roosevelt administration, consumed much valuable time and energy to no apparent end. Ironically, Roosevelt's own administrative style worsened some of the very problems he sought to address through reorganization.

But whatever the pros and cons of his administrative practices, his executive reorganization bill encountered fierce resistance. Coinciding as it did with his campaign for Court reform at home and the rise of totalitarianism abroad, executive reorganization struck some critics as a step toward dictatorship. The president's proposal, said one senator, would plunge "a dagger into the very heart of democracy."[21] In 1937 the Congress declined to act on executive reorganization. Two years later, it did approve a truncated version of Roosevelt's proposal that significantly modernized the executive branch, although the measure fell far short of his original goals.

Despite his major legislative setbacks in 1937, Roosevelt could at least take satisfaction in the performance of the economy. Since 1933, economic conditions had improved significantly. Prices, profits, and national income had risen, and the unemployment rate, while it remained high, had declined from between 20 and 25 percent to 14 percent. At long last, it seemed, the country had turned that elusive corner toward recovery. Indeed, in 1937, Roosevelt and his economic advisers feared that recovery was occurring so rapidly that uncontrolled inflation threatened and that a boom-and-bust cycle, comparable to that which had ushered in the depression, might recur. In order to cool off the economy, Roosevelt allowed the Federal Reserve Board to increase reserve requirements for member banks, which lessened the amount of credit available for investment and speculative purposes. He also attempted to balance the budget by slashing expenditures for relief and public works. In desiring a balanced budget, Roosevelt was in good company. According to public opinion polls, the vast majority of Americans, regardless of class, opposed deficit spending. In 1937, even Marriner Eccles, the administration's leading proponent of deficit spending, supported Roosevelt's decision to slash spending.[22]

Roosevelt had no sooner put his economic policies into effect than disaster struck. Between the fall of 1937 and the spring of 1938, the economy suffered one of the sharpest declines in American history, a decline that wiped out many, though not all, of the previous gains. Over a nine-month period, industrial production declined by 33 percent, wages by 35 percent, and national income by 13 percent. Four million Americans rejoined the ranks of the unemployed.[23]

As conditions worsened, there ensued a lively national debate over economic policy. Conservatives tended to blame the "Roosevelt recession" on New Deal spending, taxation, and prolabor policies, all of which, they argued, had increased the costs of doing business and forced industry to curtail production. To achieve recovery, they said, the government must establish a climate conducive to business expansion. This it could do by cutting spending, balancing the budget, reducing taxes, and in general adopting a friendlier attitude toward business. Some New Dealers countered by accusing business of deliberately causing the economic downturn. According to this argument, leaders of business and finance had failed to defeat Roosevelt at the polls in 1936, and they had lost their control over the Supreme Court, which would no longer do their bidding. So, in order to discredit the administration, they had engaged in a "political strike of capital." They had precipitated a recession by refusing to invest and expand production. A variation of this argument held that monopolistic control of industry had caused the recession and that a healthy dose of trust-busting would bring recovery. An increasing number of economists, noting that the recession had followed Roosevelt's attempt to balance the budget, believed that government spending cuts had decreased mass purchasing power and had thereby reduced the demand for goods and services. In response to this reduced demand, business had curtailed production and laid off workers. If sharp cuts in federal spending had caused the recession, these economists argued, then obviously sharp increases in spending would spur recovery. Once conditions improved, the government could then turn its attention to reducing the deficit.

In evaluating the various explanations of, and remedies for, the recession, Roosevelt had no easy task. Given the existing state of economic knowledge, none of the proposed remedies seemed risk free or guaranteed to succeed. Nor did it help that Roosevelt's top advisers were sharply divided among themselves. Henry Morgenthau, although no apologist for business, forcefully argued that the president should try to restore the confidence of business by holding the line on spending. Harry Hopkins, Harold Ickes, Marriner Eccles, and others just as forcefully made the case for increased spending. Still others championed the antimonopoly cause. All of Roosevelt's advisers pleaded with him to act, but they also wanted him to act in conformity with their own recommendations. The debate within the administration became heated at times, and tempers flared. Several meetings between Roosevelt and Morgenthau ended in shouting matches, and after one of them, the treasury secretary, who was also the president's oldest and closest friend in the government, threatened to resign.[24] Conditions, meanwhile, continued to deteriorate, and the pressure on Roosevelt to act intensified.

Finally, in April 1938, as the recession entered its eighth month, Roosevelt sided with the spenders. At his request, Congress appropriated $3.75 billion for a variety of public works and relief activities. He also encouraged the Federal Reserve Board to loosen monetary strictures and thus make more bank credit available. At the same time, he satisfied antimonopolists by calling for a congressional investigation into the concentration of economic wealth and power.

Roosevelt's antirecession measures proved only partially successful. Beginning in the summer economic conditions began to improve, but they improved so slowly as to be almost imperceptible to most Americans. Moreover, to the extent that the antirecession measures of 1938 served as an experiment in fiscal and monetary policy, the results proved inconclusive. Not only did the economic revival fall short of expectations, but it was impossible to know whether the upturn resulted from increased spending, expansive monetary policies, or a combination of the two. No wonder, then, that Roosevelt, along with the vast majority of Americans, emerged from the recession unconvinced that deficit spending on a massive scale held the key to full recovery. Deficits might be necessary to fight wars and keep people from starving, they believed, but they made no sense as a long-term policy.

Reeling from his legislative defeats and from the damage to his reputation that the recession inflicted, Roosevelt tried to regain the initiative with one bold stroke. In 1938 he attempted to purge congressional conservatives from the Democratic party. For many years he had been talking casually with Rexford Tugwell and other advisers about the benefits of realigning the two major parties along liberal and conservative lines. As it stood, the Democratic party was more liberal than the Republican party, but there were enough conservative Democrats and enough liberal Republicans to muddy the ideological waters. By purifying the parties in such a way that one became genuinely liberal and the other genuinely conservative, voters would have a clear-cut choice on election day. Moreover, realignment presumably would make less likely the situation that had developed during Roosevelt's second term, a situation in which dissident Democrats had joined with Republicans to block the president's proposals.

Roosevelt had talked about realignment before 1938, and occasionally he had supported liberal non-Democrats, such as Sen. George Norris of Nebraska, a Republican, and Sen. Robert La Follette of Wisconsin, a Progressive. With only rare exceptions, however, he had scrupulously avoided taking sides when liberal and conservative Democrats contested for the same office. As the 1938 elections approached, however, Roosevelt, angered by opposition from within his own party to court-packing and executive reorganization, decided to oppose conservative Democrats and support liberal Democrats in upcoming primaries.

But almost from the beginning, everything seemed to go wrong. Indeed, even if he had performed flawlessly, Roosevelt would have encountered formidable obstacles to party purification. As it turned out, many primary contests turned on purely state and local issues, and try as he might, he could not focus attention on broader national concerns. Nor could he counter the image of himself as an interloper, interfering in local matters and attempting to dictate to citizens how they should vote. But Roosevelt also hurt his own cause. Because he waited until the last minute to commit himself to realignment, he and his agents did not have enough time to recruit strong candidates, with the result that some of the primaries became monumental mismatches between liberal nonentities and powerful, conservative incumbents. Nor did Roosevelt clearly define his criteria for opposing particular candidates. He described as a "dyed-in-the-wool conservative" one of his chief targets, Sen. Walter F. George of Georgia, even though George had supported a half-dozen or so key New Deal measures, including the NIRA, the AAA, the Social Security Act, and the Wagner Act. Yet in other states Roosevelt supported, or at least did not oppose, candidates with records comparable to George's. In some states, heavy-handed electioneering practices imparted an unsavory odor to the president's realignment campaign. In Kentucky and Florida, workers on the WPA payroll actively campaigned for Roosevelt-backed candidates, and in other states federal bureaucrats suddenly released funds for long-delayed federal highway and bridge projects.[25]

By the end of the primary season, Roosevelt had suffered an embarrassing series of defeats. Of the 10 conservative Democrats he had opposed, all but one won renomination. Worse still, those legislators who had survived the purge now had all the more reason to battle the president. A conversation between two prominent senators who returned to Washington despite Roosevelt's opposition summed up the president's predicament: "Roosevelt is his own worst enemy," one of the senators said. The other responded, "Not so long as I am alive."[26]

The November elections brought still more bad news. Just two years before, in the aftermath of Roosevelt's great reelection victory, some political experts had sounded the death knell for the Republican party. In 1938 the GOP demonstrated that it was alive and, if not completely well, at least much recovered. It picked up 82 seats in the House of Representatives, seven seats in the Senate, and 13 governorships. Suddenly, observers started writing Roosevelt's political obituary. "Clearly," said reporter Raymond Clapper, "I think that President Roosevelt could not run for a third term even if he so desired." In as sure a sign as possible that the Roosevelt spell had been broken, some ardent New Dealers began to distance themselves from the president. "There was a time when I would have bled and died for him," said Montana Senator James Murray, "but in view of the way he has been acting I don't want to have any more dealings with him and I just intend to stay away from him and he can do as he pleases."[27]

By 1938, lots of critics had declared open season not only on the president but on his family as well. Eleanor, although still much-loved, came under attack for "running all over the country" and for embracing supposedly radical causes such as racial integration. When Eleanor prompted her husband during a Hyde Park news conference, pundits remarked that she was the brains behind the New Deal or, alternatively, that her husband was grooming her to run for the presidency. The personal lives of the five Roosevelt children also received extensive, and mostly negative, publicity. By 1938, two of the children had divorced and remarried. When son James entered the insurance business and another son, Elliott, became general manager for a chain of radio stations owned by William Randolph Hearst, critics accused the Roosevelt sons of trading on their names. Later, James prompted charges of nepotism when he became a special assistant to his father.[28]

The president's own mood reflected the downturn in his fortunes. Aides found him uncharacteristically tired and irritable. Morgenthau, who seemed to bear the brunt of the president's ill temper, suspected that Roosevelt was trying to force him out of the administration. Only a reassuring word from Eleanor Roosevelt, to whom Morgenthau confided his suspicions, eased his mind. Harry Hopkins noticed the change in Roosevelt's mood, too, but he believed that the president had simply gotten bored with his job. Even the White House press corps witnessed a rare display of the president's temper when, during one of his biweekly news conferences, Roosevelt subjected Ernest K. Lindley, a friendly reporter who had written two favorable books about him, to an angry 40-minute tongue-lashing for an article he had written.[29]

To be sure, the first two years of his second term were not completely devoid of accomplishment. In 1937 and 1938, Congress not only revived relief and public works programs but passed a major farm bill, created a public housing program, enacted a landmark child-labor measure, and established a national system of minimum wages and maximum hours. These measures were important enough to constitute a third New Deal; significantly, however, they represented not the lone triumph of the president but the results of a richly cooperative effort such as that which had produced the famous legislation of the first term.

Roosevelt could also take solace in the fact that his personal popularity survived the setbacks of his second term. Late in 1938, according to a Gallup poll, 56 percent of the public approved of his performance as president. In the course of Roosevelt's travels in 1938, an incident occurred that seemed to symbolize the relationship the president still had with a large segment of the American public. In Marietta, Ohio, an elderly woman knelt down and reverently touched the ground where Roosevelt had stood.[30] Still, no one could deny that the first half of the second term marked the low point of the Roosevelt presidency. Although popular, he seemed unable to translate his popularity into concrete achievement. As a legislative leader, he had failed to win passage of his court-packing and executive reorganization measures. As a party leader, he had failed to remold the Democratic party in his own image. Above all, he had failed to bring about economic recovery, and many people were beginning to fear that the depression might become a permanent way of life.

Then and later, political observers probed the reasons for these failures. Many of Roosevelt's contemporaries blamed the president himself. In the aftermath of his great reelection victory, they said, he became overconfident and reckless. With one stroke, court-packing, he squandered much of the goodwill he had earned from Congress and the public. His delay in responding to the recession and his ill-conceived purge attempt worsened the damage. In short, they maintained, Roosevelt had only himself to blame. Later observers, while not absolving the president from all responsibility, tended to attribute the failures of the second term to circumstances beyond his control. Roosevelt, they argued, fell victim to a constitutional system of government that so dispersed and fragmented power that even a president at the peak of his popularity and influence found himself successively thwarted by the judiciary, Congress, and an intractable party system. As two historians put it, "His failure during the second term was not simply a series of personal frustrations but the encounter of a leader with an antileadership system."[31] By focusing on some of the structural obstacles to change, historians have provided a needed corrective to the tendency to overly personalize the history of the Roosevelt era. At the same time, however, they underestimated Roosevelt's own role in shaping events during the first years of his second term. The court-packing controversy, from which much else flowed, was decidedly of Roosevelt's own doing. Had he been more forthright in explaining his objectives and had he taken the elementary precaution of consulting with legislative leaders before announcing his proposal, Congress almost certainly would have approved judicial reform of some kind. Had Roosevelt handled the Court issue more prudently, he probably would have avoided the damaging controversy over executive reorganization, for it was its juxtaposition with court-packing that imparted sinister connotations to his reorganization plans. Had there been no uproars over Court reform and executive reorganization, Roosevelt probably would not have attempted to purge his party. As for the purge attempt, it might have had a more favorable outcome if Roosevelt had more carefully planned and more skillfully executed the operation. Finally, administration policy, not institutional imperatives, brought about the damaging recession of 1937–38. In this instance at least, Roosevelt, while not completely the master of his fate, bore primary responsibility for the stalemate that had developed by 1938.

7

A THIRD TERM AND THE ROAD TO WAR, 1938–1941

If at the beginning of his presidency Roosevelt had had a choice in the matter, he almost certainly would have preferred to deal primarily with military and international affairs rather than domestic problems. The depression, however, had left him no choice but to devote most of his attention to pressing domestic concerns. But beginning midway through his second term, a series of international crises, culminating in American entry into World War II in December 1941, allowed him to assume the desired role of global strategist. Those crises, despite their underlying tragedy and the additional burden of leadership they placed upon Roosevelt's shoulders, augmented his political fortunes. Indeed, had they not occurred, he undoubtedly would have retired from office at the end of his second term with memories of the court-packing debacle still fresh in everyone's mind, with the nation still mired in depression, and with his historical reputation still very much in doubt. As it was, in 1940 he ran for and won an unprecedented third term.

Roosevelt's preference for foreign affairs did not necessarily translate into clear and consistent policies. Indeed, he was so indirect, especially as he faced the issue of American entry into the war, that he kept even his closest aides guessing at any given time about his intentions. And while some observers purported to find in Roosevelt's actions a grand design, to the very eve of the Japanese attack on Pearl Harbor Roosevelt seemed more often to be reacting to events abroad than shaping them.

Roosevelt brought to the White House an intense interest in military and international affairs. Indeed, for the sheer satisfaction he derived from a job, nothing he had done before 1933 had equaled his wartime service as assistant secretary of the navy. That service had left him with only one regret: he had missed an opportunity to duplicate Cousin Theodore's battlefield heroics. But that regret made the prospect of assuming the president's role as commander in chief all the more attractive. Roosevelt's fascination with foreign affairs reflected not only his hero-worship of Theodore Roosevelt but also his own cosmopolitan background. As far back as he could remember, he had heard tales about faraway lands, especially from his mother, who liked to recount the experiences that she and her family had had in China. His own world travels had begun as a child, and by the age of 15, he had made the Atlantic crossing eight times. By the time he became president, he had visited Europe several more times and had traveled in Latin America. Tutored in French and German as a youth, he reputedly could say "my friends" (though little else) in 11 languages. Even his favorite pastimes, stamp collecting and sailing, enhanced his interest in, and knowledge of, the world beyond American shores.

Yet Roosevelt's worldliness was in fact limited. He had traveled more extensively than most presidents, to be sure, but on most of his trips abroad he had experienced only highly selective aspects of foreign life. During their visits to Europe, he and his parents had stayed in old hotels that catered to upper-class Americans or at the country estates of dukes and earls. Roosevelt's immediate predecessor, Herbert Hoover, could lay claim to at least as cosmopolitan a background as Roosevelt. Before he entered public service, Hoover, as a mining engineer and an international businessman, had lived much of his adult life abroad, including extended stays in Australia and Asia. He had encountered a broader cross-section of foreign populations than Roosevelt, who, except for a brief, unpleasant term in a German school, had traveled primarily in the company of people of his own kind. Then, too, for all of his being at home in the world, Roosevelt remained essentially American in outlook. Like most of his fellow citizens, he believed in the universality of American values and that peoples the world over would embrace those values if only they had an opportunity to do so. In this respect he was, as Isaiah Berlin noted, a typical child of the New World.[1]

Before he became president, Roosevelt's views on foreign policy had gone through several stages. As assistant secretary of the navy, he had been the militant ultranationalist, whose speak-loudly-and-carry-a-big-stick philosophy had seemed almost a parody of Theodore Roosevelt's pronounced martial spirit. During the national debate over the League of Nations, Roosevelt made himself over as an eloquent spokesman for international cooperation. "We must open our eyes," he said as a candidate for the vice presidency in 1920, "and see that modern civilization has become so complex and the lives of civilized men so interwoven with the lives of other men in other countries as to make it impossible to avoid . . . those honorable and intimate foreign relations which the fearful-hearted shudderingly miscall by that devil's catchword, 'international complications.'"[2] During the 1920s, even as he fought his own personal battle with polio, he had helped keep alive the spirit of Wilson's brand of internationalism.

During the 1932 presidential campaign, Roosevelt retreated from his internationalist stance. Under attack from newspaper mogul William Randolph Hearst, Roosevelt issued a carefully worded statement saying that the League of Nations had strayed from the path charted by Woodrow Wilson and that he therefore no longer favored American membership in the world body. Roosevelt's abandonment of the League, coupled with his lack of specificity during the 1932 campaign, reinforced his reputation as an opportunist. "Roosevelt," wrote journalist Henry Pringle, "hauls down banners under which he has marched in the past and unfurls no new ones to the skies."[3]

Although no one had known what banner he might be marching under next, he had made one thing clear from the outset: In his administration, foreign policy would emanate from the White House. When Cordell Hull became secretary of state, Brain Truster Raymond Moley, sensing what was in store for the gentlemanly former senator from Tennessee, hoped that "Hull's capacity for bearing pain was as great as it seemed to be." From the beginning, Roosevelt subjected his secretary of state to periodic humiliations. He developed the habit of going over Hull's head to deal directly with hand-picked undersecretaries and in general of keeping Hull in the dark about foreign policy initiatives. Yet appearances could be deceiving. For Hull was a resourceful politician in his own right, and his longevity in office attested not only to his ability to bear pain but also to his usefulness to the administration. On matters relating to foreign trade, the Spanish civil war (1936–1939), and American relations with Japan, Hull exerted major influence.[4]

As his presidency unfolded, Roosevelt increasingly had to confront two facts of life. One was a deteriorating international situation; the other was a powerful desire on the part of the American people to avoid foreign entanglements. The deterioration had been going on since the early 1930s, when Japan began aggressively expanding its power and influence in Asia. Aspiring to be an industrial and military power of the first rank but lacking the natural resources and land to do so, the Japanese invaded Manchuria in 1931. In Europe, meanwhile, the rise of the fascists in Germany and Italy threatened to shatter the uneasy peace that had prevailed since World War I. In response to these developments, few if any Americans actually favored isolating the United States from the world. Nor did most Americans look upon Japanese militancy in Asia and the spread of fascism in Europe with anything but horror. But they did believe that as a depression-bound nation, the United States had enough problems of its own without taking on the problems of the world.

Moreover, by the 1930s, the vast majority of Americans—some 70 percent, according to a Gallup poll—had come to believe that the United States had made a mistake by entering World War I, and they wanted to avoid making the same mistake in the future.[5] This view of World War I rested in part upon an interpretation of history that went roughly as follows: In 1917, Britain and France had gotten the United States to enter the war on their side by deceiving Americans into thinking that democracy and civilization were at stake in the fight against Germany. In reality Britain and France were no better than Germany; all three were fighting not for principle but for territory and power. In luring the United States into war, Britain and France had received help from President Wilson, who, during the years preceding American entry, had skewed American policy in favor of the Allies. American financiers and munitions makers, who stood to make fabulous profits from the war, had also helped lure the United States into the world conflict. According to this same version of history, the Treaty of Versailles, which ended the war, had divided the spoils of war among the victors, principally Britain and France, and fastened upon Germany a settlement so cruel that it was bound to stir resentment among the German people. For the United States the war had stifled reform, enriched the few at the expense of the many, curtailed civil liberties, and contributed to the agricultural depression of the 1920s and the Great Depression of the 1930s. In short, the war had brought nothing but disaster. By the 1930s, this critical interpretation of the war and its aftermath had adherents among prominent politicians, professional historians, and, presumably, large segments of the public. And although it was by no means the only possible reading of the evidence, given the existing state of historical knowledge, this interpretation was plausible.[6]

For the first five years of his presidency, Roosevelt steered cautiously between isolationism and internationalism. In 1933, with the support of prominent business leaders in search of new markets for their goods, he extended diplomatic recognition to the Soviet Union. After an initial display of saber-rattling in Cuba, he continued the practice of his Republican predecessors of improving relations with Latin America, labeling the process his "Good Neighbor Policy." Beginning in 1934, he supported Hull's effort to lower tariff barriers by negotiating reciprocal trade agreements, and in 1935 he unsuccessfully sought American membership in the World Court.

But Roosevelt also acted in ways that reinforced isolationism. In 1935 he initiated neutrality legislation that prohibited the sale of munitions to all belligerents whenever the president declared that a state of war existed. To be sure, he had wanted discretionary power to apply the arms embargo to aggressor nations; but Congress, remembering that Wilson had skewed American policy to favor the Allies, denied Roosevelt that power, and he acquiesced. In the mid-1930s he supported the Senate investigating committee, the Nye Committee, that convinced many people that munitions makers and financiers had helped drag the United States into the war. Roosevelt fully cooperated with the committee's chairman, Sen. Gerald P. Nye of North Dakota, ordering the State Department and all other government agencies to open their files to committee inspection and assuring Nye and his colleagues that he sympathized with their efforts to clip the wings of arms manufacturers.[7] During the Spanish civil war, which began in 1936 and which pitted the republican government against fascist-supported rebels, Roosevelt assumed a more rigidly isolationist posture than some of the isolationists. Senator Nye, for example, wanted to relax neutrality policies so as to allow the United States to assist the republican forces in Spain. At the urging of Secretary of State Hull, however, Roosevelt insisted upon strict neutrality and thereby played into the hands of the rebels, who ultimately succeeded in toppling the Spanish government.[8]

Roosevelt also let it be known that if another war broke out, he would keep the United States out of it. In August 1936, he delivered his famous peroration on war. Referring to his visit to the front in 1918, he said, "I have seen war. I have seen war on land and sea. I have seen blood running from the wounded. I have seen men coughing out their gassed lungs. I have seen the dead in the mud. I have seen cities destroyed. I have seen two hundred limping, exhausted men come out of line—the survivors of a regiment of one thousand that went forward forty-eight hours before. I have seen children starving. I have seen the agony of mothers and wives. I hate war." He concluded, "We can keep out of war, if those who watch and decide . . . possess the courage to say 'no' to those who selfishly or unwisely would let us go to war." Samuel I. Rosenman, who helped write the speech, believed that the president's antiwar sentiments reflected heartfelt convictions.[9]

Roosevelt doubtless did hate war, as any rational person would. His "I hate war" speech, however, was simply the latest example of his habit of rewriting his personal past to meet the needs of the present. True enough, he had visited the front in 1918, and he had seen gruesome scenes of death and destruction. But at the time, the experience of being so close to military action had thrilled and excited him. The thrill never left him, and even as he was publicly denouncing war, he was privately regaling friends with stories about that long-ago trip to war-torn Europe. What had been a routine inspection tour of the combat zone by a government bureaucrat became, in Roosevelt's repeated tellings, a great adventure of near misses and narrow escapes. As with Theodore Roosevelt, a part of Franklin Roosevelt looked upon war as an ennobling experience.[10]

In October 1937, in his most important foreign policy speech to that time, Roosevelt sounded a strongly internationalist note. Several months earlier, Japan had intensified hostilities in China and in the process had killed thousands of civilians. In an obvious reference to Japan, but with Germany and Italy doubtless also in mind, Roosevelt said that a "reign of terror and international lawlessness" threatened "the very foundations of civilization," and that if it continued, no nation, including the United States, would be safe, for in the modern world all peoples and nations were interdependent. If offending nations failed to mend their ways, he said, then the rest of the world should combat the spread of international lawlessness as it would the spread of a life-threatening disease. "When an epidemic of physical disease starts to spread, the community approves and joins in a quarantine of the patients in order to protect the health of the community against the spread of the disease."

In the days and weeks following the speech, people waited, some with hope, others with apprehension, for Roosevelt to explain what concrete form his proposed quarantine would take.

But except for a bland statement that he would continue the search for a peaceful solution to the world's problems, nothing happened, leaving friends and critics of the administration to pore over Roosevelt's speech as they might a hieroglyphic. Eventually, there seemed to be as many interpretations as there were interpreters; some believed that Roosevelt was contemplating military action against aggressor nations, others that he was planning some kind of economic sanctions. In this instance, as in others, Roosevelt's contemporaries probably tried too hard to discern a hidden meaning in what he had said. In all likelihood, Roosevelt intended his quarantine speech not as a trial balloon for some new policy but simply as a way to focus public attention on an increasingly perilous world situation. To the extent that he had anything specific in mind, apparently it was a kind of collective cold-shoulder approach, whereby peaceful nations would cut off communications with aggressor nations.[11]

By 1938, tensions in Europe had so increased that war seemed imminent. In response, Roosevelt turned from talk of quarantines to cautious support for British and French efforts to appease Germany and Italy. Appeasement had not yet acquired a bad name. In fact, a large and respectable body of opinion on both sides of the Atlantic maintained that negotiations with Germany, with a view to rectifying some of the harshest provisions of the Treaty of Versailles, might satisfy or "appease" the Germans and avert a second world war. Not everyone favored appeasement, to be sure. In Great Britain, Winston S. Churchill, a dissident conservative, believed that concessions to Germany would only feed its appetite for further aggression. In the United States, Secretary of State Hull doubted that any good could come of attempts to pacify what he called "desperado nations."[12]

Roosevelt and most of his advisers, however, believed that appeasement was at least worth a try. In March 1938, Undersecretary of State Sumner Welles informed the British ambassador to the United States that "the President frankly recognized that certain political appeasements in Europe with which this Government had no direct concern and in which this Government could not participate were evidently an indispensable factor in the finding of bases [sic] for world peace." In April, Roosevelt issued a statement saying that the United States viewed with "sympathetic interest" an agreement between Great Britain and Italy that recognized Italy's conquest of Ethiopia, which it had brutally invaded in 1935. In September, a war scare swept Europe as Hitler demanded incorporation of parts of Czechoslovakia into the German state. When British prime minister Neville Chamberlain set out to negotiate a settlement of the crisis in Munich, Roosevelt, fully aware of the probable terms of any settlement, sent Chamberlain a two-word cablegram: "Good man." At the end of the conference, which partially dismembered Czechoslovakia, Roosevelt refrained from endorsing the specific agreements reached at Munich but told Chamberlain, "I fully share your hope and belief that there exists today the greatest opportunity in years for the establishment of a new order based on justice and on law."[13] Roosevelt's tacit support for appeasement is important mainly because it demonstrates, in retrospect, that he was no wiser or more farsighted than Neville Chamberlain and other leaders who hoped that negotiations with Germany would bring peace in their time.

Subsequent events, especially Germany's invasion of Czechoslovakia in March 1939 and Italy's invasion of Albania in early April, diminished, but did not completely destroy, Roosevelt's hopes that war might somehow be avoided. During the spring and summer of 1939, he tried to play the role of honest broker, willing to negotiate a solution to the European crisis. In April he appealed to Hitler and Mussolini to pledge that for a period of at least 10 years they would not attack any of the 31 nations of Europe and the Near East. If they promised to respect the territorial integrity of their neighbors, Roosevelt said, then the United States would participate in negotiations that might help Germany, Italy, and all other nations meet their economic needs without resorting to force. Hitler's mocking rejection of Roosevelt's appeal failed to deter Roosevelt, and between April and the outbreak of war in September, he repeatedly appealed to Germany and its neighbors to resolve their differences at the peace table. It was possible, of course, that Roosevelt fully expected Hitler to reject his appeals but issued them anyway in order to put the German leader unambiguously on record as the aggressor who had rebuffed all peace offers. Then, too, he may have wanted to make certain that no one ever blamed him for not having done everything in his power to avert war.[14] But it was even more likely that the man who had never abandoned hope that he might one day walk again still hoped that he might bring about a peaceful resolution of the European crisis. In any event, as the leader of a militarily unprepared and economically weakened nation, Roosevelt found himself powerless to effect the course of events in Europe, which had long since acquired a momentum of their own. Indicative of military unpreparedness was the fact that in September 1939, in terms of manpower, the U.S. Army ranked nineteenth in the world, behind the armies of Belgium and Greece.[15]

The one conspicuous exception to his powerlessness involved the plight of German Jews and other victims of Nazi terror. By the late 1930s, most Americans knew, however vaguely, that Jews were suffering under Nazi rule. Certainly there could be no doubt about Nazi intentions after November 1938, when, following the assassination of a German embassy official in Paris by a Jewish refugee, Nazi mobs went on a rampage, savagely beating Jews, burning their synagogues, and vandalizing their property. In response to these developments, several legislators, including Sen. Robert Wagner and Rep. Edith N. Rogers, urged Roosevelt to support revision of the Immigration Act of 1924, which had sharply restricted the number of European Jews and other nationals who could enter the country. Debate on the issue eventually centered on the so-called Wagner-Rogers bill, which would allow 20,000 children under the age of 16, most of them Jews, to enter the United States.

Roosevelt had long since outgrown the unthinking anti-Semitism that was common among members of old-stock, upper-class, Protestant American families. He had formed his administration without apparent regard for ethnic or religious affiliation, and as a result, more Jews served in the New Deal than in any previous administration. Noting the closeness to the president of Henry Morgenthau, Samuel Rosenman, Felix Frankfurter, and others, detractors spoke scurrilously of a "Jew Deal." In 1935, responding to rumors that he himself had Jewish ancestors, Roosevelt wrote a correspondent: "In the dim distant past they may have been Jews or Catholics or Protestants. What I am more interested in is whether they were good citizens and believers in God. I hope they were both." When Germany intensified its persecution of the Jews in 1938, Roosevelt said all the right things. He told reporters, "I myself could scarcely believe that such things could occur in a twentieth-century civilization."[16]

In truth, however, Roosevelt's deeds did not match his words. He tried to persuade other nations to accept Jewish refugees, but he refused to open the doors to his own country more than a crack. True enough, under existing law, more refugees from nazism fled to the United States than to any other country, including British-controlled Palestine. And yet the number who found refuge in America was but a fraction of those who wanted to emigrate but could not because of restrictive American policies. An exchange Roosevelt had with a reporter revealed much about the relative importance he attached to the issue. Did he intend to request changes in the immigration laws? the reporter asked. "That is not in contemplation," Roosevelt responded matter-of-factly. "We have the quota system." Within moments, he and reporters were laughing and joking about some other matter. As for the Wagner-Rogers bill, Roosevelt declined to take a stand. [17]

The political context in which Roosevelt operated helps explain, though not excuse, his lack of aggressive action on this issue. According to one poll, upward of 80 percent of the public opposed allowing greater numbers of European Jews to enter the country. Anti-Semitism helped shape prevailing sentiments, but so did fears that new immigrants would intensify competition for already scarce jobs and that Hitler would infiltrate their ranks with spies and saboteurs. Even many American Jews, fearful that an influx of their European coreligionists would intensify anti-Semitism, opposed changes in existing policy. Thus, from a political standpoint, Roosevelt's cautious stance on the issue was understandable, though no less regrettable. [18]

On 1 September 1939, Germany attacked Poland. Two days later, Britain and France declared war on Germany. That night, Roosevelt went on the radio to reassure the American people that he would do everything possible to keep the United States out of the war. Unlike Woodrow Wilson, however, he would not ask Americans to remain neutral in thought. "Even a neutral has a right to take account of facts," he said. "Even a neutral cannot be asked to close his mind or conscience." [19]

In addressing the European war, Roosevelt received ambiguous guidance from the public and from members of his administration. According to public opinion polls, most Americans not only wanted Britain and France to win the war but also wanted the United States to sell military supplies to the Allies. Those same polls, however, indicated that two-thirds of the public believed that it was more important to stay out of the war than it was to ensure an Allied victory. The advice Roosevelt received from his aides reflected some of these contradictions of public opinion. Some, such as Harold Ickes and Henry Morgenthau, favored all-out aid to the Allies, even at the risk of involving the United States in the war. Others, including the army and navy brass, opposed extensive aid to Britain and France for fear of depleting America's war supplies and thereby jeopardizing national defense. Still others, believing that the United States would benefit most from an outcome in which neither side won a complete victory, urged Roosevelt to help secure a negotiated settlement to the war.

Roosevelt, for his part, believed that a victorious Germany would threaten America's physical security and vital economic interests, and he moved quickly but cautiously to honor the urgent pleas from the Allies for material assistance. His first order of business was to seek revision of the Neutrality Acts. Summoning Congress into special session, he urged legislators to repeal the arms embargo and to place the sale of arms and other commodities on a "cash and carry" basis, which would require belligerent nations to pay for goods in cash, then carry those goods away from American ports in their own vessels. Since Great Britain dominated Atlantic sea lanes, the Allies would be the exclusive beneficiaries of Roosevelt's proposed changes in the law. Significantly, Roosevelt presented his plan to Congress and the public not as a measure to help Britain and France win the war but as a way of keeping the United States out of the war. During the ensuing debate, Roosevelt demonstrated that he had learned much from the court-packing debacle. This time, instead of springing his proposal on Congress at the last minute, he conferred with legislators at the earliest stages of deliberation. Then, when the measure reached the floors of Congress, he maintained a discreet silence, allowing his legislative leaders to carry the burden of the fight. In October, Congress, by wide margins in both houses, handed Roosevelt his first major victory since the court-packing defeat, and soon thereafter military supplies began to flow to the allies.[20]

Following Hitler's lightning-quick subjugation of Poland in September, an eerie calm settled over western Europe, as neither side wanted to take the offensive during the winter months. To the east, meanwhile, the Soviet Union, which had entered into a nonaggression pact with Germany in August 1939, sought to satisfy its own territorial ambitions by occupying the eastern half of Poland, establishing bases in the Baltic states, and wresting territorial concessions from Finland. All of this prompted Roosevelt to denounce Soviet aggression. "The Soviet Union," he said, "as everybody who has the courage to face the fact knows, is run by a dictatorship as absolute as any other dictatorship in the world. It has allied itself with another dictatorship, and it has invaded a neighbor . . . infinitesimally small."[21]

The lull in the fighting in western Europe—the phony war, some called it—persuaded Roosevelt once again to try his hand at peacemaking. In November he told Adolf Berle, an assistant secretary of state, that he would propose, as a basis for peace, that all countries produce all the goods they could, take what they needed, put the rest into a pool, and allow all countries to draw from the pool according to their needs.

Oddly, Roosevelt's proposal sounded very much like a global version of Upton Sinclair's End Poverty in California (EPIC) and other production-for-use plans of the 1930s. In 1935, Roosevelt had described EPIC as "perfectly wild-eyed" and "impossible, absolutely impossible" beyond the local community level. Now, apparently, he believed that such an approach might yield a peaceful world order. He never got the chance to advance his plan, however, for in February 1940, when he sent Sumner Welles to Rome, Berlin, Paris, and London to discuss the possibilities of a negotiated settlement, Welles met rebuff after rebuff. British and French leaders, especially, reacted with alarm to the Welles mission, for they feared that Roosevelt was willing to sacrifice their vital interests in the interests of a negotiated settlement.[22]

Germany's terrifying offensive in the spring of 1940 dashed the last remaining hopes of a peaceful settlement. During April and May, Hitler's armies swarmed over Norway, Denmark, the Netherlands, and Belgium. In June, the unthinkable happened: France fell to the Nazis with surprisingly little resistance. The German Führer triumphantly received the French surrender in a railway car at Compiègne, the scene of Germany's great humiliation just 20 years earlier. Suddenly Hitler stood, Napoleon-like, astride the continent of Europe, poised to attack the British Isles. Japan, meanwhile, took advantage of the fall of France to move into northern French Indochina.

Germany's spring offensive reshaped American public opinion. Most people still opposed a declaration of war, but now, for the first time, a majority of them believed that it was more important to aid Britain than to stay out of the war. Roosevelt, in turn, denounced Germany and Italy as "the gods of force and hate" and said that a victory for them would "endanger the institutions of democracy in the Western World." He also lashed out with unprecedented fury at the so-called isolationists. If they prevailed, the president hinted darkly, the United States would experience "the nightmare of a people lodged in prison, handcuffed, hungry and fed through the bars from day to day by the contemptuous, unpitying masters of other continents." To ward off such a dreadful fate, Roosevelt declared that henceforth the United States would simultaneously follow two courses of action: "We will extend to the opponents of force the material resources of this nation and, at the same time, we will harness and speed up the use of those resources in order that we ourselves in the Americas may have equipment and training equal to the task of any emergency and every defense." To these ends, Roosevelt requested and received a massive increase in defense spending. He also negotiated a spectacular destroyers-for-bases deal by which the United States gave Britain 50 destroyers in exchange for 99 year leases on British naval bases in the Western Hemisphere and a pledge that, if worse came to worst, Britain would never surrender its fleet to Germany. Roosevelt also strengthened the hand of interventionists and at the same time gave a bipartisan cast to his administration by bringing into his Cabinet two prominent Republicans, Henry L. Stimson as secretary of war and Frank Knox as secretary of the navy. Both men favored all-out aid to Great Britain.[23]

Following the fall of France, Roosevelt secretly authorized additional funding for the government-sponsored effort to develop an atomic bomb. He had first learned of the potential destructive power of nuclear energy in October 1939, when Alexander Sachs, an economist and occasional adviser to the president, approached Roosevelt on behalf of several refugee scientists, including Albert Einstein, who had fled from the Nazis. Sachs told Roosevelt that given the current state of research in the atomic field, it might be possible for an advanced nation to build a bomb of unprecedented destructiveness, and that Germany might be in the process of building such a bomb. "Alex, what you are after is to see that the Nazis don't blow us up," Roosevelt responded. The subsequent top-secret effort to develop a bomb, eventually known as the Manhattan Project, raised profound questions, not only about when and under what circumstances an atomic bomb might be deployed but also about the relationship between science and the state. But in 1940, in the aftermath of the fall of France, no one, least of all the president, was concerned about anything but beating Germany to the bomb.[24]

All in all, Roosevelt took some bold steps in 1940. But when it came to military preparedness, Congress was prepared to go even further. In September, it approved the Selective Service Act of 1940, which made all men between the ages of 21 and 45 eligible for one year of military service. Fearful of overplaying his hand, Roosevelt took almost no part in the movement that produced the first peacetime draft in the nation's history. Congress also appropriated some half-billion dollars more for defense than Roosevelt had requested.[25]

Hitler's spring offensive not only drew the United States closer to active involvement in the war; it raised the possibility that Roosevelt might run for a third term. Although the Constitution did not restrict presidential tenure, no chief executive had ever served longer than eight years, and by the 1930s, the two-term limit had long since become a fixture in the American political system. Ulysses S. Grant and Woodrow Wilson had both considered running for third terms, but they had met swift and sure rebuffs from their own parties. In 1928, the United States Senate had gone on record declaring that "the precedents established by Washington and other Presidents . . . in retiring from the Presidential office after their second term has become, by universal concurrence, a part of our Republican system of government" and that "any departure from this time-honored custom would be unwise, unpatriotic, and fraught with peril to our free institutions."[26] The rise of the European dictators, coupled with Roosevelt's own efforts to increase presidential power through court-packing, executive reorganization, and the purge of the Democratic party, seemed to strengthen the case for a limitation on presidential tenure.

As the election approached, and especially as the international situation worsened, Roosevelt came under pressure to seek reelection. Big-city party bosses, such as Chicago's Ed Kelly and Jersey City's Frank Hague, wanted the Democrats' top vote-getter once again to head their party's ticket. They urged him to run, and so did administration stalwarts Harold Ickes, Henry Wallace, and Thomas Corcoran. When France fell, opinion polls disclosed that for the first time a majority of the public supported a third term.[27]

Roosevelt, meanwhile, remained inscrutable. Indeed, no other issue during his entire career enhanced his sphinxlike image as much as the issue of whether he would seek a third term. He seemed to take sheer delight in keeping people, including his family members, guessing. Years later, Eleanor Roosevelt, in an extraordinary admission that revealed worlds about their relationship, said that Franklin had never revealed his true intentions even to her. At one time or another, he told several advisers and friends that he had no intention of running for reelection. In the summer of 1939, according to James Farley, the president said that the Democratic party should never become too dependent on him or on any one person, but that, so as not to lose his clout with Congress, he would wait until February 1940 before taking himself out of the running. But February came and went, and still Roosevelt made no announcement. In March he did tell an assembly of the party faithful, "My great ambition on January 20, 1941, is to turn over this desk and chair in the White House to my successor, whoever he may be, with the assurance that I am at the same time turning over to him as President a nation intact, a nation at peace, a nation prosperous." He also accepted a position as contributing editor to *Collier's* magazine at a salary of $75,000, to become effective the following year.[28]

Yet even as he disavowed any intentions of running for reelection, he acted in ways that virtually insured his renomination. By refusing to say, as General Sherman once had said, that he would not seek, nor would he accept, the nomination of his party for the presidency, he not only left the door to a third term wide open but also discouraged prospective candidates from organizing effective campaigns. He also failed to groom a successor. For a time, it appeared that he was positioning Harry Hopkins for a run at the presidency; but by 1940 Hopkins's persistent bad health had ruled him out. Occasionally, Eleanor asked her husband if he should not be making more of an effort to prepare someone to take his place. "Franklin," she later recalled, "always smiled and said he thought people had to prepare themselves, that all he could do was to give them opportunities and see how they worked out." Whenever anyone did emerge as a possible candidate, Roosevelt would undercut him. Thus, for example, he passed the word that Vice President Garner was too conservative, that Henry Wallace was too indecisive, that Cordell Hull was too old, that Jesse Jones was not well enough, and that Burton Wheeler, his foe in the Court fight, was so unacceptable that he, Roosevelt, would rather vote for a Republican.[29] Without Roosevelt's blessing, no one stood much of a chance.

Still, when the Democratic convention opened in July 1940 in Chicago, the scene of Roosevelt's first nomination, no one knew quite what to expect. Then came the moment when Sen. Alben W. Barkley, the convention's permanent chairman, read a statement in Roosevelt's behalf to the delegates. "The President," Barkley said," has never had and has not today any desire or purpose to continue in the office of the President, to be a candidate for that office or to be nominated by the convention for that office. He wishes in all earnestness and sincerity to make it clear to all that this convention is free to vote for any candidate."[30] The delegates listened in stunned silence. Roosevelt, it seemed, had taken himself out of the race. But slowly the implications of the statement began to dawn on them: If they were free to vote for *any* candidate, then they were free to vote for Roosevelt. Suddenly, Roosevelt loyalists poured into the aisles chanting, "We want Roosevelt." That same chant boomed out, over and over again, from loudspeakers throughout the hall.

Chicago mayor Ed Kelly, leaving nothing to chance, had stationed someone with a microphone in the basement of the convention hall to lead the cheers for the president.

Roosevelt's actual nomination the next evening came as something of an anticlimax. It also left many of the delegates with a residue of bitterness. They wanted Roosevelt, to be sure. But they believed that he had gone too far in his attempt to portray himself as the reluctant candidate responding to the call of duty. They may also have suspected that, by requiring them to come, hat in hand, to plead with him to run for a third term, he was punishing those party members who had failed to stand by him in the court-packing and purge attempts. The delegates resented even more Roosevelt's insistence that Henry Wallace replace John Nance Garner as his running mate. To many old-line Democrats, Wallace, an ex-Republican and a mystic, epitomized the impractical, starry-eyed idealists who dominated the New Deal. But Roosevelt remained adamant. "Well, damn it to hell," he reputedly told aides. "They will go for Wallace or I won't run and you can jolly well tell them so." In order to put Wallace over the top, Roosevelt not only had to issue an ultimatum, but also to send Eleanor to Chicago to assuage hurt feelings.

Finally, when all the unpleasantness was over, Roosevelt addressed the convention over a telephone hookup from the White House. Holding the pose of reluctant candidate to the end, he told the delegates that he had lain awake nights, asking himself if he had the right to call men and women into the armed forces while he himself had refused the call of duty. "I had made plans for myself, plans for a private life," he said, but "my conscience will not let me turn my back on a call to service."[31]

The Republicans, meanwhile, demonstrating how Roosevelt had turned the rules of normal political behavior topsy-turvy, nominated one of the most unlikely candidates ever to run for the presidency. He was Wendell L. Willkie, a 48-year-old Indiana native who had been a long-time Democrat, had voted for Roosevelt in 1932, had joined the GOP only the year before, and had never held an elective office. A Wall Street lawyer and president of a giant utility conglomerate, Willkie had risen to national prominence as a foe of the Tennessee Valley Authority. But even with that, most people had probably never heard of him until the Republican convention, when, on the sixth ballot, he edged out the front-runners for the nomination, Sen. Robert A. Taft of Ohio and Thomas E. Dewey the anti-racketeering district attorney of New York County.[32]

Despite, or perhaps because of, his amateur status, Willkie proved to be a surprisingly effective candidate. With his coarse voice, his wrinkled suits, and a lock of hair that seemed forever tumbling over his forehead, he looked and sounded like Jefferson Smith, the character Jimmy Stewart played in a popular movie of the time, *Mr. Smith Goes to Washington.* In fact, Willkie agreed with Roosevelt on most domestic and international issues. A supporter of extensive aid to Britain, he endorsed the destroyers-for-bases deal and thereby defused an issue that might otherwise have dominated the electoral contest. As the campaign progressed, however, Willkie, like Alf Landon four years earlier, became increasingly strident in his attacks on Roosevelt and the New Deal, even charging that the president secretly planned to dispatch American troops to Europe. In one GOP radio broadcast, the narrator said, "When your boy is dying on some battlefield in Europe—or maybe in Martinique—and he's crying out, 'Mother! Mother!'—don't blame Franklin D. Roosevelt because he sent your boy to war—blame YOURSELF, because YOU sent Franklin D. Roosevelt back to the White House!" On the defensive for one of the few times in his career, the president made his famous promise to "the mothers and fathers" of America: "I have said this before, but I shall say it again and again and again. Your boys are not going to be sent into any foreign wars." Before the campaign ended, Roosevelt had regained the offensive. Speaking in Brooklyn, he said that an "unholy alliance" of extreme reactionaries and extreme radicals who "hate democracy and Christianity" had formed within the Republican party.[33] Although some of his advisers later dismissed his harsh statements as normal campaign rhetoric, Roosevelt apparently believed that a victory for Willkie would somehow bring dangerous and undemocratic elements to power. At least, that was the thrust of a remark he made on election night, when he learned that he had won a third term with about 55 percent of the vote. Referring to the uprisings that had brought the Nazis to power in Germany, he said to a friend, "We seem to have averted a Putsch." Most people did not share Roosevelt's view of the outcome, however. Willkie had made a favorable impression on the electorate, and public opinion polls indicated that if it had not been for the war and people's natural reluctance to make a change in the midst of a world crisis, he might have won the election.[34]

Following the election, Roosevelt, looking gaunt and gray, embarked on a Caribbean cruise aboard the *USS Tuscaloosa.* For several months, friends and family members had been concerned about his health. The sea had worked as a restorative before, and so it did this time. Accompanied by Harry Hopkins and members of his personal staff—Eleanor almost never accompanied her husband on such outings—Roosevelt fished, played poker, and engaged in lighthearted conversation. Before long, he was looking tanned and rested.

While at sea, he received an urgent message from British prime minister Winston S. Churchill describing Britain's current plight. Churchill had assumed office in May 1940, but he and Roosevelt had been corresponding since the outbreak of the war. According to Churchill, a German invasion of the British Isles no longer seemed likely, as it had only a few months before; nevertheless, Britain faced two critical problems, one military and one financial. Militarily, Germany was wreaking havoc on North Atlantic shipping lanes, threatening to shut down supply routes to Great Britain. The United States could help, Churchill said, by transporting goods to Britain on American ships and by escorting British ships across the Atlantic. Financially, Churchill warned Roosevelt, Britain was running out of cash and soon would be unable to buy the supplies it needed to fight Hitler.

Addressing himself to Britain's financial plight, Roosevelt devised the idea of lend-lease. In January 1941, Roosevelt asked Congress for the power to lend, lease, sell, transfer, or exchange war materials with any nation whose defense he deemed vital to the defense of the United States. Roosevelt's admirers frequently exaggerated his legislative prowess, but there was no need to do so in the case of lend-lease. Not only did Roosevelt devise the idea, but he also staged a brilliant campaign in its behalf, expertly using fireside chats, press conferences, messages to Congress, and personal contacts with individual legislators. Using his familiar world-as-neighborhood imagery, he argued that lend-lease was as natural as one neighbor lending his garden hose to another neighbor whose house was on fire. Once the fire was out, the neighbor would return the hose.

Roosevelt also appealed to the public's concern about national security. "Never before," he warned, "has our American civilization been in such danger as now," for Hitler was bent on world domination. Already, he said, enemy agents were at work in the Western Hemisphere, trying to soften it up for the kill. Roosevelt appealed to the public's sense of idealism. The United States, he said, should help build a world in which the four freedoms prevailed: the freedoms of speech and religion, and the freedoms from want and fear. Finally, Roosevelt appealed to the public's desire to stay out of the war. He said that lend-lease although not entirely free of risk, would lessen the likelihood of the war reaching American shores. Equal to the task, Roosevelt's congressional supporters affixed to lend-lease the patriotic number 1776 and the title, a bill "to Promote the Defense of the United States." Critics of the president's proposal argued that lend-lease would deplete American arsenals and thereby weaken the nation's defenses, that it would invest the president with near-dictatorial powers, and worst of all, that it would almost certainly embroil the United States in war.[35]

In addition to defending his plan on its merits, Roosevelt attacked opponents of lend-lease in ways that did raise questions of fairness and abuse of executive power. He called his opponents appeasers and claimed that some of them were wittingly or unwittingly aiding the enemy. His supporters followed suit. Robert E. Sherwood, a distinguished playwright and presidential speechwriter, called Charles A. Lindbergh, the aviation hero and outspoken noninterventionist, "simply a Nazi with a Nazi's Olympian contempt for all democratic processes." With no evidence to substantiate his charge, Harold Ickes publicly described Lindbergh as the "No. 1 Nazi fellow traveler" and "the first American to raise aloft the standard of pro-Naziism." In addition to sanctioning attacks by his aides, Roosevelt authorized the Federal Bureau of Investigation to tap the telephones and open the mail of some of his foreign policy critics. It was clear that Roosevelt had come to regard some prominent isolationists not simply as critics of his foreign policy but as enemies of the Republic. And in dealing with enemies of the Republic, he seemed to reason, one did not adhere to legal niceties.[36]

In truth, Roosevelt's suspicions about the isolationists were unfounded. To be sure, the movement against intervention attracted its share of disreputable characters, such as Charles Coughlin, the famed radio priest who by this time had become a raving anti-Semite. It also attracted Nazi sympathizers and, during the period of the nonaggression pact between the Soviet Union and Germany, members of the American Communist party. But these were extremists, and extremists were probably no more numerous among the isolationists than they were among the interventionists. Indeed, the isolationists comprised a diverse and respectable lot. They included University of Chicago president Robert Hutchins; Socialist party leader Norman Thomas; labor leader John L. Lewis; progressive senators William Borah, Hiram Johnson, Robert La Follette, Jr., and Burton Wheeler; conservative senators Robert Taft and Arthur Vandenberg; and former president Herbert Hoover. None of the isolationists actually advocated cutting the United States off from the rest of the world. Almost all of them opposed Germany and Japan and favored some sort of aid short of war to Britain. They also favored a strong national defense. Indeed, they objected to lend-lease in part, at least, because they feared that in giving aid to Britain, Roosevelt might deplete American arsenals and leave the United States defenseless.

During the lend-lease debate, isolationists sometimes matched the rhetorical excesses of Roosevelt and his interventionist supporters. Wheeler, for example, described lend-lease as "the New Deal's triple A foreign policy; it will plow under every fourth American boy."[37] Others accused Roosevelt of being a dictator and a warmonger. For the most part, however, they raised legitimate questions about the costs and consequences of lend-lease, as well as other interventionist proposals. Significantly, the isolationists anticipated some of the themes of the so-called Realist school of American foreign relations. Isolationists argued, for example, that there were definite limits to American power and that the United States could not always bend the world to its own will. Isolationists were more likely than Roosevelt to talk in terms of a balance of power and spheres of influence. Charles Lindbergh argued that a complete victory for either Britain or Germany would leave a dangerous power vacuum in Europe, perhaps to be filled by the Soviet Union, and that American interests would best be served by a negotiated settlement.

Isolationists also pressed Roosevelt for a more specific definition of national self-interest and national security. If worse came to worst and Germany did defeat Britain, what, they asked, would be the consequences for the United States? In answer to predictions that a victorious Germany would deny the United States access to markets abroad, isolationists responded that the United States could more than compensate by expanding trade within the Western Hemisphere. In response to interventionist predictions that Hitler, once having conquered Europe, might successfully attack the United States, isolationists argued that so long as the United States maintained adequate defenses, a successful invasion was virtually impossible. For one thing, Hitler would have to keep too many troops in Europe policing occupied countries. For another, although German planes were capable of reaching sites in the Western Hemisphere, an actual invasion would require a huge naval and supply system that was beyond the capacity of Germany or any other nation.

In his eagerness to discredit the isolationists, Roosevelt brushed aside many of the questions they raised. In so doing, he passed up a golden opportunity to provide the public with a valuable lesson in the rudiments of national security and national self-interest. In any event, Roosevelt's strategy of attacking the isolationists rather than their arguments worked, in the short run, at least, and in March lend-lease became law.

During the next eight months, Roosevelt moved the United States closer to active participation in the war. But he did so in such fits and starts that observers at the time, and historians later, puzzled about his intentions. For every step forward, it seemed, Roosevelt would take a half-step backward. Thus, following the bold step of lend-lease, Roosevelt insisted that before the British could reap the benefits of the new program, they would have to divest themselves of all of their assets in the United States and agree to long-term economic and trade policies that would benefit the United States. More important, although Roosevelt had dealt swiftly with Churchill's request for financial help, he rejected the prime minister's equally urgent request to help ensure the safe passage of war supplies from the United States to Britain. German submarines were then sinking British ships faster than British shipyards could replace them. In response, Churchill had urged Roosevelt to allow the American navy to escort British ships part or all of the way across the Atlantic. But Roosevelt refused, telling aides that public opinion would not yet sanction naval escorts. In April 1941, however, he did extend the American security zone in the Atlantic to include all of Greenland and the Azores. He then ordered American ships and planes to patrol this newly expanded area and to notify British convoys of the whereabouts of enemy submarines.

Britain continued to suffer great losses, and in May, Roosevelt seemed to be on the verge of ordering escorts. In an address to the nation he vividly described the plight of the British, announced for the first time his extended patrolling policy, and pledged to take all action necessary to ensure the safe delivery of goods to Britain. "The delivery of needed supplies to Britain is imperative," he intoned. "This can be done; it must be done; it will be done." The president's speech and the initially favorable response to it raised the hopes of some, and the fears of others, that Roosevelt would authorize naval convoys or perhaps even seek revision of the Neutrality Act so as to allow American ships to carry supplies directly into British ports. Nothing of the sort happened. The next day, Roosevelt blandly told expectant reporters that he had no plans either to permit convoys or to revise the Neutrality Act. To the interventionists within his administration, Roosevelt would only say that, by his accounting, public opinion was not yet ready for convoys. But he would add cryptically that he was waiting for an incident to occur and that he expected it to occur at any time. Some of his advisers took this to mean that he was waiting for a pretext to begin convoys or possibly even to seek a declaration of war against Germany.[38]

Roosevelt's practice of advancing and then partially retreating increasingly set him at odds with his secretary of war, Henry L. Stimson. At 74, Stimson was at once the administration's senior statesman, its most outspoken interventionist, and the most perceptive critic, inside or outside the administration, of Roosevelt's response to the international crisis. By early 1941, Stimson had concluded that unless the United States did whatever was necessary to ensure the safe passage of military supplies to England, Germany would win the war. He based his gloomy conclusion in part on projections by the Navy Department that if Germany continued to sink British merchant ships at the current rate, Britain would run out of supplies within six months. Stimson believed that Roosevelt had insufficiently prepared the American public for the steps that he, of necessity, would have to take to save Britain. By portraying all of his actions, including lend-lease, as efforts to keep the United States out of the war, Roosevelt had misrepresented his intentions, which were, or should have been, to defeat Germany. During the spring and summer of 1941, Stimson urged Roosevelt to be brutally frank with the public and to explain that he had tried to keep the United States out of the war but that there now was no other way to defeat Hitler than to join forces with those nations fighting Germany. Stimson suggested to Roosevelt that he tell Congress, "It has now become abundantly clear that, unless we add our every effort, physical and spiritual as well as material, to the efforts of those free nations who are still fighting for freedom in this world, we shall ourselves be brought to a situation where we shall be fighting alone at an enormously greater danger than we should encounter today with their aid." Stimson argued, too, that it would be morally reprehensible to wait for some comparatively minor incident, say the sinking of an American vessel, to trigger American entry into the war. Enough was at stake that the country should face up to its responsibilities and enter the war directly.[39]

Stimson feared most that Roosevelt was inadvertently, and dangerously, narrowing his options. For by continuing to encourage the public to believe that Germany could be defeated without the United States entering the war, Roosevelt was foreclosing the possibility of going to Congress and getting authority to take steps that, though they might risk war, were essential to British survival and to America's national security. As for the majority of Americans who still opposed entry into the war, Stimson argued that they would support steps that might lead to war if Roosevelt told them that there was no other way to defeat Hitler. If Roosevelt, with his great powers of persuasion, would lead, Stimson assured him, "the whole country would follow." George III's mother reputedly told her son to be a king. In the spring of 1941, Stimson was telling Roosevelt to be a leader.[40]

Their respective reactions to Germany's invasion of the Soviet Union in June 1941 vividly underscored the differences between Roosevelt and Stimson. Both men understood immediately that Hitler's bold but risky decision to break the German-Soviet nonaggression pact had profoundly changed the nature of the war. But Stimson believed that Roosevelt should seize the initiative by establishing Atlantic convoys and stepping up aid to Britain. With German forces now divided between two fronts, Stimson reasoned, this was the time to strike the death blow. Roosevelt, by contrast, while ordering military aid to the Soviets, believed that the German invasion of Russia made full-scale American involvement in the war much less likely.[41]

During the summer and fall of 1941, Roosevelt reestablished his pattern of advance and partial retreat. In July, in accordance with an agreement with Denmark, he dispatched marines to Iceland as he had earlier to Greenland. He also approved a plan to provide naval escorts for British ships as far as Iceland. But before this plan could go into effect, he reversed himself, this time apparently because a convoy system would require transferring more of the Pacific Fleet to the Atlantic; Roosevelt feared that such a step would encourage Japanese expansionism in the Pacific. In mid-August, Roosevelt apparently reversed himself again. Meeting secretly with Prime Minister Winston Churchill off the coast of Newfoundland, Roosevelt, by Churchill's account, indicated his intention to convoy British ships from America to as far east as Iceland. Churchill left the so-called Atlantic Conference with the impression that Roosevelt planned to force an incident in the Atlantic that would serve as a pretext for expanded American involvement in the war.[42]

A few weeks later, such an incident did occur in the North Atlantic. On 4 September, an American destroyer, the USS *Greer*, was en route to Iceland when it received a message from a British patrol plane that a German submarine lay ten miles ahead. Instead of trying to evade the U-boat, the *Greer* set out in pursuit of it. Finally, after tracking the submarine for several hours, the American vessel established the U-boat's exact location and radioed that information to the British. A British plane promptly arrived on the scene and attacked the U-boat with four depth charges. The submarine then fired torpedoes at the *Greer,* and the *Greer* answered with depth charges. Through it all, neither vessel was hit. Moreover, by the American Navy's own account, there was no evidence that the U-boat knew the nationality of the ship with which it had exchanged shots.

Nevertheless, Roosevelt had his incident. In a highly distorted version of events, he told the public that the German submarine had initiated hostilities with the *Greer,* and, knowing full well its nationality, had fully intended to sink the American destroyer. This was piracy, pure and simple, the president said, and further proof that Germany was bent on creating a "permanent world system based on force, on terror, and on murder." Henceforth, Roosevelt announced, the navy would convoy British merchant ships in American "defensive waters." In addition United States ships and planes would no longer wait to be attacked by German vessels but would, in effect, shoot them on sight. Other incidents soon followed, allowing Roosevelt, in quick order, to gain (albeit with exceedingly narrow margins) congressional approval to arm American merchant ships and to allow those ships to transport cargo directly into Allied ports.[43]

Believing that the public was still not sufficiently alert to the dangers posed by Germany, Roosevelt matched his actions with increasingly fervent rhetoric. In one speech he claimed that the United States had come into the possession of secret maps showing that Germany planned to conquer Latin America and divide it up into five vassal states. He also claimed to have documentary proof that Germany planned to abolish all existing religions, establish "an International Nazi Church," substitute *Mein Kampf* for the Bible, and replace "the God of Love and Mercy" with "the god of Blood and Iron." The documents Roosevelt cited were, in fact, forgeries prepared by British special operations, but whether he knew that the documents were bogus is unclear.[44]

Roosevelt's effort to depict the battle against the Nazis as a quasi-religious war encountered one embarrassing obstacle: the Soviet Union. In June, after he determined that Russian armies might indeed hold out against Germany, he sought to provide aid to the Soviet Union. As a means of combating Hitler, American aid to the Soviets made perfect sense. True, in a moral sense, there was little difference between Stalin and Hitler; by 1941, Stalin already had the blood of millions of his own countrymen on his hands. True, too, in terms of democratic values, there was little difference between Germany and the Soviet Union; both were equally repressive societies. Some argued that America's best interests lay in a war of mutual self-destruction between the two European powers. Sen. Harry S. Truman of Missouri, who was no isolationist, expressed the sentiments of many when he said that if Germany appeared to be winning, the United States should help the Soviet Union, and if the Soviet Union appeared to be winning, the United States should help Germany. Still, in the circumstances then existing, Germany, as the more expansionist power, posed the greater immediate threat to American interests. Roosevelt clearly understood this, and he said as much in private. Apparently, however, he feared that a hardheaded appeal to self-interest would not be sufficiently persuasive, so in public he tried to soften the image of the Soviet Union. Once he even implied that Russians enjoyed as much religious freedom as Americans, which brought stern rebukes from American religious leaders and a suggestion from one congressman that Roosevelt invite Stalin to Washington so that the Soviet dictator might be baptized in the White House swimming pool.[45]

Roosevelt's effort to aid the Soviet Union raised one other issue, an issue that assumed increasing significance with the passage of time. Some of his advisers, including, most notably, William C. Bullitt, urged Roosevelt to seek a quid pro quo with the Soviets: in exchange for military assistance from the United States, the Soviets would relinquish the territory in eastern Europe that they had seized since 1939 and pledge not to use the war as an excuse for further territorial aggrandizement. The Russians, so the argument went, desperately needed American aid and would have no choice but to accede to American demands. Moreover, a precedent existed for making demands on the Soviets: Roosevelt had already required Britain to meet certain conditions before receiving lend-lease, and at the Atlantic Conference he had gotten Churchill to agree to a no-spoils-of-war policy. But Roosevelt declined to attach strings to American aid to the Soviet Union, perhaps for fear that if he made too many demands on the Soviets, he would drive Stalin back into the arms of Hitler, the Soviets would conclude a separate peace treaty with Germany, and as had happened during the First World War, the eastern front would collapse.[46] In any event, the initial terms of this fledgling alliance between the United States and the Soviet Union became in retrospect one of the intriguing might-have-beens of the period preceding American entry into the war.

Beyond supplying aid to Britain and Russia—serving, in Roosevelt's words, as "the great arsenal of democracy"—Roosevelt's general aims in the autumn and winter of 1941 provoked much speculation. Discerning his intentions was always a tricky business, but it was never more difficult than during this time. His on-again, off-again convoy policy, his cryptic comments to his advisers, his bold rhetoric but less bold actions—all provided the basis for any number of plausible but conflicting interpretations. Perhaps, as many isolationists believed, he had maneuvered the United States to the brink of war by stealth and guile and was simply waiting for a pretext to complete the job. Or perhaps, as many interventionists, including Stimson, believed, he was looking for ways to involve the United States in the war, not for any sinister reason, but because he viewed full American participation as essential to the defeat of Hitler. In their view, Roosevelt held back from seeking a declaration of war because he believed that isolationism still held a stranglehold on important segments of the public and Congress and because he wanted to bring the country to a greater state of military readiness before entering the war.

Yet three crucial pieces of evidence, taken together, indicate that Roosevelt still had hopes, however slim, that the United States could confine its participation in the war to supplying goods to Britain and Russia. The first was his rejection of Stimson's advice to give all-out aid to Britain and Russia and to tell the American people that such an all-out effort was the only way to defeat Germany. Roosevelt's rejection of Stimson's approach—not once, but repeatedly—suggested that Roosevelt simply did not yet share the secretary's assumption that full participation in the war was necessary to defeat Germany. The second was Roosevelt's failure to use the *Greer* sinking and subsequent incidents as a pretext for a declaration of war. He had hinted that he was waiting for such an incident to occur, but when it did, he passed up the opportunity to exploit it as much as he might have. The third piece of evidence bearing upon Roosevelt's intentions were public opinion polls, which indicated that the public was not inflexibly opposed to entry into the war. To be sure, in 1941 polls recorded that nearly four-fifths of the public was opposed to an immediate entry into the war. But that same number believed that the United States would enter the war eventually. And nearly three-fifths of those responding to the polls said that it was more important to defeat Germany than to stay out of the war. The seeming disparity in the polls was probably owing to the fact, as Stimson later argued, that no government leader, least of all the president, had told the public that entry into the war was necessary to defeat Germany.[47] In any event, on the basis of polling data, which he monitored closely, Roosevelt had reason to believe that public opinion posed no stone wall of resistance either to intensified measures to help Britain and Russia or, if he made the case, to full-scale entry into war. But he did not make the case for war to the public, because in all probability he shared the public's hope that somehow, some way, war might be avoided. To the very end, Roosevelt apparently believed that if worse came to worst and the United States did end up in the war, its participation could be limited to sending supplies and air and naval forces—but not combat troops—to Europe.

By December 1941, the very situation Stimson feared had nearly come to pass. The United States and Germany were engaged in an undeclared war in the Atlantic. But by repeatedly saying that American entry into the war was not necessary to defeat Hitler, Roosevelt had made it virtually impossible, even at this late date, to reverse himself and ask for a declaration of war. And without a declaration of war, Roosevelt might continue to send supplies to the Allies, but he could not put the economy on a war footing and throw the full weight of the nation's industrial might into the fight against Germany. By December 1941, the initiative for war or peace seemed to have passed to the Germans, and Hitler seemed in no hurry to resolve Roosevelt's dilemma by declaring war on the United States. The impasse in the Atlantic might have continued indefinitely had it not been for dramatic events in the Pacific.

It is ironic that Roosevelt's Far Eastern policies sparked far less debate than his European policies, and yet, in the short run at least, proved to be far more important. During the 1930s, as Japan had forcibly expanded its power and influence in China, Roosevelt had talked tough but still avoided a confrontation. He had offered only token assistance to China, and diplomatic and trade relations between the United States and Japan continued unabated. Even the Japanese sinking of an American gunboat, the *Panay*, in December 1937 caused only a momentary crisis in relations between the two countries.[48]

Roosevelt's approach to Japan reflected various considerations. During the 1930s, he and his advisers regarded the Far East as secondary to Europe in its importance to strategic American interests. Moreover, Roosevelt did not want to do the bidding of countries such as Great Britain, which had more at stake in Asia than the United States did. Despite

Roosevelt's sentimental attachment to China, where his mother's family had been involved in trade, and despite the traditional commitment of the United States to the territorial integrity of China, Roosevelt believed that, when all was said and done, the Chinese had to fight their own battles. To the extent that economic considerations shaped American policy during the 1930s, they probably worked to mitigate tensions between the United States and Japan, for Japan bought nearly 10 percent of America's exports, compared with 3 percent for China. Finally, the diplomats who helped guide the president's thinking on Far Eastern affairs, especially the American ambassador to Tokyo, Joseph C. Grew, argued that a policy of restraint might increase the chances that moderate Japanese statesmen would triumph over extremists for control of national policy. In sum, until well into 1940, American policy toward Japan rested upon a series of calculations about what the United States realistically might or might not accomplish in the Far East. Significantly, when Roosevelt publicly discussed relations between the United States and Japan, he did so not in the realistic language of diplomats but, as in his "Quarantine Address," in idealistic and moralistic terms.

Beginning in 1940, relations between the two countries rapidly deteriorated. In September, Japan entered into a formal alliance with Germany and Italy and occupied northern Indochina. The following summer, it moved into southern Indochina and began to cast a threatening eye on vital British and Dutch possessions in the Far East, including Singapore and the oil-rich Dutch East Indies. Roosevelt privately viewed the Japanese moves primarily in terms of their effects on the war in Europe. If Japan invaded British and Dutch colonies, Britain would have to divert military resources from the Atlantic to the Pacific, would face the loss of oil and other vital raw materials, and would be weakened in its ability to resist Germany. Similarly, if Japan attacked the Soviet Union, the Russians would have to divert men and supplies from their battle against Germany. Anything that hampered Britain's or Russia's ability to resist Germany endangered the United States; therefore, the United States had an interest in curbing Japanese expansionism in the Far East. Publicly, Roosevelt described the Japanese occupation of Indochina as additional evidence that the dictator nations intended to conquer and carve up the world.

Roosevelt sought to deter Japan from further expansion, and to do so in such a way as to avoid, or at least delay, war between the two countries. Deterrence took the form of transferring the Pacific Fleet to Pearl Harbor, of fortifying the Philippines, of increasing aid to China, and most important, of imposing upon Japan a succession of increasingly stringent economic and trade sanctions. In July 1940, the United States ceased sales to Japan of aviation gasoline and high grade scrap metal. In September, Roosevelt extended the embargo to include all types of scrap metal. Then, in July 1941, in response to the Japanese move into southern Indochina, the administration froze all Japanese assets in the United States and placed a de facto embargo on the sale of oil. During subsequent negotiations, American diplomats insisted that normal trade would resume only if Japan withdrew its forces from China and Indochina and severed its official connections with Germany and Italy.[49]

The embargo on oil served not as a deterrent but as a provocation. Faced with diminishing supplies of oil, Japanese leaders decided that unless the United States resumed shipments of oil and gave them a free hand in China, they would wage war in the Pacific to acquire new sources of oil and other raw materials. Their war plans called for a daring surprise attack on Pearl Harbor, where America's Pacific Fleet was stationed. Admiral Isoroku Yamamoto, who originated the idea of attacking Pearl Harbor, believed that America's industrial capacity would make it difficult for Japan to win a long war with the United States. But Yamamoto reasoned that if Japan, in one bold stroke, could knock out America's Pacific Fleet for at least six months, then Japan would have time to capture the Dutch East Indies, Malaya, and the Philippines and to set up a defensive perimeter in the Pacific from which to repulse an American counterattack. For this strategy to succeed, however, time was of the essence. The longer Japan waited, the more its existing supplies of oil and other products would diminish and the weaker it would become. Moreover, the longer Japan waited, the more likely it was to experience unfavorable weather conditions for a Pacific offensive. In short, Japanese leaders decided that if war was to come, they would rather fight sooner than later. In July they instructed the army and navy to begin preparations for a secret attack on Pearl Harbor. In September, officials of the Japanese government formally decided that if they did not achieve their objectives through diplomacy, they would wage war before the end of the year.

Roosevelt, meanwhile, still hoped to avert or at least postpone a showdown in the Pacific, but he held firm to his position. Applying what he believed to be the lessons of Munich, he maintained that if he yielded to Japanese demands, he would only invite more demands. He worried, too, that making concessions to Japan might weaken the will of Britain and Russia to resist Hitler. Above all, having linked Japan and Germany as moral evils and partners in world conquest for so long, he could not very easily strike a deal with Japan without inviting a great deal of public cynicism.

No one, of course, can say what would have happened if Roosevelt had relaxed the oil embargo, made other concessions to Japan, or even, as the Japanese proposed in August, met privately with the Japanese premier. Perhaps a conciliatory attitude on the part of the United States would have persuaded Japanese leaders to postpone or even rethink the idea of war in the Pacific. But such an outcome was by no means certain. If, for example, Roosevelt had rescinded the embargo, he might only have underscored Japanese dependency upon the United States; presumably, it would have been all the clearer to Japanese leaders that what the United States gave, the United States could take away. By the fall of 1941 and perhaps even earlier, most Japanese leaders seem to have concluded that their nation could not achieve greatness unless it acquired its own sphere of influence, independent of the United States or any other nation.

Speculation about what Japan might or might not do came to an abrupt end on Sunday, 7 December 1941, when wave after wave of Japanese planes attacked the American fleet at Pearl Harbor. Roosevelt had just finished lunch and was talking with Harry Hopkins when he received word of the attack. To Hopkins, the president seemed calm, even relieved that the question of American intervention in the war had now been taken out of his hands. But calm soon gave way to anger as Roosevelt learned of the dimensions of the disaster at Pearl Harbor: 18 ships either sunk or badly damaged, and nearly 200 planes lost; American casualties totaled 2,403 men dead and 1,178 wounded.[50]

The next day, Roosevelt appeared before a joint session of Congress to request a declaration of war against Japan. "Yesterday," he began, "December 7, 1941—a date which will live in infamy—the United States of America was suddenly and deliberately attacked by naval and air forces of the Empire of Japan." Congress approved Roosevelt's request with only one dissenting vote.[51]

The United States was now at war against Japan, but Roosevelt still faced the problem of Germany, which, although allied with Japan, was not required by the terms of the alliance to declare war on the United States. Stimson had urged him to include Germany and Italy in his war message. Roosevelt had declined because he feared that some legislators would argue that, because Japan and not Germany or Italy had attacked the United States, a declaration of war against all three Axis powers was unwarranted. On 11 December, Hitler and Mussolini resolved Roosevelt's dilemma by declaring war on the United States.[52]

No persuasive evidence has ever surfaced to suggest that, as some people suspected, Roosevelt knew in advance of the attack on Pearl Harbor but allowed it to proceed in order to bring a reluctant nation into the war against Germany. In fact, these suspicions provide an extreme example of the common tendency to read into Roosevelt's life a design and order where none existed. This does not mean that Roosevelt was blameless for the conspicuous lack of preparedness at Pearl Harbor. Subsequent investigations demonstrated that in the months and weeks leading up to the attack, top civilian and military leaders, from Roosevelt to his commanders in Hawaii, had made numerous errors and miscalculations. Intelligence specialists had broken Japan's secret code, and American leaders knew that war in the Pacific was imminent. But they expected the Japanese to attack British or Dutch possessions. They simply did not believe that Japan would attempt so risky a venture as an attack on Pearl Harbor. Moreover, American leaders, harboring all sorts of racist stereotypes about the Japanese, did not think that they were capable of such a feat. From this underestimation of Japanese capabilities stemmed many other errors and miscalculations, including the discounting or dismissal of clues that in retrospect seem to have offered indications of Japanese intentions.[53]

Insofar as Roosevelt was concerned, the attack on Pearl Harbor was rich in irony. If he had been bolder and more decisive, he might have led the nation into war before Pearl Harbor. But if he had done so, the populace would not have been as much in a mood to fight as it was after the Japanese attack. As it was, Pearl Harbor rallied and united the American people to an extent that even Roosevelt could never have equaled. Even in tragedy, it seemed, his luck had held.

8

WAR LEADER, PART 1, 1941–1943

For several months following the Pearl Harbor disaster, until well into 1942, bleakness clouded the war effort of both the United States and its partners. Abroad, Allied forces met one defeat after another. At home, production snags, labor shortages, and general confusion hindered mobilization. Then the tide of war began to turn in favor of the Allies. Roosevelt's performance during this first difficult stage of the war defied easy evaluation. This was in part because he involved himself, haphazardly and incompletely at times, in a vast array of matters and in part because decision making was a richly collaborative process that no one person, not even Roosevelt, dominated. Still, two things in particular about his leadership became apparent. One was his tendency, unavoidable, his admirers maintained, to focus on the needs of the moment without considering the long-range consequences of his actions. The other was his remarkable combination of personal dynamism and buoyant optimism, which bedeviled his critics, obscured the contradictions and inconsistencies in his management of the war, and once again helped banish fear from the nation.

In truth, there was much to fear in the aftermath of Pearl Harbor, as there had been during the depression. In the first place, the Allies faced a bleak military situation. Following Pearl Harbor, Japanese forces struck with lightning speed at British and American possessions throughout the Pacific. Before long, they had occupied the Philippines, Malaya, and the oil-rich Dutch East Indies. They had invaded New Guinea, from which they menaced Australia, and they had conquered Burma, from which they threatened India. Before the disaster at Pearl Harbor, American military experts had believed that Hawaii lay far beyond Japan's reach; now, fearing the worst, they worried about an attack on the West Coast of the United States. On the other side of the globe, the fight against Germany raged on three fronts—in Russia, in North Africa, and on the Atlantic—and on all three fronts, the Allies were faring badly. Despite fierce resistance, German troops had driven deep into the Soviet Union. There, by the summer of 1942, they had dispersed themselves along a 1,000-mile line running from Leningrad in the north to the Caucasus in the south. In North Africa, Axis forces threatened Egypt and the Suez Canal. In the Atlantic, German submarines continued to take a terrible toll on Allied shipping.

The United States, meanwhile, seemed ill prepared to meet the challenges of war. Having all but emptied its arsenals by providing aid to Britain and Russia, it now suffered severe shortages of everything from battleships to guns. Worse still, initial efforts to replenish military storehouses proceeded sluggishly, and when the war began, rifles were in such short supply that some draftees were drilling with broomsticks. Other problems hindered mobilization. Hitler reputedly said that the United States lacked the unity and discipline to seriously threaten Germany for another 30 or 40 years. At first, it seemed that he might be right. In the first flush of anger after Pearl Harbor, business leaders, farmers, and workers all pledged their wholehearted cooperation in support of the war effort; before long, however, they were quarreling over wages, prices, and a multitude of other issues. The nation also experienced racial and ethnic tensions. Moreover, though Pearl Harbor may have ended the debate between the isolationists and the interventionists, it did nothing to quiet partisan political bickering. To the extent that full mobilization would require a united and harmonious citizenry, the United States appeared to be headed for trouble.

In short, the United States faced a perilous situation. It seemed possible that Germany would knock Russia out of the war, turn its full fury on Great Britain, and perhaps even link up with Japan somewhere in the Near East or in Asia—all before the United States could throw the full weight of its industrial and human resources into the balance. Few people realized, Army Chief of Staff George C. Marshall later recalled, how close Germany and Japan were to winning the war.

Following Pearl Harbor, Roosevelt therefore had to address three related problems: national morale, military strategy, and economic mobilization. Morale—that elusive but undeniably important sense of common purpose and collective well-being—was his first concern. Initially, building morale posed little difficulty, for Pearl Harbor had aroused the American people to a fever pitch. But sustaining morale for the long haul—that was the greater challenge. Because the fields of battle were far from American shores, most people, even those who had loved ones in the armed services, lacked a sense of personal involvement in the war. Then, too, because the United States had emerged from World War I relatively unscathed, Americans had little understanding of the nature of modern war or of the sacrifices they might be called upon to make. For most Americans, if the Somme had any meaning at all, it was simply the name of a river in some faraway land.

Americans also seemed to hold exaggerated notions, untempered by experience, of their nation's prowess in war. Media coverage of the conflict both reinforced and reflected these notions. For example, early newspaper accounts of the fighting in the Pacific, often the products of rewrite men who were nowhere near the scene of battle, told tales of American derring-do, conveying the impression that any single American could lick 20 enemy soldiers. Confidence was a good thing—the United States could not win the war without it. But overconfidence could easily lead to complacency or, if things went badly enough on the fighting fronts, to bitter disillusionment. In either case, the war effort would suffer. Roosevelt, therefore, had to try to modulate the public temper, adjusting it in such a way as to avoid either euphoric highs or depressing lows.

He also had to contend with widespread public support for throwing the full force of American might against the Japanese. After all, it was they, and not the Germans, who had attacked the United States. But Roosevelt and his military advisers had wisely decided upon a Europe-first strategy, reasoning that Germany posed the greater threat to American interests. They reasoned further that to defeat Japan first would leave Germany standing, but to defeat Germany first would inevitably lead to Japan's collapse. People did not have to like the Europe-first strategy, but they did need to tolerate it. So in addition to everything else, Roosevelt had to redirect some of the anger that people felt toward the Japanese toward the Germans.

During the first months of the war, Roosevelt seemed to follow the promptings of a kind of sixth sense that told him when national morale needed attention. He sought, successively, to reassure, to inspire, and to explain and defend Allied strategy. First came reassurance. Thus, on a melancholy Christmas Eve two weeks after Pearl Harbor, Roosevelt, as if to say that life would go on, presided over the traditional lighting of the Christmas tree. Twenty thousand persons crowded onto the south lawn of the White House for the ceremony, and many more listened to it over a national radio hookup. Roosevelt, whose own four sons had already left for the war, gave a brief speech, then introduced Winston Churchill, who had arrived in Washington two days earlier to plot strategy. Roosevelt's listeners doubtless drew reassurance not so much from what he said as from the sound of his familiar, confident voice.[1]

Two weeks later, on the occasion of his State of the Union address, Roosevelt decided that the time had come for inspiration. He stressed national security, of course, and he emphasized the dangers inherent in an Axis victory. But, like Woodrow Wilson, though without Wilson's grand eloquence, Roosevelt defined the war in idealistic terms. "We are fighting, as our fathers have fought, to uphold the doctrine that all men are equal in the sight of God," he said. "Those on the other side are striving to destroy this deep belief and to create a world in their own image—a world of tyranny and cruelty and serfdom. . . . No compromise can end that conflict. There never has been—there never can be—successful compromise between good and evil. Only total victory can reward the champions of tolerance, and decency, and freedom, and faith." During his meetings with Churchill, Roosevelt insisted that they issue a high-sounding statement of principle, even though the prime minister was annoyed at having to take time out from plotting strategy. The resulting "Declaration by United Nations" placed the Allies, including the Soviet Union, on the side of life, liberty, independence, religious freedom, human rights, and justice; it placed the Axis on the side of savagery, brutality, and world subjugation.[2]

Although his rhetoric had a Wilsonian ring to it, Roosevelt avoided his mentor's hard-sell approach to the war. He declined, for example, to reestablish Wilson's propaganda agency, the Committee on Public Information, which had helped generate prowar hysteria. Roosevelt shunned the more strident approach not out of any particular concern for civil liberties but for practical reasons: he wished to avoid the disillusionment that would inevitably result from such an approach. More important, because fewer people opposed the Second World War than had opposed the First, selling the war required little effort.

In February 1942, after a barrage of unremittingly bad news from the Pacific, Roosevelt thought he detected the first signs of defeatism. Moreover, he had begun to hear potentially debilitating criticism of his Europe-first strategy. To counter growing public pessimism, Roosevelt delivered one of his most famous fireside chats. He began by reminding his listeners that Americans had experienced tough times before. During the Revolutionary War, he recalled, George Washington and the Continental army had faced formidable odds and recurring defeats. Moreover, some selfish, jealous, and fearful Americans—fifth columnists, Roosevelt called them—had declared Washington's cause hopeless and had called for a negotiated settlement. But Washington had persevered. Roosevelt also answered those who wanted to concentrate American forces in the Pacific rather than disperse them along several fronts. Before the broadcast, the White House had put out the word that the president wanted people to have a world map at hand during his speech. Once on the air, Roosevelt asked his listeners to follow along on their maps as he described the various battle fronts and their relation to one another. If the Americans withdrew from any one front, he argued, they would play into the hands of the Axis, which was pursuing a divide-and-conquer strategy. Finally, Roosevelt said that the enemy had described the United States as a nation of weaklings who would hire somebody else to do their fighting for them. "Let them repeat that now," he said slowly and dramatically. "Let them tell that to General MacArthur and his men. Let them tell that to the sailors who today are hitting hard in the far waters of the Pacific. Let them tell that to the boys in the Flying Fortresses. Let them tell that to the Marines." Some of Roosevelt's supporters considered his fireside chat so effective that they urged him to go on the radio more often. But Roosevelt feared that familiarity would breed, if not contempt, at least indifference. "For the sake of not becoming a platitude to the public," he wrote a friend, "I ought not to appear oftener than once every five or six weeks."[3]

To the extent that he could personally sustain public morale, Roosevelt's most effective weapon was his own coolness under fire. He knew it, too. Shortly after Pearl Harbor, he drafted a statement for the press, then affixed to it the name of his press secretary, Stephen Early. The statement had Early noting how impressed observers were that "the President seems to be taking the situation of extreme emergency in his stride, that he is looking well and that he does not seem to have any nerves." People seem to have forgotten, the statement continued, that the president had been through much the same thing during World War I, the only difference being, he added in something of an understatement, that then he had been assistant secretary of the navy, and now he was commander in chief.[4]

Roosevelt's confident, unruffled demeanor was more than an actor's pose. As during previous crises in his life—his bout with polio, the assassination attempt, the Hundred Days—people close to him watched carefully for cracks in his placid exterior. They found almost none. During the war no one, not even Eleanor, watched him more closely or saw him more often than William D. Hassett, his executive secretary. In an entry in his diary, Hassett described Roosevelt as "unruffled in temper, buoyant of spirit, and, as always, ready with a wisecrack or a laugh, and can sleep anywhere whenever opportunity affords—priceless assets for one bearing his burdens, which he never mentions." Obviously, Hassett added, Roosevelt had "no desire to be a martyr, living or dead."[5] Not even bad news seemed to dampen his spirits. In May 1942, for example, he received the expected, but still awful, news that the Philippines had fallen to the Japanese. Four days later, he was at Hyde Park, where he rose before dawn and went bird-watching. Back for breakfast, he reported excitedly to Hassett that he had identified 22 different birds, including the marsh wren, the red-winged blackbird, and the bittern.[6] Another time, he was spending the weekend at Shangri-La, his rustic retreat in the Catoctin Mountains of Maryland, when a military aide arrived from Washington with urgent news from the Pacific: the United States had sustained heavy losses in a crucial naval battle off Savo Island, near Guadalcanal. As his guests chatted in the background, Roosevelt studied a map and listened to the details of what turned out to be one of the worst defeats in American naval history. A few hours later, he was acting almost as if nothing had happened. At dinner he mentioned to his companions that things were "not going so well in the Pacific," but then quickly dropped the subject. Before long, he was regaling his guests with long and funny stories.[7] One of Roosevelt's close advisers, Samuel Rosenman, interpreted the president's serenity as a sign of complacency. Rosenman complained to Henry Morgenthau that "the President doesn't devote more than two days a week to the war. . . . I have been up at Shang-ri-la three times, and he sits there playing with his stamps." Perhaps, Morgenthau suggested, Roosevelt was thinking about weighty matters while he played with his stamps. Rosenman continued to worry, but even he had to concede that Roosevelt's remarkable composure under pressure had salutary effects on national morale.[8]

Of the two other problems that Roosevelt confronted after Pearl Harbor—military strategy and economic mobilization—military strategy commanded the greater part of his interest. Contrary to the impression Rosenman and many others had of him, he was not a passive commander in chief. To the contrary, he relished the exercise of his military responsibilities, especially during the first year and a half of the war.[9] His first task was to organize the American military leadership. When Churchill and his staff visited the White House over the Christmas holidays in 1941, they were shocked by what they found. Sir John Dill, who had just recently stepped down as head of Britain's highly structured Imperial General Staff, wrote home in dismay: "There are no regular meetings of their Chiefs of Staff, and if they do meet there is no secretariat to record their proceedings. They have no joint planners and executive planning staff." As for the president, "he just sees the Chiefs of Staff at odd times, and again no record. . . . The whole organization belongs to the days of George Washington." The United States, Dill concluded, "has not—repeat not—the slightest conception of what the war means, and their armed forces are more unready for war than it is possible to imagine." Churchill concurred. "An Olympian calm," he reported to his war cabinet upon his return to London, "had obtained at the White House. It was perhaps rather isolated. The President had no adequate link between his will and executive action."[10]

Gradually, and as need required, the American setup took on a semblance of order, although Roosevelt himself had little to do with the ordering process. In January 1942 the Americans and the British, at the urging of George Marshall, created the Combined Chiefs of Staff to coordinate Allied strategy. So as to be able to hold their own in planning sessions with their better-organized British counterparts, the American service chiefs—Marshall of the army, Henry "Hap" Arnold of the army air corps, and Ernest J. King of the navy—informally convened themselves into a Joint Chiefs of Staff. Eventually, at Marshall's urging, Roosevelt appointed Admiral William D. Leahy to serve as his personal representative on this interservice body. Thus, typical of the way things seemed to happen under Roosevelt, the Joint Chiefs of Staff, which became a fixture in the American military setup, came into being without federal statute, without executive order, and without even the formal approval of the president.[11]

Of the joint chiefs, Marshall and King carried the most influence with the president. Marshall had served as army chief of staff since 1939 and was intelligent, aloof, enormously able, and one of the few members of Roosevelt's inner circle who could resist the president's charms. Roosevelt had once tried calling Marshall by his first name, but after seeing the look of disapproval on Marshall's face, went back to calling him "General." In contrast to the stately Marshall, Admiral King had a reputation, apparently well deserved, for heavy drinking, ill-temperedness, a scandalous personal life, and a pronounced impatience with the democratic process. That reputation had almost cost him a chance to achieve his ambition to head the navy. But his masterful performance during the undeclared naval war in the Atlantic in 1941 earned him a second chance, and shortly after Pearl Harbor, Roosevelt appointed him chief of naval operations and commander in chief of the American fleet. Some military experts considered King to be one of the greatest military strategists of the twentieth century. Others believed that his narrow devotion to naval interests limited his vision. But even his detractors conceded that he possessed a keen intellect and that he deserved much of the credit for the speed with which the navy rebounded after Pearl Harbor.[12]

In addition to the joint chiefs, two other persons completed the military high command. One was Harry Hopkins, who despite declining health, reached the peak of his influence during the first two years of the war. Following the death of his second wife and before he married for a third time, Hopkins and his daughter lived in the White House, where he had unlimited access to the president. Hopkins represented Roosevelt in meetings with Churchill and Stalin and accompanied the president to all the wartime conferences. Critics exaggerated when they depicted Hopkins as a kind of Svengali who held Roosevelt under hypnotic sway, but he unquestionably wielded great power.

The final member of the military high command was Secretary of War Stimson, who occupied his position in the high command despite Roosevelt's efforts to exclude him. During the war the president declined to solicit Stimson's advice on strategy, invite him along to the wartime conferences, or include him on the distribution list for the papers of the joint chiefs. Stimson, whose pedigree could match Roosevelt's, bloodline for bloodline, and whose distinguished career had included service under four past presidents, may have been the one member of the administration who intimidated Roosevelt. Then, too, Roosevelt probably regarded Stimson as something of a scold, for almost alone among the president's civilian subordinates, the aging statesman frequently exhorted Roosevelt in blunt language to exert more forceful leadership. Whatever Roosevelt's reasons for trying to keep Stimson at arm's length, Stimson refused to be so kept. Whether the president wanted his advice or not, Stimson continued to provide it, sometimes with the encouragement of Marshall and Hopkins.

His team of military advisers in place, Roosevelt turned his attention to the war. At the outset, he had no detailed strategy in mind. Here and there, however, in his typically unsystematic way, he indicated that any plan of action must achieve four objectives. First, it must deploy the bulk of Allied forces against Germany and not Japan, for Germany was the main enemy. Second, it must put American troops into field against German troops as soon as possible and certainly before the end of 1942; for only when Americans drew German blood and vice versa would the American people put their hearts into the war effort and end their fixation on a Pacific-first strategy. Believing that successful prosecution of the war depended in part upon continued Democratic control of Congress, Roosevelt hoped that engagement in the European war would enhance his party's prospects in the November elections. Third, in order to discourage the Soviet Union from withdrawing from the war and signing a separate peace agreement with Germany, the plan must take some of the pressure off the Russians, who were then bearing the brunt of the fight against Germany. Finally, any strategy must preserve a high degree of cooperation among the Allies, especially between the United States and Great Britain, for unity was a key to victory.

Churchill was first to get the president's ear with a specific plan of action. During his visit to the White House in late 1941 and early 1942, the British prime minister proposed a joint Anglo-American offensive to drive Axis forces from North Africa. Given the strategic importance of the North Africa–Mediterranean area of the world, Churchill's plan had much to recommend it. Moreover, in varying degrees, it met each of Roosevelt's objectives. Consequently, without consulting his military advisers, Roosevelt reacted favorably toward Churchill's plan.

Most of those same military advisers were dead set against a campaign in North Africa, and Churchill had no sooner left town than they sought to change the president's mind. Acting as their spokesman, Marshall argued that such a campaign entailed many risks, that success was by no means certain, and that even a successful outcome would have but slight impact on the course of the war. Worst of all, as a peripheral theater of action, North Africa would waste precious resources that the United States could put to better use elsewhere. Behind Marshall's criticism of the North African venture lay a suspicion, widespread in military circles, that the British were trying to use the United States not only to defeat Germany but also to preserve the British Empire.

For the 64-year-old army chief of staff, who stood firmly in the tradition of Ulysses S. Grant, the principles of modern warfare called for a direct assault at the heart of the enemy, not a series of harmless pinpricks along the periphery. As an alternative to Churchill's plan, Marshall proposed that the United States and Britain amass men and supplies in the British Isles, then launch a massive cross-Channel invasion of Nazi-controlled France. Allied forces would then fight their way through France and the Low Countries and into Germany itself. Eventually, Marshall recommended to Roosevelt three separate but related operations: first, the immediate buildup of men and materiel in the United Kingdom; second, depending upon conditions on the Russian front, a small-scale, cross-Channel invasion of France in the fall of 1942; and third, a full-scale, cross-Channel invasion of France sometime in 1943.[13]

With the exception of some of the navy brass, who preferred a Pacific-first strategy, Roosevelt's top military advisers not only endorsed Marshall's recommendations but believed that any other course of action would lead to disaster. The Soviets supported the opening of a second front in Europe, and as far as they were concerned, the sooner the better, for an invasion of France would force Hitler to divert some of his forces from the Russian front. The only dissent came from the British, who argued that a direct attack on the European continent before the Allies had assured themselves of overwhelming superiority in men and supplies, would degenerate into the kind of awful but indecisive bloodletting that had characterized the fighting during World War I. The British also believed that a campaign in North Africa accorded more closely with their goals of preserving their empire and of assuring themselves a favorable position in the postwar world.

During the first six months of 1942, with his most trusted military advisers and the Russians on one side and with the British on the other, Roosevelt vacillated. In mid-January, after meeting Churchill, Roosevelt favored an invasion of North Africa. By early March, after Marshall and others had had a chance to make themselves heard, Roosevelt wrote Churchill that he was becoming "more and more interested" in opening a front in France, perhaps as early as the upcoming summer. The opening of a European front, Roosevelt conceded, would exact great losses, "but such losses will be compensated by at least equal German losses and by compelling Germans to divert large forces of all kinds from Russian fronts."[14] By the end of March, however, when he met with his chief military advisers, Roosevelt seemed to have cooled to the idea of a European front. According to War Secretary Stimson, the president went off "on the wildest kind of dispersion debauch," suggesting possible military operations in the Middle East and Mediterranean. But then Marshall held forth, and by the end of the meeting, Roosevelt once again sounded as though he would support a cross-Channel invasion. Two days later, with the encouragement of Marshall and Hopkins, Stimson sought to stiffen Roosevelt's resolve by writing the president one of his periodic leadership letters. "John Sherman said in 1877," Stimson wrote, "'the only way to resume specie payments is to resume.' Similarly, the only way to get the initiative in this war is to take it."[15] By April, Roosevelt was positively enthusiastic about a cross-Channel invasion. That month, he dispatched Hopkins and Marshall to London to present a detailed invasion plan to Churchill and wrote the prime minister that the plan had his, Roosevelt's, "heart and *mind* in it."[16] But before Hopkins and Marshall had returned from London, political developments in France momentarily raised the possibility that French forces in North Africa might go over to the Allies, and Roosevelt then suggested that a North African campaign, which he seemingly had rejected, was at least worth discussing.[17] By this time, Roosevelt's advisers may have felt as though they were watching a tennis match of sorts, but one in which Roosevelt was playing on both sides of the net.

There was more to come. Between 29 May and 1 June, Roosevelt met with Soviet foreign minister Vyacheslav M. Molotov, the man who gave his name to the incendiary cocktail, and received from the Russian a firsthand report about the horrors of the eastern front. Roosevelt not only promised Molotov a second front in Europe, he promised him the second front before the end of the year—this over the objections of General Marshall, who was then projecting the spring of 1943 as the most suitable time for a full-scale invasion of the Continent. But the second front was no sooner on again than it was off again. With the British continuing to oppose any kind of offensive in Europe in 1942, no matter how limited, and continuing to push for a landing in North Africa, Roosevelt backed away from his promise to Molotov, although he did not repudiate it. At the same time, he appeared to be no closer to committing himself, or staying committed, to a specific course of action. One time, he would talk about invading North Africa. Another time, he would revive talk of a cross-Channel attack in 1942 or early 1943. Still other times, he would talk about sending troops to the Middle East.

Meanwhile, his military aides fumed. At the end of one particularly long and difficult day of negotiations with the British, Roosevelt suggested to Marshall the possibility of sending American forces to the Middle East. Marshall, fearful of losing his temper, excused himself for the night. The usually self-contained general was angry because he saw his cherished plans for the cross-Channel invasion going up in smoke and because he believed that Roosevelt was approaching the strategy-making process frivolously, like a child playing war games.[18]

Roosevelt's apparent vacillation over strategy during the first six months of 1942 raised many questions. Did he lack decisiveness? Or were Marshall and Stimson right in thinking in their moments of frustration that Roosevelt failed to comprehend the seriousness of the situation? Was he, as others believed, too susceptible to the charms and wiles of Winston Churchill? Or was it just possible, as some historians later suggested, that Roosevelt possessed a more sophisticated understanding of the global situation than his chiefs, that he had certain clear objectives in mind, and that in his own patented way, he was manipulating men and events to achieve his objectives?[19]

Save during the months immediately preceding Pearl Harbor, the private thoughts of this very public man had never been harder to discern. Yet in all probability, the explanation for Roosevelt's seeming inability to settle upon a strategy was threefold. First, he was genuinely torn between opposing plans of operation for the simple reason that the choice between a cross-Channel invasion and a North Africa campaign was not as clear-cut as either Roosevelt's military advisers or Churchill made it seem. Each course of operation had advantages and disadvantages, and each offered particular risks and opportunities. Long after the war and with the full advantage of hindsight, military experts continued to disagree about the comparative merits of an early cross-Channel as opposed to a North Africa campaign. Therefore it was not surprising that Roosevelt should have difficulty choosing from among various strategies. Second, Roosevelt did not see it as his responsibility to have to choose between conflicting proposals, because he approached the matter of strategy as he would have approached a political problem. With his trusted military advisers and the Russians on one side and Churchill, a man whom he greatly respected and admired, on the other side, the politician in Roosevelt sought to mediate between competing interests, to serve as a broker of sorts. In the company of his own advisers, he would talk up the advantages of the British proposals; in the company of the British, he would sometimes enumerate the advantages of the American proposal. In a sense, he treated his chiefs and their British counter-parts as the military equivalents of his celebrated high- and low-tariff proponents: he was trying to get them into a room to work out a compromise.

But the third and most important reason for Roosevelt's apparent vacillation over strategy was simply that he was doing what he usually did in such situations: he was maintaining his flexibility, keeping his options open, and above all trusting in the future. Faced with what those around him considered to be the most important decision of his life—a decision upon which hinged the fate of the Western world—he experienced no apparent anguish, no Hamlet-like inner turmoil. While his aides fussed and fretted, Roosevelt cheerily went about his daily routine, filled his spare moments with bird-watching, stamp-collecting, and lighthearted conversation with friends and aides, and apparently never missed a good night's sleep—all the while confident that something would turn up.

Finally, it was not Roosevelt but Marshall who brought things to a head. Early in July, he and Admiral King, with the support of Stimson, said in essence to the president that if the Allies were unwilling to go all out against Germany, that is, to launch a cross-Channel invasion, then the United States should shift the bulk of its resources to the Pacific and go all out against Japan. In June, in one of the key battles of the war, American naval and air forces had halted the Japanese advance at Midway Island, and now Marshall and King recommended that the United States follow up this important victory by taking the offensive in the Pacific. Marshall later claimed that he had intended the Pacific-first recommendation as a bluff, which he hoped would force the British to reconsider their opposition to an invasion of France. Faced with the prospects of fighting the Germans alone, Marshall reasoned, Churchill and his advisers just might embrace the second-front strategy.[20] Marshall never admitted it, but given his increasing frustration with the president, he almost certainly aimed his bluff not only at the British but also at Roosevelt.

To the extent that Marshall had hoped to end the stalemate between the Allies over strategy, he succeeded, although not before he received a rare dressing-down from his commander in chief. For their Pacific-first recommendation, Roosevelt sternly rebuked Marshall and King. Their proposal, he wrote them, "is exactly what Germany hoped the United States would do after Pearl Harbor. Secondly it does not in fact provide use of American troops in fighting except in a lot of islands whose occupation will not affect the world situation this year or next.

Third: it does not help Russia or the Near East. Therefore it is disapproved as of the present." He signed his order, "Roosevelt, C in C."[21]

Marshall's bluff had brought forth from his commander in chief a vigorous assertion of authority. But more important, it moved Roosevelt to end the deadlock over strategy, if not in a way that particularly pleased the army chief of staff. In mid-July, Roosevelt dispatched Marshall, King, and Hopkins to London to meet with the British and to reach immediate agreement over plans for the duration of 1942. Roosevelt's instructions to his trio of advisers virtually ensured the adoption of Churchill's original proposal for an invasion of French North Africa, and that, indeed, was what happened. Marshall and his team of military planners continued to believe that the agreed-upon North Africa strategy, although perhaps better than no strategy at all, was fundamentally flawed. They continued to believe, too, that if Roosevelt had stood foursquare behind them, they might have prevailed in negotiations with the British. Gen. Dwight D. Eisenhower, Marshall's right-hand man and the one who had overseen the drafting of plans for the now-postponed cross-Channel invasion, expressed the mood of his colleagues. The day the Allies agreed to invade North Africa, Eisenhower said, was "the blackest day in history."[22]

That day also marked the nadir in relations between Roosevelt and his commanders. As the decision stage ended and the planning and execution stages began, however, their relations improved. Having finally approved a course of action, Roosevelt now left it to his generals and admirals to carry it out. Unlike his fellow warlords Churchill, Stalin, and Hitler, Roosevelt did not bully or badger his military subordinates. He did not spend his time poring over maps, devising battle plans, and summoning his chiefs to his side at all hours of the day and night. Marshall, Eisenhower, Stimson, and others still thought that Roosevelt was wrong about North Africa, and they would never become accustomed to his disorderly ways; but as they began preparing for their first major offensive, which at Roosevelt's urging was scheduled for November, complaints about their commander in chief's conduct of the war, for the time being at least, abated.

While Roosevelt and his chiefs were debating strategy, Roosevelt had also been overseeing economic mobilization. For the fate of the Allied forces, whether in North Africa or in the Pacific, depended as much on the productivity of American farms and factories as on military leadership, strategy, and tactics. After Pearl Harbor, Congress granted Roosevelt sweeping powers to reorganize the economy for war. He, in turn, dispersed these powers throughout the executive branch. As a result, most of the key wartime debates over public policy took place not in Congress, or between Congress and the executive branch, but within the executive branch.

Roosevelt's management of the mobilization process closely resembled his earlier management of the New Deal. Once again, he sparked ideas in others rather than originated ideas himself. Once again, he shunned long-range planning, preferring to concentrate on one problem at a time, and then only when it reached the crisis stage. When crises arose, as they did in the production of war supplies during 1942, he created new agencies—often without abolishing the old ones—to deal with the crises. Roosevelt, one reporter noted, went through production agencies and production chiefs faster than Lincoln went through generals. And once again, Roosevelt blurred lines of responsibility, assigning the same task to many different individuals and agencies. In 1942 alone he created six new agencies, including the War Production Board, which along with a half-dozen or so already-existing agencies, dealt with the problems of economic mobilization. A nation that had just about mastered the names of one set of alphabet agencies now had to master the names of another. Between crises, Roosevelt gave his subordinates freedom to run their bailiwicks as they saw fit, but he maintained his habit of occasionally intervening in their affairs at the most unexpected moments and in the seemingly most trivial of matters. At any moment—no one could ever predict when—his attention might fix upon an obscure personnel matter or a minor item in some department's budget request.

On the whole, Roosevelt appointed able and honest persons to head his mobilization agencies. They included most notably Donald M. Nelson of the War Production Board and James F. Byrnes of the Office of Economic Stabilization and later of the Office of War Mobilization. None of Roosevelt's civilian chiefs shone as brightly as his military chiefs, in part because of their own limitations, in part because of the limitations Roosevelt placed upon them, and in part because, unlike their military counterparts, they had to perform their less glamorous, but equally complex, tasks in the full glare of public scrutiny.

Roosevelt's untidy management style confirmed his reputation among contemporaries as a bad administrator. In entries in his diary and in letters to friends, Stimson summed up the indictment: "He wants to do it all himself. . . . the poorest administrator I have ever worked under in respect to the orderly procedure and routine of his performance. . . . I often wish the President wasn't so soft-hearted towards incompetent appointees. . . . Today the President has constituted an almost innumerable number of new administrative posts, putting at the head of them a lot of inexperienced men appointed largely for personal grounds and who report on their duties directly to the President and have constant and easy access to him. . . . The lines of delimitation between these different agencies themselves and between them and the departments is very nebulous. . . . the Washington atmosphere is full of acrimonious disputes over matters of jurisdiction."[23] Roosevelt's defenders once again argued that his administrative practices, especially his habit of delegating the same task to different individuals and agencies stimulated creative competition and allowed him, as the broker among competing governmental units, to keep his own hands on the reins of power.

On one point his critics and defenders agreed: Roosevelt pushed his subordinates, civilian and military alike, to achieve goals they themselves thought lay beyond their reach. In the final accounting, this was his most significant contribution to the civilian side of the war effort. Early in 1942, when military experts presented him with carefully prepared estimates of the upcoming year's production of planes, tanks, and ships, Roosevelt simply crossed out their figures, substituted higher figures of his own, and released these higher figures to the public.[24] Military and civilian authorities alike reacted with dismay, for they felt certain that the president's production goals were totally unrealistic and that the failure to reach those goals would damage public morale. But Roosevelt brushed aside all objections, saying to Harry Hopkins, "Oh—the production people can do it if they really try." Another time, he dismissed labor–management strife as an obstacle to mobilization. Almost as if to say that the labor turbulence of the preceding decade had been a mirage, he told a delegation of laborites and industrialists that there was little difference between workers and their bosses. "It's like the old Kipling saying about 'Judy O'Grady an' the Colonel's Lady.' They are both the same under the skin."[25]

To their disappointment, liberals, especially those who wanted to use government to more evenly redistribute wealth and power, found that Roosevelt's all-things-are-possible spirit did not extend to their causes. Some liberals had initially supported World War I in hopes that the discipline of war would spur reform at home. They had no such illusions as they entered World War II. They did hope, however, to hold their own. Roosevelt, for his part, wanted to preserve as many New Deal reforms as possible, and from time to time he talked about the need for bold new initiatives. But he also maintained that winning the war took priority over everything else, or as he later put it, "Dr. New Deal" gave way to "Dr. Win the War." In this spirit, he offered little resistance as Congress dismantled his beloved Civilian Conservation Corps and other New Deal agencies such as the Works Progress Administration and the National Youth Administration. True enough, the war drastically re-duced unemployment and with it the need for work relief; but some lib-erals wanted to preserve agencies such as the CCC, the WPA, and the NYA, at least in skeletal form, to help smooth the process of reconver-sion from war to peace and to help stabilize the economy thereafter. These concerns left Roosevelt unmoved, however. Nor did he try to prevent Congress from emasculating two other New Deal programs, rural electrification and aid to sharecroppers and tenant farmers.

Nothing disturbed some liberals, such as La Follette and his ilk, as much as what appeared to them to be Roosevelt's excessive courting of the business community. For one thing, they objected to the administra-tion's recruitment of large numbers of corporate executives, many of whom had pronounced anti-New Deal sympathies, to serve in govern-ment war agencies. Citing the potential for conflicts of interest, liberals also objected to the administration's practice of allowing executives—the so-called dollar-a-year men—to remain on corporate payrolls while serving in Washington. Lax enforcement of the antitrust laws and the awarding of military contracts to firms that had long histories of anti-union practices drew fire from liberals as well. In Congress, liberals and conservatives alike protested that the lion's share of war work was going to a few corporate giants at the expense of medium- and small-size en-terprises. Although Roosevelt frequently expressed annoyance with the complainers, whom he suspected of harboring partisan motives, he pri-vately agreed with some of their complaints. Nevertheless, he took the position that reform would have to await, if not the end of the war, at least a definite turning of the tide.[26]

Roosevelt took much the same position in matters relating to civil rights and civil liberties. The struggle for civil rights for blacks, in par-ticular, required of him a tricky balancing act between black militance and white intransigence that he would just as soon have postponed in-definitely. The war itself did much to bring race relations to the forefront of the nation's consciousness. It accelerated certain forces, including economic expansion, urbanization, and industrialization, that loosened the ties that bound blacks to the cotton culture of the South. In unprecedented numbers, blacks moved during the war. Some moved from rural to urban areas within the South; others moved out of the South altogether, migrating to the North and Far West, where they sought employment in war plants. Even if nothing else had happened during the war, black migration alone, most of it to predominantly white areas, would have upset the racial status quo. But much more did happen. For blacks, the war dramatized in particularly vivid fashion the gap between America's democratic rhetoric and the reality that governed race relations. After all, the United States was fighting Germany, in part at least because Americans considered Nazi theories of Aryan supremacy as dangerous. Yet most white Americans acted as though they shared Hitler's belief in white supremacy. During the war, black leaders proclaimed as their goal the "Double V": victory over Hitler abroad, and victory over racism at home.

Roosevelt, for his part, sympathized with the victims of racial prejudice, and he deplored racial hatred and violence. When specific instances of injustice came to his attention, frequently through Eleanor's efforts, they could move him to anger and action. He understood, too, that racial strife at home played into the hands of America's enemies abroad. But he also believed that progress in race relations would require time, patience, and better educational opportunities for blacks and whites; above all, he believed that war was no time for radical experiments in racial equality. Accordingly, he sought to do just enough to mollify blacks but not enough to disturb large numbers of whites.

As it turned out, Roosevelt had already set the pattern for his wartime handling of civil rights issues before Pearl Harbor. Late in 1940 and early in 1941, civil rights proponents, including Eleanor, urged the president to desegregate the armed forces and prohibit discriminatory practices in defense industries. In response, Roosevelt issued a few statements strongly condemning racism. But when he asked his military and civilian chiefs to comply with black demands, he met stiff resistance. Stimson, Marshall, and others believed that blacks lacked the ability to fill other than menial roles in the armed services and, moreover, that mixing the races would cripple the morale of America's fighting forces. Secretary of the Navy Knox said that he would resign before he would oversee integration of his service. Roosevelt's civilian chiefs proved equally recalcitrant. To force war plants to hire blacks would cripple production, they warned. In the face of such resistance within his own administration,

Roosevelt did not persist. Civil rights activists did persist, however, and when their entreaties to the president brought no results, they raised the stakes. Led by A. Philip Randolph, the dynamic head of the Brotherhood of Sleeping Car Porters, they threatened a mass march on Washington. On the eve of American entry into the war, Roosevelt was trying to project an image of national unity and national resolve; the idea of a hundred thousand blacks—the figure mentioned by Randolph—descending on the nation's capital doubtless conjured up in him visions of the Bonus March and worse. For Washington remained a Jim Crow town, whose restaurants and hotels were closed to blacks and whose all-white police force could not be counted on to show restraint in its dealings with black protestors.

Roosevelt tried to avert the march, first by dispatching his wife and several advisers to persuade black leaders to drop their plans for the protest, then by meeting himself with march organizers. Finally, when personal intercessions failed to produce results, Roosevelt partially met the demands of blacks. In June 1941 he issued Executive Order 8802, banning discriminatory employment practices in defense industries and in the federal government. He also established the Fair Employment Practices Committee (FEPC) to investigate violations of the order. Six days before the march was scheduled to begin, Randolph called it off, claiming victory. Some of his followers correctly pointed out that the FEPC lacked enforcement power and that Roosevelt's executive order said nothing about desegregation of the armed forces. They accused Randolph of selling out to the president. Most of Randolph's followers, however, hailed the executive order as a great step forward in the struggle for racial equality and as an example of the power of mass action, or at least the threat of mass action.[27]

Much the same pattern prevailed during the war except that more often than not, military necessity, rather than pressure from blacks, forced the president's hand. For example, when severe labor shortages threatened to interrupt the flow of munitions to the war zones, Roosevelt and his production chiefs sought to lower discriminatory barriers to black employment. Similarly, when it became clear that the confinement of blacks to menial positions in the armed services was wasting manpower, Roosevelt nudged, but never pushed, his service chiefs to make more effective use of black recruits. Clearly, if Roosevelt had been inclined to do so, which he was not, he could have done more to advance the cause of racial equality. As commander in chief he had it within his power to desegregate the armed services; and having created the FEPC, he could have strengthened that agency as a weapon against job discrimination. But Roosevelt declined to take these or other steps, in part because he feared a backlash of white resentment. As it was, racial disturbances rocked several cities, including Detroit, where 25 blacks and nine whites died before federal troops restored order. Almost all of these disturbances were started by whites who resented the influx of blacks into their communities. Roosevelt doubtless feared, not unreasonably, that a mounting number of disturbances could well hinder the war effort.

Political considerations also deterred Roosevelt from taking bolder action; indeed, politics may have been paramount in his thinking. For better or worse, white southerners remained a vital component of the New Deal coalition, and Roosevelt believed that he could not afford to alienate them. Lest Roosevelt need any instruction on this score, southern Democrats were quick to supply it. As one of them put it, without the South "there would be no Democratic Party now and President Roosevelt would not have his position as President and I would not be in Congress. It will be very difficult to break up a solid South and there is only one thing that will really do it, and that is this race question."[28] In short, the war had presented Roosevelt with the unwelcome problem of racial tension; but the war also provided him with an excuse for postponing the day of reckoning.

A significant sidelight to Roosevelt's involvement in civil rights matters was the way in which Eleanor served as a lightning rod, deflecting criticism from her husband to herself. Many whites believed that the administration deliberately encouraged blacks to think of themselves as equals. But for this disturbing tendency, whites tended to blame the president's wife rather than the president. One rumor that made its way through the South warned that black women were no longer willing to work as maids but were forming "Eleanor Clubs," whose goal was to put "a white woman in every kitchen by 1943." Secretary of War Stimson, who considered civil rights a dangerous diversion from the war effort, complained in his diary about Mrs. Roosevelt's "intrusive and impulsive folly."[29] But if Eleanor could deflect criticism from her husband, she could also deflect praise. Although the president remained popular among blacks, some civil rights leaders believed that Eleanor deserved most of the credit. "I have always felt that F.D.R. was overrated as a champion of the Negro," Roy Wilkins, an executive of the NAACP, said years later. "He was a New York patrician, distant, aloof, with no natural feel for the sensibilities of black people, no compelling inner commitment to their cause." But to Wilkins, Eleanor Roosevelt was a "loyal and effective friend" of the NAACP.[30]

The most serious breach of civil rights during the war occurred when the government interned some 112,000 Americans of Japanese descent. Like his role in so many other things, Roosevelt's role in the events leading up to this sad episode in American history was ambiguous. In public he preached tolerance. A week after Pearl Harbor, on the hundred and fiftieth anniversary of the ratification of the first 10 amendments to the Constitution, he took time from a busy schedule to proclaim Bill of Rights Day and to pledge, "We will not, under any threat, or in the face of any danger, surrender the guarantees of liberty our forefathers framed for us in the Bill of Rights." A few weeks later, when he learned that some employers were firing foreign-born workers, he denounced the practice as stupid, unjust, and harmful to the war effort.[31]

But even as he made these pronouncements, pressure was mounting on the administration to eliminate the threat to national security supposedly caused by the presence of Japanese-Americans on the West Coast. Roosevelt neither encouraged nor resisted this pressure, which increasingly took the form of demands that the government round up and incarcerate all Japanese-Americans. Instead, he turned the problem over to his subordinates. During January and February 1942, there ensued within the administration a fierce debate over the proper course of action. On one side stood the new attorney general, Francis Biddle, who had surveyed constitutional law and pored over FBI reports that discounted threats of espionage and sabotage and could find no grounds for incarcerating Japanese-Americans. On the other side stood officials in the War Department who argued that Japanese-Americans belonged to an "enemy race" and therefore posed a potential threat to national security. On the West Coast, meanwhile, newspaper editors, public officials, and self-proclaimed protectors of the American way, such as the American Legion, were fanning the flames of anti-Japanese-American sentiment. It was not conducive to calm reflection that the debate over internment coincided with the terrifying Japanese advances in the Pacific, with the first reports of Japanese cruelty to American captives in the Philippines, and with false sightings of Japanese submarines off the California coast.

Still and all, internment was by no means inevitable. For one thing, identifying, rounding up, removing, and incarcerating such large numbers of persons presented logistical problems of enormous magnitude. For

Father and son, 1883. *(Courtesy FDR Library)*

Mother and son, 1893. *(Courtesy FDR Library)*

FDR in white turtleneck, center, on Groton's second football team, 1899. *(Courtesy FDR Library)*

The Assistant Secretary of the Navy and his family, Washington, D.C., 1919. The children (left to right) are: Anna; Franklin, Jr.; James; John; and Elliott. *(Courtesy FDR Library)*

The Democratic vice presidential candidate and his running mate, Governor James M. Cox of Ohio, Dayton, Ohio, 1920. *(Courtesy FDR Library)*

In 1925, four years after the attack of polio, FDR standing with support of his long-time valet, LeRoy Jones, and his doctor, William McDonald. (*Courtesy FDR Library*)

Soup line during the Great Depression. (*Courtesy FDR Library*)

With daughter Anna and Eleanor during 1932 campaign. (*Courtesy FDR Library*)

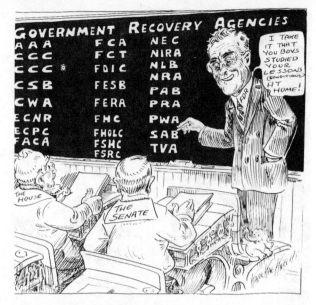

Cartoonist Karl Kae Knecht conveys widespread impression of FDR's dominance of Congress during New Deal, 1934. *(Courtesy Evansville Courier)*

FDR signs Social Security bill, August, 1935. Standing (left to right): Rep. Robert L. Doughton (D-N.C.); Edwin Witte, Director of the President's Social Security Committee; Sen. Robert F. Wagner (D-N.Y.); Sen. Robert M. La Follette, Jr., (Prog.-Wisc.); Sen. Augustine Lonergan (D-Conn.); Sec. of Labor Frances Perkins; Sen. William H. King (D-Utah); Rep. David J. Lewis (D-Md.); and Sen. Joseph F. Guffey (D-Penn.). *(Courtesy AP/Wide World Photos)*

Ross Lewis cartoon, *Milwaukee Journal*, 1939–40. *(Courtesy Milwaukee Journal)*

"MOTHER, WILFRED WROTE A DIRTY WORD!"
Dorothy McKay, *Esquire*, Nov. 1938. *(Courtesy of the Hearst Corp.)*

Presidential press conference, 1939. *(Courtesy FDR Library)*

Returning home from Casablanca Conference, FDR celebrates his 61st birthday aboard Boeing Clipper, January 30, 1943. With FDR (left to right): Adm. William D. Leahy, Harry Hopkins, and Capt. John M. Cone. (*Courtesy FDR Library*)

At Yalta Conference, with Churchill and Stalin, February, 1945. (*Courtesy FDR Library*)

In Philadelphia during last presidential campaign, 1944. *(Courtesy FDR Library)*

another, even within the War Department, which was much more jittery about the potential for sabotage and espionage than the Justice Department, some influential officials, most notably Secretary Stimson, had scruples about the constitutionality of internment. But gradually, a few determined officials in the War Department and in the army managed to tip the scales of bureaucratic opinion in favor of internment. That settled the matter as far as Roosevelt was concerned, and on 19 February 1942 he signed Executive Order 9066, which authorized military officials to remove "any or all persons" from so-called military zones in the United States. It remained for Roosevelt to determine the extent to which he would implement the order. Would he permit the internment of all Japanese-Americans, or only those who happened to live near military installations and defense plants? On this question, too, Roosevelt deferred to his subordinates, telling Stimson to do what he thought best but adding, in his typically cryptic way, to "be as reasonable as you can."[32]

So it was that Roosevelt helped set in motion the events that forced some 112,000 Japanese-Americans, some two-thirds of them American citizens, from their homes on the West Coast and into dreary internment camps scattered throughout the interior of the country. Through it all, he displayed striking indifference not only to the constitutional ramifications of internment but also to the human tragedy involved. In this, he was not alone. With practically no debate and by voice votes in both houses, Congress established criminal penalties for those unfortunate Japanese-Americans who dared resist incarceration. Later, the Supreme Court made assent unanimous among the branches of government by upholding the constitutionality of the president's executive order. Outside the government, meanwhile, no significant opposition to internment developed. Publications normally outspoken in defense of civil liberties, such as *The New Republic*, *The Nation*, and *The Progressive*, remained conspicuously silent. The American Civil Liberties Union later called internment the worst violation of civil rights in the United States since slavery, but when it counted, the ACLU was weak and ineffective in its defense of Japanese-Americans.[33]

Internment notwithstanding, by no means everything that happened on the home front was bad. Indeed, the war brought some great unexpected benefits, chief among them being economic recovery. It became a cliché to say that the war ended the depression, but the actual mechanism of recovery was massive government spending during the war for war purposes. In any event, by the end of 1942 unemployment had ceased to be a major problem; indeed, labor shortages in strategic industries became a more serious concern. Before long, Americans were enjoying the highest standard of living in their history, even though the uncertainties of war, coupled with various shortages and inconveniences, prevented them from appreciating their good fortune. The war not only ended the depression, it also pointed to government fiscal policy—spending, borrowing, taxation—as an antidote to future economic downturns. The great English economist John Maynard Keynes had been saying as much for many years, but it required the crisis of war to persuade many of the skeptics.

Roosevelt, however, remained skeptical. As his conversations with Budget Director Harold Smith, faithfully recorded in Smith's diary, made clear, the president retained his fairly orthodox fiscal views. His predecessors in the White House, he told Smith, had helped cause the depression by failing to retire more of the national debt following World War I. He would not make the same mistake, Roosevelt further informed his budget director, for upon completion of the current war, he would seek to commit the government to debt reduction at the earliest possible time.[34]

In addition to stimulating the economy, the war brought about one of the few downward redistributions of wealth in American history. A combination of high wages, overtime pay, and graduated income tax rates shifted a portion of the national income from wealthy Americans to middle- and lower-class Americans. Because an excessive concentration of wealth in the hands of a few had probably helped cause the depression, the leveling effects of the war, though modest, benefited the entire nation.

Roosevelt could claim little credit for these favorable economic developments. True, he did request the federal expenditures that stimulated the economy. But in doing so, he encountered little significant opposition, for no responsible public leader, no matter how fiscally conservative, dared argue that the United States could not afford to build planes, tanks, and battleships because the resulting expenditures might throw the budget into imbalance. The real issue was how to pay for the war, and on that issue Roosevelt occupied the middle ground between those who favored heavy borrowing and those who favored heavy taxation.

In the fall of 1942, Roosevelt anxiously awaited the invasion of North Africa. Finally it came. On 8 November, American troops under the command of General Eisenhower waded ashore at Casablanca in Morocco, and at Oran and Algiers in Algeria. As Roosevelt awaited the first reports out of North Africa, he was uncharacteristically nervous. Finally, the phone call came through from the War Department. As his secretary handed him the receiver, his hands shook. The news was encouraging: The troops were ashore, casualties lower than expected. "Thank God!" Roosevelt said. "Thank God!"[35]

The landing in North Africa went well from a military standpoint, but almost immediately the United States found itself unexpectedly bogged down in a political and diplomatic quagmire. This precarious situation had its origins in Franco-American relations following the fall of France. In 1940, Germany had set up a puppet regime, with headquarters in Vichy, to govern those parts of France unoccupied by Nazi soldiers. In response, French general Charles de Gaulle denounced the Vichy regime, left France, and formed in London a government-in-exile. Meanwhile, hoping eventually to draw Vichy into the Allied orbit, Roosevelt had established ties with the French government, even though many of its officials were out-and-out Nazi sympathizers. Roosevelt had also given De Gaulle the cold shoulder, in part because Roosevelt simply disliked the strong-willed French general and in part because he doubted that De Gaulle commanded much support among the French people. All this had occurred before the Allied invasion of French North Africa, which was under the control of the Vichy government.

As the date for invasion approached, Roosevelt and his advisers hoped that their courting of the Vichy regime would pay dividends in the form of active cooperation between French forces and Allied forces, at best, or nonresistance on the part of French forces, at worst. In fact, however, as Allied soldiers scrambled ashore, they encountered unexpected resistance from the French. At that point, General Eisenhower, acting on behalf of the Allies and after an incredibly complicated series of maneuvers, concluded an agreement with the ranking Vichy military official in North Africa, Admiral Jean Darlan. According to the agreement, Darlan promised to order French forces to lay down their arms, and Eisenhower promised to recognize Darlan as the legitimate civil authority in French North Africa. Since Eisenhower had to deal with the Vichy government, he probably had no choice but to deal with Darlan. Still, the American general could not have found a more odious figure than the French admiral with whom to strike a deal, for Darlan was a Nazi sympathizer and a notorious anti-Semite. He was, furthermore, thoroughly unreliable. He had sold out the Third Republic to the Nazis, and now, for the right price, he seemed perfectly willing to sell out the Nazis to the Allies.

The so-called Darlan deal ignited a firestorm of protest in Great Britain and in the United States. Some of Roosevelt's closest aides, including Henry Morgenthau, expressed anguish. To collaborate with Nazi collaborators, critics said, mocked the Four Freedoms, the Atlantic Charter, and all of Roosevelt's other noble pronouncements. Moreover, if the Allies could consort with the likes of Darlan, then what was to prevent them from doing business at some point with Hitler or Hirohito?[36] Journalist Walter Lippmann, who was in the process of fashioning an incisive critique of certain tendencies in the conduct of American foreign policy, was less concerned with the morality of the Darlan deal than with more fundamental issues. Conceding the military usefulness of some kind of arrangement with Darlan, Lippmann argued that the United States had given too much to the French admiral and had received too little in return. Worse still, Lippmann argued, Roosevelt had failed to consider the long-range implications of his policy. By embracing Vichy and shunning De Gaulle, the president was creating potential problems for the United States in the postwar world. Peace would eventually come, Lippmann said, and when it did, the United States would need the support of a strong and united France. But what the Allies were doing in North Africa made that prospect less likely.[37]

The furor over the Darlan deal shocked and surprised Roosevelt. The invasion had gone well, and now suddenly, a political controversy threatened to overshadow America's first successful action in the European war. Roosevelt defended his actions on grounds of military necessity. A temporary arrangement with Darlan had been necessary, he argued, to save American lives. To drive home the point, he quoted an old Bulgarian proverb: "My children, you are permitted in time of great danger to walk with the Devil until you have crossed the bridge." But critics would have none of it, and they flung back at Roosevelt his own idealistic statement of war aims. Attacks on Roosevelt's policies were hardly new, but one of his longtime aides said that he could not remember a time when criticism had affected the president more deeply. Fortunately for him, the controversy came to an abrupt end on Christmas Eve 1942, when a member of a French resistance group assassinated Darlan in Algiers. Who, if anyone, had ordered the assassination was never clear, although any number of people, including the Americans, the Germans, members of the French resistance, even Vichy associates, had a motive.[38]

In the long course of the war, the Darlan controversy had no tangible effect on the outcome. The whole episode remains significant, however, if for no other reason than that it reveals something about Roosevelt's way of waging war and diplomacy. Not only had Roosevelt authorized Eisenhower to deal with Darlan, he probably contributed to the subsequent controversy by neglecting to prepare the American public in advance for his first major exercise in realpolitik. If, for example, he had cited his Bulgarian proverb before the Darlan deal rather than after it, he might have prepared Americans for his North Africa policy, as well as for other steps the Allies would of necessity have to take during the war. The first shipments of lend-lease materials to the Soviet Union, for example, had offered a perfect opportunity for explaining how national self-interest sometimes requires a walk with the devil. But instead of providing lessons in realpolitik, Roosevelt had glossed over some unpleasant facts about the Soviet Union and had then gone on to depict the war in highly idealistic terms. And in North Africa, like Woodrow Wilson at Versailles he got caught in a moral backlash. Fortunately for Roosevelt, the backlash was less debilitating to him than it had been to Wilson, from whose experiences, incidentally, Roosevelt continued not to learn. Ultimately, however, it was probably fruitless to expect Roosevelt to square his rhetoric with his actions, for he probably saw no gap between the two. In other words, he did not carefully calculate his policies on the basis of national self-interest and then cloak them in idealism for public consumption. For him, as for most Americans, self-interest and idealism were inseparable.

The Darlan controversy also underscored Roosevelt's tendency to focus on short-term rather than long-term goals. In his dealings with the Vichy regime, his nearly exclusive concern was to facilitate the invasion of North Africa. Facilitating the invasion obviously deserved the highest priority. But Lippmann argued that the Allies might have formulated a policy that both increased the chances of military success in North Africa and addressed the long-term postwar interests of the Allies. Not that Roosevelt was oblivious to the future; indeed, already taking shape in his mind was a vision of a postwar world, a world without colonies or trade barriers, a world along the lines of the Four Freedoms, a world in which four nations—the United States, Great Britain, the Soviet Union, and China—policed the globe and kept the peace. But Roosevelt failed to relate his North Africa policy, or most other specific policies for that matter, to his plans for the future. Still, present-mindedness was not exclusively a Rooseveltian trait; to a greater or lesser degree, it characterized the thinking of the entire high command, from the commander in chief to the secretary of state to the military commanders in the field.

When Roosevelt found himself on the defensive, he usually tried to regain the initiative by creating a diversion, some dramatic action often unrelated to the source of his troubles. In late 1942 and early 1943, Roosevelt found himself on the defensive. First came the November elections, in which the Republicans picked up 44 seats in the House of Representatives and nine seats in the Senate. Then came the Darlan episode. In January came Roosevelt's dramatic response. With the fighting still going on in North Africa, Roosevelt decided to travel into the war zone to meet Churchill in Casablanca. The ostensible purpose of the conference was to formulate strategy, but the two leaders could have carried out this task through their staffs, especially since Stalin had declined to attend because the epic Battle of Stalingrad was then at its peak. But Roosevelt and Churchill decided to meet anyway. What was more, they decided to meet in one of the most dangerous places in the world, for Casablanca, although ostensibly under Allied control, was rife with rumor, intrigue, and the threat of violence. Roosevelt doubtless reveled in all the "firsts" that he would be making—being the first president to fly in an aircraft, the first president to leave the country during wartime, the first president since Lincoln to visit a war zone.[39]

On a Saturday evening in January 1943, three weeks before his sixty-first birthday, Roosevelt and his aides left Washington on the first leg of a 7,000-mile journey. From Washington, they went by train to Miami; there they boarded a Pan American Clipper, which could take off and land on water. From Miami, they flew to Trinidad, then to Belem, Brazil, then across the South Atlantic to Bathhurst, British Gambia, which was located on the west coast of Africa. Along the way, Roosevelt's aides worried about one thing or another: Admiral Leahy became ill and had to stay behind at Trinidad; John McCrea, the president's naval aide, complained of an earache, which probably came from flying in the unheated, unpressurized cabin; Harry Hopkins, who hated flying, had to ward off airsickness; Admiral Ross T. McIntire, the president's physician, worried that the flight would be bad for the president's heart; and in an age when air travel was still far from common, to say nothing of air travel over an ocean during wartime, everyone aboard the flying boat doubtless worried about crashing or getting shot down. Every one, that is, except the president, who seemed to be having the time of his life. Excerpts from Harry Hopkins's travel journal captured Roosevelt's mood: "I sat with him, strapped in, as the plane rose from the water—and he acted like a sixteen-year-old, for he has done no flying since he was President; the President still treats it as a first-class holiday; the President slept late, his first night on an airplane, and woke up in the best of spirits; the President missed nothing."[40]

Shortly after the president's plane landed off the west coast of Africa, his traveling companions received a brief but jolting reminder of his disability. As Roosevelt was being hoisted from a whaleboat to the deck of an American cruiser, where he and his party were to spend the night, one of the men carrying him slipped, and Roosevelt fell to the deck. He suffered no apparent harm, and as he usually did in such circumstances, he went on about his business as though nothing had happened. The next day, the sixth since Roosevelt had left Washington, an army C-54 transport flew the presidential party across deserts, snow-capped mountains, and fertile black fields, then touched down on an airstrip 15 miles outside Casablanca. Worried about a possible assassination attempt, Secret Service agents were waiting for the president, and they quickly got him into a car and out of the area. Roosevelt had no sooner arrived at the old Anfa Hotel, the site of the conference, than he was having cocktails and dinner with Churchill and their combined staffs. "Much good talk of war—and families—and the French," Hopkins noted in his journal. "I went to bed at 12 but I understand that the Pres. and Churchill stayed up till two." Only an air-raid warning ended the festivities.[41]

During the ensuing 10-day conference, the Allies tentatively agreed to follow the campaign in North Africa with an invasion of Sicily and possibly Italy. They agreed, too, to delay a cross-Channel invasion until sometime in 1944. The conference occasioned Roosevelt's declaration that the Allies would demand from Germany and Japan unconditional surrender, a declaration that, some critics later argued, needlessly prolonged the war. Roosevelt probably issued the declaration to counter the impression left by the Darlan deal that the Allies might consort with the enemy. He also wanted to reassure the Soviet Union that, despite the latest postponement of the cross-Channel invasion, the United States and Great Britain would fight to the end. Too, Roosevelt may have sought to prevent either the Japanese or the Germans from claiming that they had lost the war not on the battlefield but at the peace table, as the Germans had claimed after World War I. But whatever his reasons for the timing of the declaration, it was consistent with everything Roosevelt had said about the war thus far.

In retrospect, the Casablanca conference took on added significance because it marked the high point of relations between the United States and Great Britain. Among the world powers, the United States was on the rise, Great Britain on the decline, and at Casablanca their representatives met more or less as friendly equals. But all of these things would have transpired if the Allies had met in Washington, London, or some other place. As far as Roosevelt was personally concerned, the most notable thing about the conference was that he had gone to such great and dangerous lengths to attend it. In doing so, he once again demonstrated a fascinating contradiction in his behavior: On matters of policy he could be maddeningly cautious and indecisive, as he had been in formulating war strategy; in personal matters, he could be bold, daring, even foolhardy.

Soon after the Casablanca conference, the Allies rejoiced in a series of heartening developments. Early in February 1943 the Battle of Stalingrad, which had raged for two and a half months, ended, with the Russians winning one of the great victories not only of the war but in the history of warfare. In May, the United States and Great Britain finally drove the Axis from North Africa and turned their attention toward Sicily and Italy. May also brought a stunning reversal of fortunes in the Atlantic, where the Allies finally gained naval ascendancy. During that month alone, Allied vessels destroyed nearly a third of all German U-boats at sea; thereafter, Germany never again seriously threatened to disrupt the ever-widening flow of men and supplies from America to Europe. By spring, American and British bombers were pounding German cities and industrial centers, although with results less decisive than Allied military experts had hoped. On the other side of the world, meanwhile, the United States had already turned back the Japanese at Midway, held Guadalcanal in the Solomon Islands, and taken the offensive in the Pacific. The war was far from over, but by mid-1943, the tide had turned in favor of the Allies.

Sometime in 1943—it is impossible to say exactly when—the tide also turned in the struggle to mobilize the American home front. To be sure, problems aplenty remained. Labor shortages and labor-management disputes occasionally interrupted production; bureaucratic infighting on a grand scale persisted, as Roosevelt's subordinates in the executive branch fought among themselves over taxation and labor policies, the distribution of resources between military and civilian sectors of the economy, and a multitude of other matters. There was still too little coordination between strategic needs and the allocation of vital resources, in part because of Roosevelt's aversion to long-range military planning. Widespread dissatisfaction with wage and price controls and with the rationing of everything from butter to tires eroded public morale. And racial and ethnic tensions continued to hinder national unity. Despite all of these problems, by the end of 1943, the American economy was achieving astonishing feats of production. Shipbuilding led the way. Before Pearl Harbor, it had taken 355 days to build one vessel; by 1943, American shipyards had slashed that time to 56 days. In fact, one of Henry J. Kaiser's famous yards even built a ship in 14 days.[42] Of course, speed and quantity meant a certain sacrifice in quality. One of Kaiser's ships—not the 14-day wonder—capsized at the pier. But speed and quantity were what the Allies needed most in 1943. The aircraft industry performed another impressive feat of production. In 1940, when Roosevelt called for 50,000 planes, production experts had scoffed. In 1943 alone, aircraft plants turned out 85,433 planes.[43]

A story circulated during the war that suggested the importance of American industrial productivity. An American soldier, it seemed, was guarding a German prisoner of war who had been taken captive during the fighting in Italy. The American, with mocking reference to German theories of Aryan superiority, asked the German why, if he was such a superman, he was now in the hands of an inferior species. The German POW took the question seriously and went on to explain the circumstances of his capture. It so happened, he said, that he had been a battery commander stationed on a hill with six 88-millimeter antitank guns. Over the course of many hours, American tanks approached the hill, and one by one he and his men fired upon the tanks and blew them up. In the end, however, he explained, the Germans ran out of antitank shells before the Americans ran out of tanks. The story conveyed an important truth. In the final accounting, America's greatest contribution to the war effort was its tremendous productive capacity, which ranked second only to Russian manpower as the most decisive factor in the final outcome.[44]

So in November 1943, as Roosevelt prepared to set off for another wartime conference, this one in Tehran, where he would meet Stalin for the first time, the tide had turned in the Allies' favor, both abroad and at home. This decisive shift in the fortunes of war had come sooner and with much less sacrifice on the part of the Americans than any objective observer, surveying the world situation in the immediate aftermath of Pearl Harbor, could have predicted.

Things turned out better than anyone had any right to expect, Roosevelt's admirers argued, because Roosevelt had planned it that way. Historian A.J.P. Taylor later said that of all of the warlords, only Roosevelt knew what he was doing.[45] In truth, his personal contribution to the favorable situation in which the Allies found themselves at the close of 1943 is difficult to assess. To be sure, he had surrounded himself with talented commanders, such as Marshall and King, who had in turn contributed much to the war effort. There were some exceptions, the most notable among them being the flamboyant Douglas MacArthur, whom Roosevelt had once described as one of the two most dangerous men in America, whom the public vastly overrated, and whom Roosevelt kept on because of his undeserved popularity, though at a safe distance from Washington. But on the whole, Roosevelt's appointees served him and the Allied cause well. He had helped forge a close personal relationship with Churchill, and that relationship, perhaps unprecedented among world leaders, had aided the Allied cause. And his goal-setting and morale-sustaining skills doubtless had helped speed economic mobilization. Certainly his insistence on a Europe-first emphasis was sound, even if he was only reflecting the near-unanimous sentiment of his advisers.

But an evaluation of his major contribution to strategy, his belated support for the campaign in North Africa, involves a bewildering series of might-have-beens. What, for example, would have happened if the Allies had invaded France in 1942 instead of North Africa? With the advantage of hindsight, it becomes clear that a cross-Channel invasion of France in 1942 or even in 1943 would have entailed enormous risks. On the other hand, an early invasion might have brought great rewards, namely a shortening of the war in Europe and a more advantageous position for the United States in postwar Europe. Moreover, if the Russians had lost the Battle of Stalingrad, as seemed possible at the outset, the decision to invade North Africa rather than France probably would have spelled disaster for the Allied cause. But as 1943 drew to a close, Roosevelt was unconcerned about such imponderables. All he knew was that once again, events had borne out his optimism.

9

WAR LEADER, PART 2, 1944–1945

In 1944 and early 1945, with the end of the war in sight, Roosevelt turned his attention to the postwar world, at home and abroad. Although he was as reluctant as ever to commit himself to a future course of action, he nevertheless set forth certain broad goals. At home, he wanted the adoption of a far-reaching bill of economic rights that would guarantee to every American a job, decent housing, education, and protection from many of the vicissitudes and uncertainties of life. Internationally, he sought the creation of a peaceful world order in which the United States, acting under the auspices of a new world organization, would play a prominent role in global affairs. Roosevelt increasingly lacked the energy to put up much of a fight for his goals, especially at home. But it probably did not matter, for by the time he had gotten around to planning for the future, events seemed to have acquired a momentum of their own. Even if he had been at his best, he would have had great difficulty altering their course.

In January 1944, in his State of the Union address, Roosevelt announced his domestic goals, both for the duration of the war and for the postwar era. In the short run, he wanted Congress to reduce the cost of the war for future generations by raising taxes and to enact various measures to keep down the cost of living. He also urged Congress to enact a national service law, which would make every able-bodied adult eligible to work in war plants or in any other essential capacity. Just as the government could draft young men to serve in the army, so under Roosevelt's proposal, the government could draft citizens to work, say, in an aircraft factory in Los Angeles or in a shipyard in Mobile. National service, which Stimson had supported since the beginning of the war but which organized labor, and, to a lesser extent, big business, had bitterly opposed, aimed in large part to prevent strikes that might hinder the flow of supplies to the fighting fronts. Immediately following Pearl Harbor, leaders of the nation's two major labor organizations, the American Federation of Labor (AFL) and the Congress of Industrial Organizations (CIO), had pledged on behalf of their members to forsake work stoppages for the duration of the war. But some workers refused to relinquish the main weapon with which they might force employers to bargain in good faith, and they defied the no-strike pledge and walked off the job. In 1943 alone, there occurred some 3,700 work stoppages involving nearly 2 million laborers. At no time, however, did strikes significantly curtail war production or jeopardize the war effort. Roosevelt described his proposal not as a slap at insurgent laborites, which it was, but as a call to patriotic service. Citizens summoned to duty in aircraft factories, he said, could proudly tell their grandchildren that during the great war, they had served their country by helping make fighting planes.[1]

As for postwar America, Roosevelt called in ringing terms for the adoption of an economic bill of rights. The first Bill of Rights, he said, had secured for Americans their political rights. But in the modern industrial age, political rights were not enough, he maintained. True freedom now required economic security and independence. "Necessitous men," he said, "are not free men." He went on to enumerate a series of economic rights to which people were entitled, "regardless of station or race or creed." They included the right to a job and the right to earn enough money to provide food, shelter, clothing, and recreation; the right to adequate medical care and a good education; and the right to be protected from the economic ravages of old age, sickness, accidents, and unemployment. In addition, farmers had a right to sell their products at a price that would afford them a decent living, and businessmen had a right to trade in an atmosphere free of unfair competition and monopolistic control.

Roosevelt's economic bill of rights had far-reaching implications. Economic security, he was saying, was not only a desirable goal but the right of every citizen. Presumably, then, the federal government had an obligation to guarantee the right to economic security, in much the same

172

way that it had an obligation to guarantee the rights enumerated in the first 10 amendments to the Constitution. Thus, if the private economy failed to generate enough income to provide individual citizens with the basic necessities of life, a decent education, recreation, adequate medical care, and all the rest of the things Roosevelt enumerated, then the government would step in and make up the difference. Yet in subsequent speeches, it became clear that Roosevelt envisioned no great expansion of government. He seemed confident that the free enterprise system would be able to make the economic bill of rights a reality, with government limiting itself to a supporting role. "I believe in free enterprise— and always have," he said. "I believe in the profit system—and always have. I believe that private enterprise can give full employment to our people."[2]

As a summation of liberal goals, Roosevelt's State of the Union message had one revealing omission. Nowhere did he invoke the rhetoric of economic egalitarianism with which he had at least occasionally punctuated his speeches a decade earlier. During the 1930s, some prominent political figures, such as Robert La Follette, Jr., George Norris, and Huey Long, had advocated the redistribution of wealth along more equitable lines. They had argued that the concentration of wealth in relatively few hands not only undermined democracy but, because it eroded mass purchasing power, had helped cause the depression. Many of these liberals also had advocated strict enforcement of the antitrust laws and other curbs on the power of big business. To be sure, in the case of a La Follette or a Norris, it sometimes seemed as though the vision of a bygone age of family farms, small towns, and corner grocery stores inspired their opposition to the concentration of wealth and power that characterized modern life. But whatever their particular frame of reference, these leaders had represented an important, although minority, element within American liberalism. And although Roosevelt had never fully shared their vision or endorsed their programs, his rhetorical attacks on "money changers" and "economic royalists" and his call for a wealth tax act had reflected their influence.

By the 1940s, the redistributionist liberals were in decline. Huey Long was dead; George Norris was out of office; and La Follette, though still a member of the Senate, bore the heavy burden of his prewar isolationism. Moreover, although the obvious lack of mass purchasing power during the depression had lent plausibility to proposals for a downward redistribution of wealth, the experience of war suggested alternatives to such distribution as an antidote to the nation's economic ills. The most important of these alternatives was massive government spending, which, by 1944, had raised the country out of depression and was holding out the promise of continued economic growth. Similarly, the war dealt a blow to the movement to restrict the power of big business. With the Allied war machine heavily dependent on the output of American factories, with big businesses holding the lion's share of war contracts, and with workers supposedly enjoying the protections afforded by unions, there seemed little need for, and indeed some danger in, a major reorganization of the corporate structure.

So Roosevelt's address provided unmistakable evidence of the declining influence of the redistributionist, anticorporate faction of liberalism. Aside from making a perfunctory and purely ritualistic condemnation of monopolies, and a call for the taxation of "unreasonable" profits, he said nothing about narrowing the gap between the rich and the poor. True, his economic bill of rights would increase the standard of living of the poor. But that increase would presumably come from economic growth rather than the pockets of the rich. Nor did he say anything that even the most sensitive millionaire could legitimately construe as personally threatening, aside, that is, from a general condemnation of selfish, but unnamed, "special" groups. Indeed, his only major proposal that seemed punitive was national service, and that proposal he directed at American workers. Throughout his career, Roosevelt had always reflected, more than he had shaped, the dominant tendencies of his time. So now, during 1944, as he stressed economic security and deemphasized economic egalitarianism, he was reflecting the changing nature of modern American liberalism.

Still, Roosevelt had proposed an ambitious agenda for the upcoming session of Congress. But having proposed the agenda, he encountered stiff opposition from legislators. In the end, Congress rejected his proposals, including the one for national service.

The fate of Roosevelt's program reflected an increasingly tense relationship between the executive and the legislative branches of government. Actually, on most war-related matters, Congress had proved exceedingly accommodating to the president. Legislators had, for example, granted Roosevelt broad authority to manage the war and the economy as he and his agents in the executive branch saw fit. Non-war-related matters proved to be a different matter, however, and since Pearl Harbor, Congress had defeated most of Roosevelt's recommendations. "The Congress is in a state of revolt against the President," one Senate veteran wrote. "In all the years I have been in and around Washington

I have never seen a Congress so bitter toward the president." By 1944, relations between Roosevelt and Congress had deteriorated still more. Journalist Allen Drury, who reported on the United States Senate, later recalled that "there was an ugly hostility, a bitter jockeying for political advantage and power, a mutual mistrust and dislike that constantly clouded his relations with Congress." It was no exaggeration to say, Drury concluded, that the president and Congress "despised each other."[3]

Roosevelt was not solely to blame for this state of affairs. Republican legislators, confined to what increasingly appeared to be permanent minority status, lashed out at the president in frustration. Southern Democrats, worried that administration policies would undermine white supremacy in the South, fought the president even on trivial matters. Other legislators were concerned about the precipitous decline in the power and prestige of Congress during the war, and they fought desperately to prevent a further erosion of legislative prerogative. In all of this, Roosevelt became a scapegoat for the accumulated frustrations of Republicans, southern Democrats, and members of Congress generally.

But Roosevelt had made a bad situation worse by neglecting his Democratic base of support and by ineptly handling legislative matters. To the dismay of Democratic party leaders, during the war he assumed a nonpartisan public stance, refusing to campaign on behalf of or even endorse most of his party's congressional candidates. The memory of Woodrow Wilson's ill-fated attempt to influence the outcome of the 1918 election doubtless contributed to Roosevelt's above-the-fray approach to electoral politics. But just as Wilson had paid a heavy price for involving himself in legislative races, so Roosevelt paid a heavy price for remaining aloof. In the midterm elections of 1942, many Democrats, including several loyal New Dealers, had gone down to defeat, and party officials had blamed the reversals on Roosevelt's failure to intervene. Actually, Roosevelt had behaved no differently in 1942 than he had throughout most of his presidency. Except for his abortive purge attempt in 1938, he had never made a concerted effort to build ideological majorities conducive to reform; nor, besides allowing Democratic candidates to hold on to his long coattails, had he ever done much to support his fellow party members during campaigns. By 1944, he was paying the price for past neglect.[4]

Roosevelt further hurt his own cause by needlessly offending his legislative leaders. Periodically over the years, he had subjected them to embarrassment. His failure to inform them of his court-packing plan and his intervention in the Senate leadership fight, both in 1937, were but two examples. Another incident occurred in February 1944, at the very time he was asking Congress to consider his economic bill of rights. Both houses had passed a tax bill, which in Roosevelt's view raised insufficient revenue and contained gaping loopholes favoring well-to-do interest groups. In fact, Roosevelt stood on solid ground in criticizing the bill. But the way in which he expressed his displeasure—a stinging veto message that called into question the integrity of the Democratic congressional leadership—prompted his Senate majority leader, the usually loyal and pliable Alben Barkley, to resign his leadership post in protest. In truth, Barkley had already acquired the dubious reputation of being Roosevelt's errand boy in the Senate, and he probably was looking for an opportunity to assert his independence. In any event, Congress issued a double rebuke to the president. It promptly overrode his veto of the tax bill, and Barkley's Democratic colleagues in the Senate reelected the Kentuckian to the majority leader's post. The controversy over the tax bill, coupled with the Barkley affair, doomed any chance that Roosevelt would get favorable consideration of his legislative initiatives.[5]

But he probably would not have succeeded in gaining his legislative objectives under any circumstances, for the tax bill–Barkley episode was more a symptom than a cause of the troubled relationship between the executive and legislative branches of government. The whole episode underscored one of the paradoxes of Roosevelt's presidency. Despite his unquestioned skill as a politician, he frequently displayed striking weaknesses as a legislative leader. Only in the years immediately before Pearl Harbor, when he had steered lend-lease and the revisions in the Neutrality Act through Congress, had his legislative performance matched the brilliance of his performance in certain other aspects of the presidency.

Only when it came to veterans' benefits did Roosevelt score a major legislative success in 1944. Two years earlier, he had authorized members of his administration and outside experts to formulate plans to help returning GIs readjust to American life, and in 1943 he had transmitted those plans to the Congress. But final passage of the Servicemen's Readjustment Act of 1944, known as the GI Bill of Rights, owed less to Roosevelt's legislative generalship than to a massive lobbying campaign by the American Legion and to patriotic fervor. After all, who would deny benefits to the brave young men who had risked their lives for their country? No one, as it turned out, and the measure unanimously passed both houses of Congress. With its education subsidies, medical benefits, unemployment insurance, and low-interest home loans, the GI Bill of Rights had enormous and largely positive long-range consequences.[6]

Debate over the two bills of rights took place against the backdrop of the 1944 presidential campaign. Despite Roosevelt's periodic claim that he yearned to retire to Hyde Park, few people doubted that with the war still in progress, he would run for a fourth term. Moreover, by still failing to groom a successor, he once again ensured that the Democrats had no choice but to turn to him. It therefore came as no surprise when the Democrats nominated Roosevelt for the fourth time that July.

Only the selection of a running mate generated suspense during what was otherwise a cut-and-dried convention. That selection took on special significance because Roosevelt's vice president presumably would enjoy an advantage over the competition in the race to succeed Roosevelt in the White House four years later. Normally the incumbent, in this case Henry Wallace, would have remained on the ticket. Why, after all, break up a winning team? But by 1944, Wallace had fallen into disfavor with many southerners, city bosses, and party leaders, although he retained the support of liberals and laborites within the Democratic coalition. Roosevelt, therefore, led Wallace to believe that he would be on the ticket, but he cast about for an alternative. There ensued a series of maneuvers that were complicated and confusing even by prevailing Rooseveltian standards. In the end, Democratic delegates, with Roosevelt's behind-the-scenes support, selected Harry S. Truman, an able, moderate, but relatively unknown senator from Missouri who owed his selection primarily to the fact that no one could think of a particularly good reason for opposing him. The convention ended on a note of harmony. Nevertheless the vice-presidential selection process had temporarily exposed ideological and regional fault lines in the Democratic party and, moreover, provided a disturbing glimpse of what might be in store for the party in a future without Roosevelt.[7]

The Republicans, meanwhile, selected as their standard-bearer Thomas E. Dewey, the incumbent governor of New York. Before assuming Roosevelt's old seat in Albany, the 42-year-old Michigan native and Columbia Law School graduate had attracted national attention as the crusading prosecutor who had put the likes of Lucky Luciano and other notorious gangsters behind bars. In addition to their Albany connection, Dewey and Roosevelt had something else in common. Both of them were political descendants of Theodore Roosevelt—Franklin Roosevelt in the obvious ways, and Dewey as a member of the liberal, internationalist wing of the GOP. Linked though they were by ties of political kinship, the two men presented strikingly different public images. To a nation accustomed to Roosevelt's warm and reassuring manner, Dewey seemed cold and aloof, more of a patrician than even his patrician opponent. For example, Dewey was so fearful of picking up germs that during prison and hospital inspections, he would pull out a handkerchief and delicately place it over doorknobs before touching them. His austere manner and diminutive size made him the butt of many jokes. He was the groom on the wedding cake, said one pundit; he spent election night pacing the floor underneath his bed, said another. In fact, the jokes obscured Dewey's impressive intellectual and administrative credentials, as well as his thoughtfulness on most issues.[8]

Like his predecessors, Landon and Willkie, Dewey found himself in an almost impossible situation. He supported the basic thrust of Roosevelt's policies at home and abroad, but he had to convince voters that he could execute Roosevelt's policies better than Roosevelt. Dewey also faced the difficult task of criticizing the president without seeming to undermine public confidence in the commander in chief during wartime. As the campaign progressed, Dewey, like Landon and Willkie before him, succumbed to desperation and dredged up the time-worn charge that Communists had infiltrated the government.

Only one issue had the potential to cost Roosevelt the election, but political etiquette and fear of a backlash prevented Dewey from discussing it publicly. The issue was Roosevelt's health. In truth, by 1944, the president was a sick man. Despite his apparent equanimity under pressure, he seemed to have aged dramatically since the beginning of the war. His face had become drawn and lined; the circles under his eyes had darkened; and his complexion had acquired a grayish pallor. Now, when he was going over the mail with his secretary, he would occasionally nod off to sleep. In March 1944, after a long bout with the flu, he checked into the naval hospital in Bethesda, Maryland, for a physical examination. Doctors were shocked by what they found. Their famous patient was suffering from hypertension, hypertensive heart disease, a degree of congestive heart failure, and bronchitis. In retrospect, Roosevelt was a prime candidate for heart disease. His father had died of a heart attack, his disability made regular exercise difficult, he was a chain-smoker, and he had a highly stressful job. His condition, although not immediately life-threatening, was serious enough to raise doubts about his ability to meet the demands of high office for another four years.

Surprisingly, neither during the physical examination nor later did Roosevelt ask the attending physicians about his condition. His lack of inquisitiveness stood in sharp contrast to his earlier relentless interrogations of doctors and therapists following his attack of polio. More surprising still, his physicians, including his personal doctor, Admiral Ross McIntire, told him nothing about their findings except that he had to lose weight, rest more, cut down on cigarettes, and take some medicine.[9] Actually, the failure of Roosevelt's doctors to inform him of the severity of his condition or even of the fact that he had a heart condition in the first place conformed to a long-standing pattern in his life. People had always been reluctant to confront him with bad news. During the many years that he underwent treatment for his paralysis, even when Roosevelt pressed his physicians and therapists for details, they apparently never told him what they knew to be true: that he was unlikely ever to walk again. That in itself was probably not unusual, for the doctors were simply reluctant to remove the last shred of hope from their patient. But the practice of withholding bad news from Roosevelt had also extended into his political life. Not until the very end of the court-packing controversy had anyone told him directly that he was backing a lost cause. Then, in response to Roosevelt's request for a frank appraisal of the situation, Vice President Garner had confronted him with the political realities. Throughout his life, it seemed, Roosevelt had built up around himself a nearly impenetrable wall of optimism that kept out the bearers of bad news.[10]

But Roosevelt's appearance and behavior increasingly betrayed his illness. In late July and August, after the Democratic convention, he sailed to Hawaii, where he conferred with his Pacific commanders. In the past, sea voyages had worked as a restorative to his health. But not this time. Upon his return, he looked drawn and weary. Worse still, his report to the nation, in the form of a live radio address from the deck of a destroyer anchored off Seattle, was a near disaster. Roosevelt had prepared the address in haste and without the assistance of speechwriters. The result was a rambling speech delivered in an uncharacteristically halting manner. No one knew it at the time, but Roosevelt later revealed that during the first part of the speech he experienced sharp chest pains, probably caused by an insufficient supply of oxygen to the heart muscles.

Other incidents occurred. In late August, at a state dinner for the president of Iceland, Roosevelt proposed a toast to his honored guest. The president of Iceland then rose, spoke briefly, and sat down. But then Roosevelt offered the very same toast he had offered earlier. "Everyone was so stunned," Henry Morgenthau noted in his diary, "that hardly anybody got up when he proposed the toast the second time."[11]

Because of Roosevelt's faltering performance, his appearance at a dinner sponsored by the International Brotherhood of Teamsters in late September took on special significance. Everyone at the dinner had earlier heard rumors, some of them wildly exaggerated, about Roosevelt's health. Now they would have a chance to see for themselves. The speech was important, too, because of the presence of a large contingent of labor leaders. Stung by Roosevelt's call for national service legislation, laborites wanted Roosevelt to reassure them of his continued support; and although there was no danger that the union chieftains would defect to the GOP, expectations of a low voter turnout in the upcoming election meant that Roosevelt would need a strong showing from organized labor to guarantee victory.

As Roosevelt prepared to speak, even his friends and family members in the audience felt apprehensive. His daughter, Anna Roosevelt Boettiger, leaned over to speechwriter Sam Rosenman and said, "Do you think that Pa will put it over? . . . If the delivery isn't just right it'll be an awful flop." She need not have worried, for her father delivered one of the most effective political speeches of his career. Employing a gifted stage actor's full range of facial expressions and voice inflections, he defended his own record and skewered that of the GOP. Republicans, he said, attacked labor three and a half out of every four years. But then, just before election time, they discovered that they actually loved labor after all. The highlight of the speech came when he confronted charges by some Republican leaders that during his recent trip to the Pacific, he had left his dog, Fala, behind in the Aleutian Islands, and then, at taxpayers' expense, had sent a destroyer back to retrieve the Scottish terrier. Slowly and deliberately, he delivered his lines: "These Republican leaders have not been content with attacks on me, or my wife, or my sons. No, not content with that, they now include my little dog Fala. Well, of course, I don't resent attacks, and my family doesn't resent attacks, but Fala does resent them." Roosevelt's listeners were now laughing so hard that he had to pause for several moments. Playing out the scene to the end, Roosevelt slowly sipped a glass of water and dabbed at his mouth, all the while feigning indignation at having to defend the honor of the falsely maligned Fala.[12]

More followed, but his speech was already a spectacular success. Of course, insofar as Roosevelt's remarks concerned Dewey, they were unfair, for he had not spread the false Fala story. Moreover, elsewhere in the speech Roosevelt associated Dewey with the most reactionary elements in his party and in so doing misrepresented the New York governor's position on most issues. Then, too, just because Roosevelt had risen to this occasion did not alter the fact that he was seriously ill and that the severity of his illness could potentially impair his performance as president. But fair or not, the "Fala" speech was a brilliant performance, and it had an immediate impact on the campaign. For one thing, Roosevelt's backers received a great boost in morale. They had been waiting for a sign that "the old man" was back and in top form, and Roosevelt had given it to them. For another thing, Dewey now realized that he had a fight on his hands, and he abandoned his responsible but dull issue-oriented campaign in favor of a bare-knuckled attack on Roosevelt and the New Deal. Thus, it was after the "Fala" speech that the Republican challenger began to engage in red-baiting. Roosevelt, for his part, followed the speech with physically grueling campaign appearances in New York City, Philadelphia, and Chicago, and thereby eased, though by no means eliminated, concerns about his health.[13]

In addition to the personal duel between Roosevelt and Dewey, the 1944 presidential contest featured two notable developments in the evolution of modern campaign techniques. One was an unprecedented reliance on public opinion polls; the other was a novel use of radio for political purposes. Roosevelt had been reading poll results since the late 1930s, and while he was not slavishly devoted to them, he considered polling an indispensable source of information about public attitudes. Dewey placed even more faith in them. "Never argue with the Gallup Poll," he had once said. During the 1944 campaign, the two candidates, but especially Dewey, made more extensive use of polls than any previous contenders for the presidency.[14]

The candidates also made unprecedented use of radio in a presidential race. It was not the amount of programming devoted to electioneering that was significant, but its nature, particularly an innovative one-hour tribute to Roosevelt on election eve. Sponsored by the Democratic National Committee and produced, written, and directed by the master of radio production, Norman Corwin, the program featured songs

and skits praising Roosevelt and lampooning Dewey. Nearly 50 Holly-
wood celebrities stepped up to the microphone to endorse Roosevelt.
They included Judy Garland, Humphrey Bogart, James Cagney, Rita
Hayworth, Jane Wyman, Groucho Marx, Lana Turner, Edward G. Robinson, and Frank Sinatra. Also appearing on the broadcast were writers
Edna Ferber and Dorothy Parker, artist Waldo Pierce, playwright Elmer
Rice, and philosopher John Dewey (who emphasized that he was no relation to the other Dewey). Interspersed with the celebrity endorsements
were testimonials by Americans from all walks of life, including wounded
GIs, wage-earners and union members (AFL and CIO), housewives,
businessmen, and farmers. Members of the Democratic National Committee later credited the broadcast with adding upward of 2 million votes
to Roosevelt's total. But whatever its immediate impact on the outcome
of the election, the Democratic radio program with its merging of Hol-
lywood production values, radio, and politics, signified a new stage in
the commercialization of presidential campaigns.[15]

On Election Day, Roosevelt once again prevailed, with 53.5 percent of the popular vote to 46 percent for Dewey. Roosevelt's margin of
victory was not only the narrowest of his four elections but the narrowest
margin since Wilson's reelection in 1916. Roosevelt won the electoral
college by a more comfortable margin of 432 to 99. As a percentage of
eligible voters, fewer persons went to the polls in 1944 than in any presidential election since 1924. The low turnout probably hurt Roosevelt
more than it did Dewey, for the decline in voting was apparently heaviest
among lower-income groups, which had been voting Democratic since
1932. Roosevelt could take solace from the fact that some of his old
isolationist foes, including Sen. Gerald P. Nye, had gone down to defeat.
On the other hand, the conservative coalition of Republicans and conservative Democrats remained intact.[16]

Following the election, planning for the postwar world took center
stage, for by then, the end of the war was in sight, at least in Europe. In
June, American and British forces had successfully launched the much-
delayed cross-Channel invasion of France. By December 1944, the Allied advance had slowed in the wake of a fierce German counterattack.
Nevertheless, Allied troops were regrouping, and it seemed only a matter
of time before they regained the offensive. On the eastern front, meanwhile, Russian armies had driven the Germans from the Soviet Union
and most of eastern Europe and were fast approaching German borders.

Roosevelt never developed a particularly clear or coherent plan for the postwar world. To be sure, he wanted to prevent a third world war, and he wanted to keep the United States from retreating into isolationism after the cessation of hostilities. To these ends, he favored creation of a new world organization, to be known as the United Nations. But as he privately made clear, some members of this organization would be more equal than others. Specifically, the four victorious Allied powers— the United States, Great Britain, the Soviet Union, and China—would police the globe and enforce the peace for an indefinite period after the war. Believing that colonialism sparked international conflict, Roosevelt also wanted to phase out British and French colonies in Asia and Africa.

Beyond these broad objectives, however, Roosevelt's views, although always confidently expressed, were replete with uncertainties and contradictions. Exactly how and under what circumstances the big four would act, for example, he did not say. Nor was it clear what role the United States would play in this policing system. At the Tehran Conference in December 1943, he told Stalin that if trouble broke out in Europe, the United States might send planes and supplies, but Britain and the Soviet Union would have to provide the armies. On the other hand, in July 1944, when Charles de Gaulle visited the White House, Roosevelt told him that the United States would maintain forces at military outposts around the world. He was similarly ambiguous on the subject of postwar Germany.[17]

Sometimes, especially in private discourse, Roosevelt sounded like a realist who believed that power played a central role in international affairs and who harbored no illusions about the difficulties of maintaining peace in the postwar era. Thus, he frankly acknowledged in private that the real power in the postwar world would reside with the big four. He also recognized that the great powers would maintain certain spheres of influence after the war. In October 1944, when Churchill and Stalin met in Moscow and divided the Balkan states between them, assigning to each state a percentage to indicate the degree of British or Soviet influence, Roosevelt gave his assent. Then, too, Roosevelt disclaimed any utopian goals. About the best anyone could hope for, he wrote a friend, was the passage of 25 years or so before another war broke out.[18]

But just as often, he seemed to ignore, or at least minimize, certain pressing realities of international life. With indefatigable optimism he talked of bringing together in harmony Arabs and Jews in the Middle East, Communists and anti-Communists in China, and Hindus and Moslems in India. Nor did he foresee any major obstacles to U.S.-Soviet friendship after the war. "The Russians are perfectly friendly," he said in off-the-cuff remarks in March 1944. "They aren't trying to gobble up all the rest of Europe or the world. They didn't know us, that's the really fundamental difference. They are friendly people."[19] Then there were the pet schemes with which Roosevelt liked to regale aides and visiting diplomats, such as his global production-for-use plan or his proposal to create a new nation, to be called Wallonia, out of parts of Belgium, Luxembourg, and France. To British foreign secretary Anthony Eden, who sat in on planning sessions with Roosevelt during the war, he was anything but realistic. Although Roosevelt displayed an impressive knowledge of world history and geography, Eden noted, the opinions Roosevelt built upon that knowledge "were alarming in their cheerful fecklessness. He seemed to see himself disposing of the fate of many lands, Allied no less than enemy. He did all this with so much grace that it was not easy to dissent. Yet it was too like a conjuror, skillfully juggling with balls of dynamite, whose nature he failed to understand."[20]

Eden's depiction of Roosevelt captured the expansive, freewheeling, rather imperious side to his personality. Here, obviously, was the same man who, as a candidate for the vice presidency in 1920, had boasted of writing the Haitian constitution, only now he was doing his boasting in private and not in public. And yet to the extent that Eden portrayed Roosevelt as a kind of monarch, who with the flick of a wrist determined the fate of peoples and nations, he was misleading. Despite his brash talk, Roosevelt proved to be extremely cautious in specific situations. In fact, he seemed so eager to preserve Allied unity and to avoid any controversy that might jeopardize American membership in the United Nations that he avoided taking a firm stand on the most sensitive issues involving the shape of the postwar world.

The problem that arose from his cautious approach, however, was that the longer he avoided issues, the less control he had over them. His desire to phase out European colonialism offered a case in point. Almost alone among Western leaders, Roosevelt understood that the sun was finally setting on the old European colonial empires. At the beginning of the war, Roosevelt had hoped to persuade Britain to take the first tentative steps toward granting independence to India. He had also insisted that France relinquish control of Indochina, for he believed that the French had badly mismanaged their Asian wards. "France has had the country—thirty million inhabitants—for nearly one hundred years," he wrote Hull in January 1944, "and the people are worse off than they were at the beginning. . . . The people of Indo-China are entitled to something better than that."[21] Roosevelt did not favor immediate independence for colonial peoples, whom he regarded as much too backward to assume the reins of self-government. Instead, he wanted to grant colonies such as Indochina trusteeship status, with the United States and other nations managing their affairs until such time as they were able to govern themselves. A strong element of national self-interest inspired Roosevelt's anticolonialism, for the United States presumably would benefit if all of the old colonies were opened up to commercial trade.

Early in the war, when Roosevelt had pressed Churchill for concessions on India, Churchill had adamantly refused to concede anything. Indeed, the colonial issue, which the British thought was none of the president's business, ranked second only to the dispute over the second front as the major source of friction between the two Allies. In the face of British resistance, Roosevelt declined to employ measures other than moral suasion, but he declined to use even that as time wore on. He refused, for example, to follow the advice of diplomat William Phillips, who, upon his return from a fact-finding mission to India, urged Roosevelt to issue an ultimatum to the British: either they take definite steps toward granting self-government to the Indians, or the United States would withdraw its forces from that military sector. By early 1945, however, even if Roosevelt had wanted to press the matter, he had little if any leverage with which to exact concessions from the British. By 1945, too, Roosevelt had lost the means and the will to resist France's return to Indochina. Roosevelt's first instincts had proved sound. Colonialism was on the wane; nationalism was on the rise. The opportunity for Roosevelt to align the United States with this inexorable movement in history, it seemed, had passed.

By 1945, it was also too late to avert the greatest tragedy of a tragic war, the Holocaust. In 1942 German officials had decided to exterminate all the surviving European Jews they could get their hands on. Soon thereafter, officials in the State Department received evidence of German intentions. So, too, did several American Jewish leaders, including Rabbi Stephen Wise. As the Germans began to implement their plans for mass murder, American and British intelligence agents learned the location of the concentration camps where the executions were to take place. Many factors contributed to the failure of the United States to try harder to prevent the murder of some 6 million Jews: anti-Semitism among some officials in the State Department; bureaucratic foot-dragging; continued public opposition to relaxation of the immigration laws; the absence of strong public pressure; and disbelief, even in the face of mounting evidence, that the Nazis could be guilty of so great a crime against humanity. But surely a major factor that impeded efforts to rescue the Jews was a conspicuous lack of presidential leadership. By December 1942 Roosevelt unquestionably knew about the Nazi extermination program. Yet, as one leading student of the Holocaust accurately observed, the president had "little to say about the problem and gave no priority at all to rescue." Throughout the war Roosevelt had frequently questioned the advice of his military advisers. When those same advisers rejected, with little explanation, a proposal to bomb the rail lines leading to the concentration camps, Roosevelt raised no objection. To be sure, in 1944, when Henry Morgenthau presented him with a blunt report documenting American culpability in the murder of the Jews, Roosevelt established a War Refugee Board that did save thousands of persons from the gas chambers. But by that time, it was too late to save the millions more who had already perished.[22]

In February 1945, Roosevelt traveled, once again at considerable hazard, to the Black Sea resort of Yalta in the Soviet Union. By that time, if it was not yet too late to alter significantly the emerging shape of Eastern Europe, it was at least late in the day. For by then, Russian armies, having driven the Germans from the Soviet Union, held a commanding position in Poland and elsewhere in Eastern Europe. In truth, however, that part of the world was not uppermost in Roosevelt's mind when he went to Yalta to confer with Churchill and Stalin. Five months earlier, after talking with Roosevelt, W. Averell Harriman, the American ambassador to the Soviet Union, had noted that the president "consistently shows very little interest in Eastern European matters except as they affect sentiment in America."[23] Nothing had changed in the interim.

At Yalta, Roosevelt's first priority was to get Stalin to reaffirm the commitment he had made at the Tehran Conference to enter the war against Japan after the defeat of Germany. In February 1945, Japan still occupied Manchuria, Korea, Indochina, the Dutch East Indies, and the entire coast of China. The atomic bomb remained in the planning stage, and military strategists were predicting a long campaign—perhaps as long as eighteen months—and heavy American casualties in the drive to force Japan into final surrender. Those same military strategists believed that Russian assistance would shorten the war in the Pacific and save American lives. Roosevelt also sought at Yalta both to reaffirm Stalin's commitment to participate in the United Nations and to clarify details of the new organization's structure. As for Poland and Eastern Europe, Roosevelt wanted, at the very least, a face-saving arrangement which would satisfy the Soviets but also appease some six to seven million Americans of Polish ancestry, who feared for the fate of their homeland.

In the final accounting, Roosevelt achieved most of what he wanted. Stalin pledged to enter the war against Japan two or three months after the defeat of Germany. In exchange, Roosevelt and Churchill acknowledged certain Soviet territorial interests in Asia. Stalin also confirmed Soviet intentions to participate in the United Nations. Unwilling to jeopardize Soviet entry either into the Pacific war or into the UN, Roosevelt settled for a pledge from Stalin to include non-Communist Poles in a provisional Polish government. Stalin also signed a Declaration on Liberated Europe in which he agreed to allow the nations of Eastern Europe to hold free and unfettered elections and to form democratic governments.[24]

Roosevelt undoubtedly knew that the Yalta accords would not bring freedom and democracy to Eastern Europe. When Admiral Leahy told Roosevelt that the agreement on Poland was "so elastic that the Russians can stretch it all the way from Yalta to Washington without ever technically breaking it," Roosevelt replied, "I know. But it's the best I can do for Poland at this time."[25] Nor did he necessarily trust Stalin to abide by the letter of the Declaration on Liberated Europe. Roosevelt had, after all, been suspicious enough of Stalin to have withheld information about the atomic bomb from him. At the same time, however, Roosevelt did not believe that he was consigning Eastern Europe to perpetual subjugation by the Soviet Union. For him the future was fluid, not fixed. He probably believed that in time he could persuade Stalin to relax his grip on Eastern Europe. He also seemed to believe that once the Soviets began participating in the United Nations, they would achieve a greater sense of their own security and be more willing to grant a measure of independence to their neighbors.

Critics later claimed that Roosevelt had handed Poland over to the Soviet Union. In fact, Roosevelt did not give Stalin anything that was in his possession. Soviet troops, not American or British troops, occupied Poland and much of Eastern Europe. The critics might have been on firmer ground if they had argued that Roosevelt should have brought pressure to bear on Stalin early in the war—say, in 1941, when the Russians desperately needed American aid to survive. And yet it would have required almost miraculous foresight to have predicted that within two years the Soviets would have turned back the German invasion, much less assumed a commanding military position in Eastern Europe. Moreover, in 1941, Roosevelt still feared that the Soviets might conclude a separate peace with Germany. Still, Roosevelt had less excuse for failing to attach conditions to continued lend-lease assistance during and after 1944, by which time the Soviets had repulsed the threat to their home-land. He had still less excuse for having acquiesced in Churchill's secret agreement with Stalin, concluded in December 1944, whereby the two leaders divided Europe into spheres of influence. In short, by the time of the Yalta Conference, Roosevelt's options were severely limited.

As it turned out, Roosevelt's most serious error occurred not during the Yalta Conference but in its aftermath, when he painted for the American people too rosy a picture of the future, especially as it pertained to Soviet-American relations. There was irony here, too, for Roosevelt believed deeply that he must avoid raising expectations to unrealistic levels, as Woodrow Wilson had done. Consequently, in his discussion of the proposed United Nations, he scrupulously avoided any hint of the utopian. During his post-Yalta address to Congress, he conceded, in reference to the blueprint for the United Nations, that no plan was perfect and that no one could say how long that or any other blueprint for world peace could last. And yet in that same speech, he could not bring himself to present a similarly realistic assessment of Soviet-American relations. But then, he was probably incapable of presenting such an assessment because he did not believe it. He believed instead that he could preserve cooperation among the victorious Allies into the postwar world. Once the Soviet Union ended its traditional isolationism by joining the United Nations and thus becoming part of the community of nations, it might be amenable to friendly persuasion and world opinion. Roosevelt was not alone in his optimism. The Russian experts in the State Department, including Roosevelt's interpreter at Yalta, Charles E. Bohlen, who had few illusions about the Soviet Union, believed that the Allies might yet work out an equitable settlement of the situations in Poland and Eastern Europe generally. One of the few dissenters was George F. Kennan, whose gloomy assessment of the chances of Soviet-American cooperation proved prophetic.[26]

By February 1945, Roosevelt who had recently turned 63, was a sick man, and there was no hiding it. At Yalta, Churchill's personal physician, Lord Moran, thought that Roosevelt displayed all of the symptoms of hardening of the arteries of the brain and had only a few months to live. When he reported to Congress on the conference, he spoke for the first time to that body from a seated position, and he made a rare reference to his infirmity: "I hope that you will pardon me for an unusual posture of sitting down during the presentation of what I want to say, but I know that you will realize that it makes it a lot easier for me in not having to carry about ten pounds of steel around on the bottom of my legs; and also because I have just completed a fourteen-thousand-mile trip."[27]

Roosevelt's physical appearance seemed to deteriorate by the day. One time, in fact, his personal secretary, Grace Tully, noticed that he looked worse after an absence of only two hours from his office. "We had been waiting for the Boss in the Oval Study," she later recalled, "and when he was wheeled in I was so startled I almost burst into tears. In two hours he seemed to have failed dangerously. His face was ashen, highlighted by the darkening shadows under his eyes and with his cheeks drawn gauntly." Roosevelt partisans insisted that he had lost nothing of his mental acuity, but the overall testimony was mixed. In March, Major General Albert C. Wedemeyer briefed the president on Far Eastern affairs over lunch. It had been several months since Wedemeyer had seen Roosevelt, and he was shocked. Roosevelt's "color was ashen, his face drawn, and his jaw drooping," Wedemeyer recalled. "I had difficulty in conveying information to him because he seemed in a daze. Several times I repeated the same idea because his mind did not seem to retain or register." Even though Roosevelt must have been able to read the concern in other people's faces, he never asked his doctors about his condition. And his doctors, for their part, apparently never raised the subject themselves.[28]

At the end of March 1945, in the hope of regaining his strength, Roosevelt decided to visit his retreat in Warm Springs, Georgia. It was there, after all, that he had gone 20 years before in search of a cure for his paralysis. Warm Springs had not fulfilled its promise in that regard, but for Roosevelt, a stay at his "Little White House" in the Georgia countryside had almost always worked as a restorative. To his disappointment, wartime security considerations had forced him to forsake trips to Warm Springs. But now, with the war in Europe drawing to a close and with safety no longer a major concern, Roosevelt instructed his staff to pack up for the trip south.

Eleanor, who maintained a schedule only slightly less demanding than the president's, as usual did not accompany him to Warm Springs. Joining him instead, in addition to his staff members, were his cousins Laura Delano and Margaret Suckley. Also joining him at Warm Springs was Lucy Mercer Rutherfurd, the woman with whom he had had an affair some 25 years before. Following the breakup of their relationship, she had married a wealthy widower, Winthrop Rutherfurd. Upon his death in 1941, she and Roosevelt had once again begun to see each other. Occasionally, when Eleanor was out of town, Lucy would join Roosevelt and others for dinner at the White House. Few persons knew of their history together, and most White House insiders thought that Mrs. Rutherfurd was simply one of the president's many friends.

On 30 March, Good Friday, Roosevelt and his party arrived in Warm Springs. Roosevelt quickly settled into a routine. He slept until late in the morning, then read the newspapers, then went over the mail, which his secretaries, fearful of tiring him, parceled out in small quantities. Once in a while a messenger would arrive from Washington with the latest dispatches from the war fronts. But at this advanced stage of the war, few matters any longer required his immediate attention.

By Thursday, 12 April, nearly two weeks after his arrival, Roosevelt seemed to have regained some of his strength. His color had improved, and he was relaxed and in good humor. He spent the better part of that morning in bed reading the *Atlanta Constitution*. When he got up, he went over the mail and chatted with his cousins and Lucy Rutherfurd. At noon, Elizabeth Shoumatoff, a portrait artist, arrived to work on a watercolor she was doing of him. The president, she later recalled, "seemed so absorbed, his gaze had a faraway aspect and was completely solemn."[29] At one o'clock, he glanced up and said, "We have fifteen minutes to work." Some 15 minutes later, he raised his hand and passed it over his forehead several times. "I have a terrific headache," he said softly. Then he slumped forward in his chair. By the time his doctor arrived, he was unconscious and breathing heavily. Soon thereafter, the breathing ceased. All attempts to revive Roosevelt failed, and at 3:35 P.M. the doctor pronounced him dead of a cerebral hemorrhage.

For the sake of his place in history, the timing of Roosevelt's death was probably fortunate. To his admirers, of course, it was unthinkable that if he had lived, anything could have diminished the heroic stature of the man who had fought his way back from polio, who had inspired a nation in the depths of the Great Depression, and who had led the nation from the brink of disaster at Pearl Harbor to the threshold of victory in the spring of 1945. Roosevelt had beaten the odds many times in the past. Surely, if he had lived, he would have beaten the odds again.

But what Roosevelt's admirers overlooked was his health. By April 1945, his condition had deteriorated to such an extent that, if a cerebral hemorrhage had not claimed his life, he almost certainly would have suffered the same fate as Woodrow Wilson and become physically incapacitated before completing his term in office. In such circumstances, the consequences for the nation probably would have been worse in Roosevelt's case than they had been in Wilson's, if only because the nation might have been left leaderless for much longer. When Wilson suffered his paralyzing stroke in October 1919, one and a half years remained on his term; as of April 1945, nearly four full years remained of Roosevelt's term. Moreover, because of Roosevelt's habit of dividing authority, assigning overlapping responsibilities, and pitting subordinates against one another, there was no one in the administration with the stature to step in and assume the ailing president's responsibilities. Harry Hopkins might have served that function five years earlier, but in 1945 he too was a dying man. George Marshall could have handled military affairs, but he would have been out of his depth managing the intensely political civilian side to government operations. In all likelihood, bureaucratic warfare on a grand scale would have broken out, as presidential aides and cabinet secretaries, their ambitions long held in check, fought one another to fill the leadership vacuum. If these things had come to pass, and it seems inevitable that they would have, Roosevelt's historical reputation would surely have suffered. At the very least, his decision to run for a fourth term would have come under intense scrutiny.

Even if Roosevelt had avoided the worst and had completed his term in a weakened but not incapacitated state, he would have faced some enormous challenges to his reputation. How, for example, would he have responded to the stiffening of Soviet control over Eastern Europe? Would he have ordered the use of atomic bombs on Japan? How would he have managed the reconversion of business and industry from war to peace? How would he have made good on his promise of an economic bill of rights?

Even in the short run he would have confronted great challenges, such as persuading two-thirds of the United States Senate to approve the United Nations charter. Before he died, ratification was by no means certain. True enough, in 1943 a majority of senators had gone on record in favor of American membership in a world organization. But in 1919, during the early stages of the debate over the League of Nations, the odds had favored American membership in the League. Moreover, Cordell Hull, whom senators trusted much more than Roosevelt, had been instrumental in gaining Senate acceptance of the idea of a new international organization. But Hull had resigned his post in November 1944 because of poor health, and he would not have been available to lead the fight for the United Nations.

On the day Roosevelt was buried, journalist Allen Drury, who covered the Senate, wrote in his private journal that because of the bitter feelings between Roosevelt and the Senate, any proposal to join the United Nations under his sponsorship "would have had heavy going; too many antagonisms would have been riding with it." Drury added, "It is no untruth to say, and everyone who knows the Senate knows it, that the chances for American participation in the world organization are considerably better under Harry Truman than they ever could have been under Franklin Roosevelt."[30] As it turned out, internationalism gained momentum from Roosevelt's death, as Truman skillfully channeled public grief over Roosevelt's passing into support for the United Nations. In this instance, at least, Roosevelt may have wielded more power in death than he would have in life.

10

REPUTATION AND LEGACIES

Franklin Roosevelt was as confident about his place in history as he was about everything else. He would not have been disappointed with his posthumous reputation. The reputations of most former presidents tend to fluctuate with changing circumstances and new perspectives. Thus, for example, Roosevelt's mentors, Theodore Roosevelt and Woodrow Wilson, have had their ups and downs in ratings of chief executives. But not Franklin Roosevelt. In 1948, three years after his death, a poll of prominent historians ranked him the third greatest president in American history, after Abraham Lincoln and George Washington. Thirty-five years later, despite changing ideological and methodological currents in the study of history, and despite persistent efforts by detractors to chip away at his reputation, Roosevelt moved up a notch in the ratings, edging out Washington for second place.[1] Yet in one key respect, Roosevelt's lofty stature is misleading, for it conceals sharp disagreement among commentators about the wisdom of many of his actions and about the nature of his legacies.

Roosevelt possessed an extraordinarily keen sense of his own place in history. Perhaps he acquired this sense from his mother, who not only saved his boyhood letters for posterity, but also corrected them for grammar and spelling before putting them away. Whatever its origin, Roosevelt, as historian Allan Nevins once noted, "regarded history as an imposing drama and himself as a conspicuous actor."[2] As early as his Harvard years, according to Rexford Tugwell, he began saving his correspondence, apparently in the belief that it would be of interest to future generations. (Oddly enough, had he not preserved his letters from Lucy Mercer, Eleanor might never have found out about their affair.) As governor and as president, he directed his staff to preserve for the benefit of historians all incoming and outgoing mail and all documents originating in his office, no matter how insignificant a particular item might seem to be. To store the resulting mass of papers, which eventually numbered in the millions, he might have made arrangements with the Library of Congress, which housed the manuscript collections of other presidents. But Roosevelt, who probably believed that he would have a place in history as large as or larger than that of any of his predecessors, wanted a library of his own, where scholars could come to study his life and times. So in November 1939, on 16 acres of the family estate that were donated to the federal government by his mother, he laid the cornerstone for the first presidential library.[3]

In all of this letter-saving and library-building, there was a large measure of calculation. Roosevelt was confident that he would enjoy a favorable historical reputation, to be sure; but just to be on the safe side, he took certain precautions. Thus, for example, he deliberately planted evidence for future scholars, such as the note he affixed to a handwritten copy of his first inaugural address that falsely claimed that he had written the address himself and that it had taken him only four and a half hours to compose it. In fact, the writing process had involved numerous aides and had stretched out over several days. Rexford Tugwell believed that the very act of preserving such a large mass of documents was an attempt by Roosevelt to shape his historical reputation. "The elaborate and successful actor while alive prepared a gigantic trap for historians," said Tugwell, who suspected that historians would be too busy exploring documents "to ask embarrassing questions."[4]

The documentary record of his life constitutes one basis for an assessment of Roosevelt's role in history. His complicated legacies are the other. His most important legacies were an enlarged role for the federal government in the economy, the political coalition that had formed under his leadership, and a revitalized presidency. The federal government had been assuming new economic responsibilities at least since the turn of the century. But the New Deal and the war greatly increased government intervention in the economy, the purpose of which was to compensate for deficiencies and self-destructive tendencies in capitalism.

New Deal programs such as Social Security, unemployment compensation, the minimum wage, public housing, bank deposit insurance, regulation of the stock market, and farm subsidies became fixtures in the
economic and social life of the nation. So, too, did the GI Bill of Rights
and, for good or ill, the close relationship that developed between the
defense industries and the federal government—what President Dwight
D. Eisenhower, in his farewell address to the nation in 1961, dubbed
"the military-industrial complex."

Roosevelt's critics complained that his administration ushered in
the welfare state, and they denounced the New Deal in the abstract; but
even the critics came to accept most specific New Deal programs. For
example, nothing did more to turn large segments of the business community against Roosevelt than the creation in 1934 of the Securities and
Exchange Commission, which was set up to regulate the stock exchange.
The idea of the federal government policing the citadel of the free enterprise system drove some financiers into states of near-apoplexy. In
time, however, the SEC became so thoroughly entrenched that in the
early 1980s, when members of the Reagan administration suggested that
the SEC should be abolished in the interests of deregulation, a howl of
protest went up on, of all places, Wall Street. The financial establishment had learned not only to live with the SEC but even to depend on
the once-despised agency to maintain the confidence of investors. Indeed, by the 1980s, a more frequent and telling criticism of the SEC and
other regulatory agencies was not that they undermined the free-enterprise system but that they maintained too cozy a relationship with the
interests they supposedly regulated.

Roosevelt also bequeathed to future generations a powerful political
coalition. Although it was not as durable as the legislative heritage, it
nevertheless helped shape the contours of American politics for many
decades. During the 1930s, the party of Roosevelt replaced the party of
Lincoln as the majority party. As late as 1988, the coalition, although
battered and bruised, was still discernible, especially at the congressional, state, and local levels of government. At that time, too, more
Americans still classified themselves as Democrats than Republicans.

Roosevelt's third important legacy, and the one for which he was
most personally responsible, was a revitalized presidency. He did not create the modern presidency. Rather, he built upon the solid foundation
laid by his illustrious predecessors Theodore Roosevelt and Woodrow
Wilson. Even Herbert Hoover, by his unprecedented efforts to combat
the depression and by unwittingly becoming the scapegoat for hard

times, helped make the executive department the centerpiece of national government. But it was during Roosevelt's long tenure that the presidency became, of the three branches of government, first among equals. And that was as it should be, a host of commentators concluded. During World War II, the distinguished journalist Raymond Clapper defended presidential ascendancy by saying that "the ignorance and provincialism of Congress render it incapable of meeting the needs of modern government." At the same time, historian Henry Steele Commager claimed that "democracy apparently flourishes when the Executive is strong, languishes when it is weak."[5] An opposing tendency, which regarded the expanded powers of the modern presidency with alarm, also emerged from the Roosevelt years, finding expression in 1951 in the passage of the Twenty-second Amendment to the Constitution, which limits the tenure of presidents to two consecutive terms. This tendency also found expression in the periodic, but largely unsuccessful, attempts by Congress to modernize its procedures and reassert itself as a coequal branch of government.

But during the 1950s and early 1960s, celebrants of a strong presidency gained the upper hand. Among liberals, especially, it became an article of faith that a strong and active president was vital to the progress and security of the nation. Indeed, in the view of journalist Theodore H. White, whose best-selling account of the 1960 presidential contest did much to glamorize the presidency, nothing less than the "destiny of the human race" rested upon the shoulders of the American chief executive.[6] A spate of books appeared from both academic and commercial presses describing and extolling the rise of the modern presidency. One influential student of the office, Clinton Rossiter, even rendered obsolete Lord Acton's famous dictum that power corrupts and absolute power corrupts absolutely, at least insofar as American chief executives are concerned. "The Presidency," Rossiter wrote, "is a standing reproach to those petty doctrinaires who insist that executive power is inherently undemocratic" and "no less a reproach to those easy generalizers who think that Lord Acton had the very last word on the corrupting influences of power." If Lord Acton did not have the last word on the chief executive, another Englishman very nearly did, according to Rossiter, who approvingly quoted John Bright's paean to the American presidency: "To my mind," Bright had said in 1861, "there is nothing more worthy of reverence and obedience, and nothing more sacred, than the authority of the freely chosen magistrate of a great and free people; and if there be on earth and amongst men any right divine to govern, surely it rests with a ruler so chosen and so appointed."[7] In celebrating the presidency, commentators such as Rossiter clearly took Franklin Roosevelt as their model.

For his successors in the White House, the Roosevelt presidency, with its enlarged powers and more greatly enlarged prestige, became both an inspiration and a burden. The experience of Roosevelt's first successor, Harry S. Truman, demonstrated some of the burdensome aspects of the Roosevelt legacy. During his first years in office, nearly everyone, including Truman himself, seemed to ask in every situation, "What would Roosevelt have done?" But no matter how hard Truman tried to emulate his illustrious predecessor, he never measured up to the great man in the eyes of Roosevelt loyalists, some of whom could not bring themselves to address Truman as "Mr. President." Roosevelt partisans even took some of the luster off Truman's come-from-behind victory in the 1948 presidential election, arguing, with some justification, that the outcome owed more to the strength of the New Deal coalition than to Truman's popularity.[8]

For another of Roosevelt's successors, Lyndon B. Johnson, the Roosevelt memory served more to inspire than to intimidate. Indeed, of all of Roosevelt's successors during the half-century after his death, Johnson took the example of FDR most to heart. Some of Johnson's friends and advisers believed that he viewed the former president as a father figure. In any event, Johnson sought not only to match the accomplishments of Roosevelt but to surpass them. At one time or another, even presidents who had maintained a low opinion of Roosevelt while he was president, such as Eisenhower and Richard M. Nixon, or who had been indifferent to him, such as Jimmy Carter, had to confront the expectations created by the Roosevelt presidency.

Ironies aplenty have attended the efforts of Roosevelt's successors to emulate his feats. For one thing, he did not actually do all that his legend credits him with doing. He was not, for example, the legislative master of the New Deal. Some scholars have made this point, of course, apportioning credit (and sometimes blame) to members of Congress, to powerful interest groups, and to other participants in the richly collaborative effort that had produced the New Deal. But the image of Roosevelt as legislative mastermind, bending a docile Congress to his will, persists. "In the first Hundred Days he gave Congress a kind of leadership it had not known before and still does not care to have repeated," wrote Clinton Rossiter. "In the golden days of the New Deal he initiated a

dozen programs designed to save a society from the defects of its virtues."
Or as one of Roosevelt's popular biographers described the Hundred
Days: "In the meantime, bills originating in the White House were
passed almost daily. This was presidential power without precedent—
FDR could dream up an idea, something that had never been tried, and
set the huge machinery of government in motion to implement it." "Ever
since Roosevelt's day," President John F. Kennedy remarked to a friend,
"all the laws have been pretty much written downtown," meaning in the
executive departments.[9] Actually, encomiums to Roosevelt's legislative
craftsmanship more accurately describe the work of his faithful protégé,
Lyndon Johnson. Although his Great Society programs were collaborative efforts, Johnson played a much more direct role than Roosevelt in
the formulation and passage of legislation. But so dominating has the
Roosevelt legend been that Johnson did not get credit for—or perhaps
himself realize the magnitude of—his achievement. Thus, to the extent
that Johnson and other presidents have sought to duplicate Roosevelt's
feats as legislative leader, they not only lived in his shadow, but they
were chasing shadows.

Ironic, too, was the fact that even though presidents tried to emulate Roosevelt, his record offered scant guidance to his successors when
it came to the two great issues they faced in the postwar world, the cold
war abroad and the black civil rights movement at home. Such was the
ambiguity of Roosevelt's intentions regarding the Soviet Union that two
of his vice presidents and political heirs, Harry Truman and Henry Wallace, could propose strikingly different approaches to the Soviet Union,
each in the belief that he was following in the footsteps of the master.
Truman favored taking a hard-line approach, Wallace a conciliatory one,
but neither seemed to doubt for a moment that he was doing what Roosevelt would have done in his place. Because the nations of Asia and
Africa, which were emerging from European colonial rule, formed the
principal battleground for the cold war, Roosevelt's successors had to
grapple with problems relating to those parts of the world. But there,
too, Roosevelt provided uncertain guidance. On the all-important subject of French Indochina, for example, he bequeathed to his successors
eloquent anticolonial preachments, his belief that Indochina should one
day achieve independence, but also, by the time of his death, acquies-
cence in continued French domination of its Southeast Asian colonies.
Indeed, Roosevelt's contradictory views on Indochina foreshadowed the
muddled thinking of subsequent administrations that eventually in-

volved the United States in the longest and least successful war in its history.[10]

On the great domestic issue of postwar America, race relations, Roosevelt offered almost no help, except for a vague, general sympathy for the victims of racial oppression. The experience of President Kennedy in particular suggests the limited usefulness of Roosevelt's example. Just as black leaders had threatened a march on Washington in 1941 to draw attention to their plight, so too, in the summer of 1963, they planned a mass protest in the nation's capital. In 1941, Roosevelt had urged protest organizers to call off the march for fear of stirring a backlash of white resentment; they had heeded Roosevelt's request in exchange for the president's promise to create the Fair Employment Practices Committee, an agency that had more symbolic than substantive value to the cause of racial justice. Like Roosevelt, Kennedy, in 1963, tried to persuade black leaders to cancel their march on Washington; but unlike Roosevelt, he found that expressions of goodwill and symbolic gestures, even from a president, no longer sufficed to quell black protest. Civil rights organizers not only went ahead with their march, but they also forced Kennedy to endorse the most comprehensive civil rights proposals since Reconstruction. It was not only Kennedy who found Roosevelt's legacy deficient in the area of civil rights. Presidents who had to grapple with violent resistance to integration, urban riots, and complex issues, such as busing and affirmative action, could draw little inspiration from the Roosevelt record.

Nor despite his seemingly long reach, did Roosevelt provide much guidance on the peculiar set of economic problems that beset the nation during the 1970s and after. In the depths of the depression, the nation had needed above all to restart the engines of commerce and industry. People needed to buy and sell, to spend and consume. In 1933, a few weeks after Roosevelt's first inaugural address, a businessman made this point when he exhorted his employees: "President Roosevelt has done his part: now you do something. Buy something—buy anything, anywhere; paint your kitchen, send a telegram, give a party, get a car, pay a bill, rent a flat, fix your roof, get a haircut, see a show, build a house, take a trip, sing a song, get married."[11] Although Roosevelt was a devoted conservationist, the central thrust of the New Deal involved not conservation and belt-tightening but stimulating the production and consumption of natural resources to the point of wastefulness. That was why Harry Hopkins's speedy, almost reckless, approach to relief and public works was so much more effective as an economic stimulus than Harold Ickes's slow, scrupulous, carefully planned approach. Hopkins attempted to get as much money into as many hands as quickly as possible. Similarly, during the war, the nation needed most urgently to produce huge numbers of tanks, planes, guns, and ships. Military production was wasteful and inefficient, but it did not matter. Speed, not efficiency, was the key to victory.

To be sure, during World War II, Roosevelt had to ask Americans to make sacrifices. But though the deprivations were bitterly resented by many, they were relatively minor: the public had to endure shortages of such things as meat, sugar, gasoline, heating oil, rubber, and household appliances. But because these shortages occurred against the backdrop of economic recovery and because everyone knew that they were only temporary, they effected no basic changes in American habits. The only real sacrifice Roosevelt asked during the war was contained in his national service proposal. But he made that proposal very late in the war, when the need for national service had passed and when there was virtually no chance that Congress would accept it.

Roosevelt's successors faced fundamentally different economic problems. In the 1970s, in order to mitigate the environmental impact of growth, the country had to pay as much attention to conservation as to production and consumption. This required actually reversing Roosevelt's widely shared belief that material security could be achieved without any particular sacrifice. One of Roosevelt's "most irritating and most successful qualities," historian David Potter once observed, "was his habit of assuming that benefits could be granted without costs being felt—an assumption rooted in his faith in the potentialities of the American economy."[12] As one of Roosevelt's successors, Jimmy Carter, discovered, however, calling upon the public to sacrifice could have politically disastrous results.

A third irony of presidents' using Roosevelt as a model was that not all of his actions were worthy of emulation. Especially in his treatment of critics of his foreign policy, he set a bad example for his successors. Before and after Pearl Harbor, he and his supporters had smeared isolationists with the brush of nazism and in other ways misrepresented the views of those who opposed American entry into the war. Against the isolationists, he unleashed the FBI, the Internal Revenue Bureau, and other government agencies. In the end, he not only defeated the isolationists, he destroyed them. "Not only was the once great power of isolationism shattered," noted a student of the movement, "its public image was so tarnished that 'isolationist' became (then and later) a smear word used to connote much that was evil and even subversive in America and foreign affairs."[13]

It was a short step from Roosevelt's treatment of noninterventionists to the abuses of presidential power that occurred in the name of national security during the Johnson and Nixon presidencies. It was a short step, too, from the exaggerations and distortions of fact that accompanied Roosevelt's efforts to aid Britain before Pearl Harbor to the systematic deception of the American public that occurred throughout the war in Vietnam. Roosevelt and his successors apparently reasoned that Americans needed to be emotionally aroused before they would assume their responsibilities in the world. Perhaps Roosevelt and his heirs were right. But there is no way of knowing for sure, because they never tried as an alternative a sustained, honest, straightforward campaign to educate the public—the type of campaign that Henry Stimson had urged Roosevelt to wage. Of course, Roosevelt was not the first president to deceive the public, to discredit legitimate critics, or to abridge civil liberties in times of national crisis. Indeed, he was no worse in these respects than other wartime presidents, especially Abraham Lincoln. Nevertheless, he did make it easier for future presidents to abuse their powers in the name of national security. Roosevelt's no-holds-barred campaign against the isolationists had one other long-term effect: it denied to future generations a perspective on international affairs that emphasized the limitations of American power—a perspective that might have proved useful as the nation confronted crises in Korea, Vietnam, and elsewhere in the world.

Roosevelt bequeathed to future generations a presidency laden with great, indeed unrealistic expectations. As Godfrey Hodgson and other perceptive students of the modern presidency have pointed out, this has inevitably led to frustration, as one president after another has failed to live up to those expectations.[14] But paradoxically, in one important respect, Roosevelt also left a legacy of lowered intellectual expectations. Roosevelt's most pronounced personal characteristic and the source of his greatness was his radiant personality. Oliver Wendell Holmes, Jr., delivered the classic verdict: "A second-class intellect, but a first-class temperament!" In fact, Holmes's characterization may have been a case of mistaken identity. He was probably referring to Theodore Roosevelt and not to Franklin.[15] Nevertheless, most observers then and later have agreed that Holmes's characterization fit FDR to a tee. But, generalizing from Roosevelt, they also have seemed to argue, at least implicitly, that

in a president a first-class temperament is preferable to first-class intellect.[16] The comparison between Roosevelt and Herbert Hoover, with his
superior intelligence but dour personality, seems to clinch the case. Of
course, a brilliant intellect has seldom been a prerequisite for the presidency, given the strain of anti-intellectualism that runs through American history.[17] Yet it was not until Roosevelt's tenure and after that
personality and the related matters of image and style began to figure so
prominently in the selection and evaluation of presidents.

Of all the presidents who followed Roosevelt into the White House
in the half-century after his death, the one who most fully embodied this
particular Rooseveltian legacy was Ronald Reagan. During the 1980
presidential campaign, both Reagan partisans and Roosevelt partisans
were chagrined when Reagan frequently and admiringly invoked Roosevelt's name. Roosevelt's admirers protested that Reagan was exploiting
FDR's heritage for selfish political purposes. And indeed, Reagan did
have a penchant for quoting Roosevelt selectively and out of context.
Then, too, great differences separated the two presidents: Roosevelt advocated the expansion of government, Reagan its contraction. Roosevelt
involved himself in the day-to-day operations of his administration; Reagan, as no president since Calvin Coolidge, delegated responsibility to
his subordinates. It is inconceivable, for example, that a major initiative
in foreign policy like the Iran-Contra episode could have taken place
without Roosevelt's knowledge. Roosevelt was a master of the give-and-
take of the press conference; Reagan, despite intensive coaching, often
seemed hesitant and fumbling, and he was prone to major misstatements.
Roosevelt presided over enduring legislative achievements and the for-
mation of a lasting political coalition. There was no such outpouring of
constructive legislation from the Reagan administration; moreover, for
all the talk about a Reagan revolution, he failed to bring about a voting
realignment comparable to the New Deal coalition.

Yet in matters of personality and style, there are some striking sim-
ilarities between Roosevelt and Reagan. "Though Reagan's politics ultimately would evolve into opposition to some of the most enduring
legacies of the New Deal," journalist and Reagan biographer Lou Cannon noted, "his style has remained frankly and fervently Rooseveltian
throughout his life. His cadences are Roosevelt's cadences, his metaphors
the offspring of FDR's."[18] This was no accident, for Reagan once admitted that he had carefully studied Roosevelt's gestures and inflections and
tried to make them his own. The elaborate measures Reagan's media
advisers took to ensure that Reagan appeared in the best possible light,

even to the point of choreographing his every move, recalled the elaborate steps Roosevelt and his aides took to conceal the extent of his disability. During their final reelection campaigns, both had to confront doubts about their physical and mental capacity to continue to meet the demands of high office, Roosevelt during the 1944 campaign and Reagan after a faltering performance in the first televised debate in 1984. Roosevelt responded with his famous Fala speech and Reagan with a quip about the youthfulness of his opponent during the second televised debate. "Never mind that the answer was a dodge and as empty of content as an air bubble," two reporters wrote. "It signaled the answer they [the president's supporters] wanted to hear: the old man wasn't slipping after all."[19] The reporters were writing about Reagan, but they could just as easily have been writing about Roosevelt.

Above all, Roosevelt and Reagan were indefatigable optimists who instilled confidence in large segments of the public. Especially during his first term, Roosevelt's optimism helped yield an unprecedented outpouring of constructive legislation that, with all of its shortcomings, bought time until the war and the government spending that accompanied it rescued the United States from the depression. During the 1980s—in the context of mounting deficits, an eroding industrial base, growing inequities in the distribution of wealth, trade imbalances, and potential environmental disasters—that same kind of Rooseveltian optimism, as exhibited by Ronald Reagan, served more to divert attention from problems than to confront them.

There is much to admire about Roosevelt, including his high spirits and the courage with which he faced adversity. Yet, as the experience of his successors helped confirm, his greatness was too deeply rooted in the circumstances of his own times to be easily or even wisely duplicated. Among presidents, alas, Franklin Roosevelt was not a man for all seasons.

CHRONOLOGY

1882   Franklin D. Roosevelt born 30 January in Hyde Park, New York.

1896–1900   Attends Groton preparatory school in Groton, Massachusetts.

1900   Father, James, dies at age 72.

1900–1904   Attends Harvard University.

1904   Enters, but does not complete course of study at, Columbia Law School.

1905   Marries Anna Eleanor Roosevelt, 17 March.

1906   First child, Anna Eleanor, born.

1907   Admitted to New York bar; serves as junior clerk in firm of Carter, Ledyard, and Milburn, New York City. Second child, James, born.

1909   Third child, Franklin Delano, Jr., born in March and dies in November.

1910   Elected to the New York State Senate. Fourth child, Elliott, born.

1912   Campaigns for Woodrow Wilson; reelected to New York State Senate with 62 percent of vote.

1913   Appointed assistant secretary of the navy.

1914   World War I breaks out. FDR defeated in Democratic primary for U.S. Senate seat by James W. Gerard. Fifth child, the second Franklin Delano, Jr., born.

1916   Sixth and last child, John Aspinwall, born. FDR begins affair with Lucy Mercer.

1917   United States enters World War I in April.

1918   World War I ends in November.

1920   Nominated for vice president on Democratic ticket with James N. Cox; resigns navy post. Cox-Roosevelt ticket defeated by Warren G. Harding and Calvin Coolidge.

1921   In August is stricken with poliomyelitis at summer home on Campobello Island, New Brunswick, Canada.

1924   Makes first major public appearance since being stricken with polio as he nominates New York governor Al Smith for the presidency at the Democratic National Convention.

1927   Founds Georgia Warm Springs Foundation as treatment center for polio victims.

1928   Elected governor of New York with 50.3 percent of the vote.

1929   In October stock market crashes; Great Depression begins.

1930   Reelected governor with 63 percent of the vote.

1932   Elected president over Republican opponent Herbert Hoover with 57.4 percent of the vote, 8 November.

1933   Survives assassination attempt in Miami, 15 February. Inaugurated as thirty-second president on 4 March. Delivers first of 27 "fireside chats" on 12 March. London Economic Conference, 12 June to 28 July.

March–June 1933   First Hundred Days

June–August 1935   Second Hundred Days

1935–1936   Supreme Court invalidates National Industrial Recovery Act, Agricultural Adjustment Act, and other New Deal measures.

1936   Reelected president over Alfred M. Landon with 60.8 percent of the vote, 3 November.

1937   "Court-packing" controversy, February–July. Delivers "Quarantine" speech, 5 October. "Roosevelt Recession" begins in September, lasts until June 1938.

1938   Attempts to "purge" Democratic party.

1939   Nazi-Soviet Pact, August. Germany invades Poland in September; France and Great Britain declare war on Germany; World War II begins. FDR takes first step toward development of atomic bomb in October. In November United States modifies Neutrality Act to allow cash-and-carry trade with belligerent nations.

1940   April–June: Germany conquers Denmark, Norway, Holland, Belgium, Luxembourg, and France. Winston Churchill becomes prime minister of Great Britain. FDR announces "destroyers-for-bases" deal in September; signs Selective Service Act of 1940. Elected to third term, over Republican Wendell L. Willkie, with 54.8 percent of the vote, 5 November.

1941   Signs Lend-Lease Act, 11 March. Germany attacks the Soviet Union, 22 June. United States freezes Japanese assets in July. FDR meets Churchill at Atlantic Conference, Placentia Bay, Newfoundland, 9–12 August. Mother, Sara Delano Roosevelt, dies at age 85 on 7 September. Japan attacks Pearl Harbor, 7 December; United States declares war on Japan, 8 December; Germany declares war on United States, 11 December. FDR meets Churchill in Washington in first Allied war council, December to January 1942.

1942   Issues Executive Order 9066 authorizing internment of Japanese-Americans, 19 February. American forces land in North Africa, 7 November.

1943   Meets Churchill at Casablanca Conference, 14–24 January; calls for Axis powers' "unconditional surrender." Battle of Stalingrad ends in Soviet victory, 31 January. Allies successfully conclude North African campaign in May and invade Sicily and Italy, July through September. FDR meets Churchill and Joseph Stalin at Tehran Conference, 28 November to 1 December.

1944   D-day, 6 June: Anglo-American forces invade Normandy. FDR travels to Hawaii for conferences with commanders of Pacific theater, July–August. Elected to fourth term, over Thomas E. Dewey, with 53.5 percent of the vote, 7 November.

1945   Meets with Churchill and Stalin at Yalta Conference, 4–12 February. Dies at Warm Springs, Georgia, 12 April. Buried at Hyde Park, New York, 15 April. Germany surrenders, 8 May. Japan surrenders, 15 August.

1962   Eleanor Roosevelt dies, 7 November.

NOTES AND REFERENCES

INTRODUCTION

1. Robert E. Sherwood, *Roosevelt and Hopkins: An Intimate History* (New York: Grosset & Dunlap, 1950 [1948]), 9; Rexford G. Tugwell, *The Democratic Roosevelt: A Biography of Franklin D. Roosevelt* (Baltimore: Penguin, 1969 [1957]), 11–12.

CHAPTER 1

1. The description of the Vanderbilt mansion is from a brochure for visitors prepared by the National Park Service. On the Hyde Park area, see F. Kennon Moody, "F.D.R. and his Neighbors: A Study of the Relationship Between Franklin D. Roosevelt and the Residents of Dutchess County" (Ph.D. dissertation, State University of New York at Albany, 1981).

2. James quoted by FDR in William D. Hassett, *Off the Record With FDR* (New Brunswick, N.J.: Rutgers University Press, 1958), 124. Unless otherwise indicated, this account of FDR's family background, youth, and upbringing is based primarily upon information in Frank Freidel, *Franklin D. Roosevelt: The Apprenticeship* (Boston: Little, Brown, 1952), 3–96; Kenneth S. Davis, *FDR: The Beckoning of Destiny, 1882–1928* (New York: Putnam, 1971), 16–223; and Geoffrey C. Ward, *Before the Trumpet: Young Franklin Roosevelt, 1882–1905* (New York: Harper & Row, 1985).

3. Memo, James Roosevelt, 5/13/nd., Roosevelt Family Papers Donated by the Children, Franklin D. Roosevelt Library, Hyde Park, New York.

4. Quoted in Sara Delano Roosevelt (as told to Isabel Leighton and Gabrielle Forbush), *My Boy Franklin* (New York: Ray Long & Richard R. Smith, 1933), 13–14.

5. James Roosevelt to FDR, 30 January 1898; Sara Roosevelt to FDR, 30 January 1904; and Sara Roosevelt to FDR, 14 May 1899, Roosevelt Family Papers Donated by the Children.

6. Sara Roosevelt to FDR, Wed. afternoon, Aug. 1901, Roosevelt Family Papers Donated by the Children.

7. Sara Roosevelt, *My Boy Franklin*, 4; Sara Roosevelt to FDR, Wed. afternoon, Aug. 1901, Roosevelt Family Papers Donated by the Children.

8. Elliott Roosevelt, ed., *F.D.R.: His Personal Letters* (hereinafter referred to as *Personal Letters*) (New York: Duell, 1947–1950), vol. 1: 29–34 and passim.

9. FDR to Parents, 1 February 1900, *Personal Letters*, vol. 1:382–383.

10. FDR to Parents, 14 May 1897, *Personal Letters*, vol. 1:96–98.

11. Davis, *Beckoning of Destiny*, 115.

12. On James Roosevelt Roosevelt and James Roosevelt, Jr., see Ward, *Before the Trumpet*.

13. Quoted in Davis, *Beckoning of Destiny*, 116.

14. Joseph Alsop, a distant relative of FDR's, believed that FDR's rejection by Porcellian, in addition to his earlier failures to achieve the popularity he sought at Groton and Harvard, may have contributed to his later decision to enter politics. For FDR desired "to stake out his own territory, where he would not be in competition with other young men of his own sort." Joseph Alsop, *FDR: 1882–1945: A Centenary Remembrance* (New York: Viking, 1982), 27. Eleanor Roosevelt later said that the Porcellian episode gave FDR greater sympathy for those who were down and out.

15. FDR editorial, *Harvard Crimson*, 2 November 1903, in *Personal Letters*, vol. 1: 512–513. See also FDR editorial, 30 September 1903, ibid., 502–503.

16. On Eleanor, see Joseph P. Lash, *Eleanor and Franklin* (New York: W.W. Norton, 1971); and Ward, *Before the Trumpet*, 258–316.

17. Arthur M. Schlesinger, Jr., *The Age of Roosevelt: The Crisis of the Old Order 1919–1933* (Boston: Houghton Mifflin, 1957), 330.

18. A detailed account of FDR's entry into politics is contained in Freidel, *The Apprenticeship*.

CHAPTER 2

1. On the Sheehan fight and FDR's legislative career generally, see Ernest K. Lindley, *Franklin D. Roosevelt: A Career in Progressive Democracy* (New York: Blue Ribbon Books, 1931), 77–114; and Freidel, *The Apprenticeship*, 97–156.

2. Quoted in Davis, *Beckoning of Destiny*, 259.

3. For an example of the disparity between Roosevelt's later claims and reality, see the discussion of the 54-hour bill in George Martin, *Madam Secretary: Frances Perkins* (Boston: Houghton Mifflin, 1976), 99, 495–96.

4. The Troy speech is extensively quoted in Nathan Miller, *FDR: An Intimate History* (Garden City, N.Y.: Doubleday, 1983), 89–90.

5. Quoted in ibid., 86.

6. Frances Perkins, *The Roosevelt I Knew* (New York: Viking, 1946), 11–12.

7. Quoted in Schlesinger, *Crisis of the Old Order*, 341.

8. On the navy years, see especially Freidel, *The Apprenticeship*, 157–373.

9. Ibid., 232, 275.

10. Quoted in Miller, *FDR*, 106. On the relationship between Roosevelt and Daniels, see Freidel, *The Apprenticeship*, 286–317.

11. Quoted in *Personal Letters*, vol. 2: 269–70.

12. FDR to Eleanor, October 1914, in ibid., 256–57.

13. Eleanor Roosevelt, *This Is My Story* (New York: Harper & Bros., 1937), 149.

14. Quoted in Geoffrey C. Ward, *A First-Class Temperament: The Emergence of Franklin Roosevelt* (New York: Harper & Row, 1989), 313.

15. FDR to Eleanor, 18 July 1917, *Personal Letters*, vol. 2: 349. The *New York Times* interview is reprinted in the note following this letter.

16. On the Lucy Mercer affair and, more generally, on the personal relationship between Franklin and Eleanor, see especially Lash, *Eleanor and Franklin*, and Alsop, *A Centenary Remembrance*, 40–50. See also Ward, *A First-Class Temperament*.

17. Quoted in Frank Freidel, *Franklin D. Roosevelt: The Ordeal* (Boston: Little, Brown, 1954), 71.

18. FDR quoted in ibid., 71; Harding quoted in Schlesinger, *Crisis of the Old Order*, 365.

19. Quoted in Richard Hofstadter, *The American Political Tradition and the Men Who Made It* (New York: Alfred A. Knopf, 1948), 325. On Roosevelt's business activities during the 1920s, see Freidel, *The Ordeal* 138–51.

20. Quoted in Miller, *FDR*, 183.

21. The most complete treatments of Roosevelt's bout with polio are Hugh Gregory Gallagher, *FDR's Splendid Deception* (New York: Dodd, Mead, 1985); and Richard Thayer Goldberg, *The Making of Franklin D. Roosevelt: Triumph Over Disability*. (Cambridge, Mass.: Abt Books, 1981). See also Ward, *First-Class Temperament*.

22. Hugh Gregory Gallagher, "FDR's Cover-Up: The Extent of His Handicap," *Washington Post*, 24 January 1982, D1,3.

23. Quoted in Freidel, *The Ordeal*, 217.

24. Quoted in Gallagher, *FDR's Splendid Deception*, 73.

CHAPTER 3

1. Schlesinger, *Crisis of the Old Order*, 386.

2. Quoted in Miller, *FDR*, 258.

3. Lindley, *Franklin D. Roosevelt*, 237.

4. On the early role of radio in politics, see Kathleen Hall Jamieson, *Packaging the Presidency: A History and Criticism of Presidential Campaign Advertising* (New York: Oxford University Press, 1984), 18–29.

5. FDR to Howe, 1 December 1929, in *Personal Letters*, vol. 3: 92.

6. Quoted in Hofstadter, *American Political Tradition*, 327.

7. James MacGregor Burns, *Roosevelt: The Lion and Fox* (New York: Harcourt Brace Jovanovich, 1956), 143.

8. Lindley, *Franklin D. Roosevelt*, 333.

9. Samuel I. Rosenman, ed., *The Public Papers and Addresses of Franklin D. Roosevelt* (New York: Random House; Macmillan; Harper and Bros., 1938–1950), vol. 1: 75–76, 15–16 (hereinafter referred to as *Public Papers*).

10. Ibid., 330, 453.

11. Ibid., 14–15.

12. Ibid., 96.

13. Frank Freidel, *Franklin D. Roosevelt: The Triumph* (Boston: Little, Brown, 1956), 225.

14. *Public Papers*, vol. 1: 20.

15. On Hyde Park and FDR's plans for it, see, F. Kennon Moody, "F.D.R. and His Neighbors."

16. Quoted in Miller, *FDR*, 236.

17. On Raskob and on the nomination battle in general, see David Burner, *The Party of Provincialism: The Democratic Party in Transition, 1918–1932* (New York: Alfred A. Knopf, 1968) and Elliot A. Rosen, *Hoover, Roosevelt, and the Brains Trust* (New York: Columbia University Press, 1977).

18. Quoted in Freidel, *The Triumph*, 269.

19. Quoted in Miller, *FDR*, 246.

20. Ronald Steel, *Walter Lippmann and the American Century* (Boston: Little, Brown, 1980), 287–98.

21. Miller, *FDR*, 258.

22. Milton MacKaye, "Profiles: The Governor—II," *New Yorker* (22 August 1931), 28; Edmund Wilson, "The Hudson River Progressive," *The New Republic* (5 April 1933), 219–20.

23. *Public Papers*, vol. 1: 647–49.

24. Quotations in William E. Leuchtenberg, *Franklin D. Roosevelt and the New Deal, 1933–1940* (New York: Harper & Row, 1963), 10; Burns, *The Lion and the Fox*, 138: and Freidel, *The Triumph*, 328.

25. Quoted in David Burner, *Herbert Hoover: A Public Life* (New York: Alfred A. Knopf, 1979), 151.

26. British journalist quoted in ibid., 314; Borglum quoted in Leuchtenburg, *Roosevelt and the New Deal*, 13.

27. Burner, *Herbert Hoover*, 315.

28. Rosen, *Hoover, Roosevelt, and the Brains Trust*, 336. In fact, as Rosen points out, the tariff issue was enormously complicated and had broad implications for fighting the depression. Moreover, Roosevelt was hardly alone in trying to hedge the issue. Several prominent Democrats urged him to avoid a firm commitment so as to maintain maximum flexibility.

29. Miller, *FDR*, 285.

30. "The Week," *The New Republic* (16 November 1932): 1.

31. Quoted in James Roosevelt and Sidney Shalett, *Affectionately, F.D.R.*, (New York: Avon Books, 1959), 225.

32. Frank Friedel, *Franklin D. Roosevelt: Launching the New Deal* (Boston: Little, Brown, 1973), 169–74; Schlesinger, *Crisis of the Old Order*, 466.

CHAPTER 4

1. Quoted in Donald Richberg, *My Hero* (New York: G.P. Putnam's Sons, 1954), 157.

2. On proposed solutions to the depression, see R. Alan Lawson, *The Failure of Independent Liberalism, 1930–1941* (New York: Putnam, 1971), 63; Schlesinger, *Crisis of the Old Order*, 182, 201–2; "Congress Considering National Economic Planning," *Congressional Digest* 11 (April 1932): 97–118.

3. On FDR's initial analysis of the depression, see Freidel, *Launching the New Deal*, esp. 60–82; FDR quoted in James A. Farley, *Jim Farley's Story: The Roosevelt Years* (New York: Whittlesey House, 1948), 36.

4. *Public Papers*, vol. 2:11–16.

5. For a detailed overview of the Hundred Days, see Leuchtenburg, *Roosevelt and the New Deal*, 41–62.

6. Quoted in Schlesinger, *Coming of the New Deal*, 21.

7. Quoted in Leuchtenburg, *Roosevelt and the New Deal*, 61.

8. Quoted in Schlesinger, *Coming of the New Deal*, 22.

9. Donald Day, ed., *The Autobiography of Will Rogers* (New York: Avon Books, 1975), 221–22.

10. Charles A. Beard, "In Defense of Congress: Citadel of Our Freedom," *American Mercury* 55 (November 1942), 529–35.

11. For a discussion of works on Congress, see the bibliographic essay.

12. This account of the history of FERA is based on Patrick J. Maney, "*Young Bob*" *La Follette: A Biography of Robert M. La Follette, Jr.*, *1895–1953* (Columbia: University of Missouri Press, 1978), 95–114.

13. On the FDIC, see Leuchtenburg, *Roosevelt and the New Deal*, 60; on the origins of the TVA, see Preston Hubbard, *Origins of the TVA: The Muscle Shoals Controversy, 1920–1932* (Nashville: Vanderbilt University Press, 1961) and Richard Lowitt, *George W. Norris: The Persistence of a Progressive, 1913–1933* (Urbana: University of Illinois Press, 1971).

14. Leuchtenburg, *Roosevelt and the New Deal*, 50, 55; Maney, "*Young Bob*" *La Follette*, 115–16.

15. On the origins of the AAA, see Christiana McFadyen Campbell, *The Farm Bureau and the New Deal* (Urbana: University of Illinois Press, 1962) and Van L. Perkins, *Crisis in Agriculture: The Agricultural Adjustment Administration and the New Deal, 1933* (Berkely: University of California Press, 1969); on the NIRA, see Robert F. Himmelberg, *The Origins of the National Recovery Administration* (New York: Fordham University Press, 1975) and Ellis W. Hawley, *The New Deal and the Problem of Monopoly* (Princeton: Princeton University Press, 1966).

16. Alsop, *A Centenary Remembrance*, 76.

17. Quotations in Sherwood, *Roosevelt and Hopkins*, 1–2.

18. Wilson quoted in William E. Leuchtenburg, "The Achievement of the New Deal," in Harvard Sitkoff, ed., *Fifty Years Later: The New Deal Evaluated* (New York: Alfred A. Knopf, 1985), 214–15. On the role of women in the New Deal, see Susan Ware, *Beyond Suffrage: Women in the New Deal* (Cambridge: Harvard University Press, 1981).

19. Quoted in Freidel, *Launching the New Deal*, 5–6.

20. *Public Papers*, vol. 2: 155–57, 379–82; vol. 7: 74.

21. Quoted in Schlesinger, *Coming of the New Deal*, 553.

22. Quoted in Freidel, *Launching the New Deal*, 377.

23. For a detailed account of Roosevelt's role in the World Economic Conference, see Freidel, *Launching the New Deal*, esp. 470–89.

24. Leuchtenburg, *Roosevelt and the New Deal*, 121–24; J. Joseph Huthmacher, *Senator Robert F. Wagner and the Rise of Urban Liberalism* (New York: Atheneum, 1968), 156–57.

25. On Wagner and the fate of his initiatives, see Huthmacher, *Senator Robert F. Wagner*, 160–80.

26. Quoted in Robert H. Zieger, *American Workers, American Unions, 1920–1985* (Baltimore: Johns Hopkins University Press, 1986), 34.

27. Quoted in Huthmacher, *Robert F. Wagner*, 176.

28. On blacks and the New Deal, see, for example, Nancy J. Weiss, *Farewell to*

the Party of Lincoln: Black Politics in the Age of FDR (Princeton: Princeton University Press, 1983); Harvard Sitkoff, A New Deal for Blacks: The Emergence of Civil Rights as a National Issue (New York: Oxford University Press, 1978); Raymond Wolters, Negroes and the Great Depression: The Problem of Economic Recovery (Westport, Conn.: Greenwood, 1970); and John B. Kirby, Black Americans in the Roosevelt Era; Liberalism and Race (Knoxville: University of Tennessee Press, 1980).

29. On these insurgent movements, see Leuchtenburg, Roosevelt and the New Deal, 95–117; and Alan Brinkley, Voices of Protest: Huey Long, Father Coughlin, and the Great Depression (New York: Alfred A. Knopf, 1982).

30. Quoted in Schlesinger, The Politics of Upheaval (Boston: Houghton Mifflin, 1960), 8.

31. Perkins quoted in Leuchtenburg, Roosevelt and the New Deal, fn. 23, 150–51, and in Perkins, The Roosevelt I Knew, 239. On FDR's role in the banking bill, see Leuchtenburg, 158.

32. Maney, "Young Bob" La Follette, 163–69; Leuchtenburg, Roosevelt and the New Deal, 154.

33. Quoted in Schlesinger, Politics of Upheaval, 325–26.

34. Quoted in Frank Freidel, Franklin D. Roosevelt: A Rendezvous with Destiny (Boston: Little, Brown, 1990), 150.

35. For the wide range of New Deal activities, see Leuchtenburg, "The Achievement of the New Deal," in Sitkoff, Fifty Years Later, 211–31.

36. The Gallup Poll: Public Opinion 1935–1971 (New York: Random House, 1972), 1: 1.

37. George F. Kennan, Memoirs: 1925–1950 (New York: Bantam Books, 1969 [1967]), 4.

CHAPTER 5

1. Quoted in Schlesinger, Coming of the New Deal, 572.

2. Charles T. Abshire to FDR, 6 July 1936, President's Personal File 9, Gifts A, Roosevelt Library (hereinafter President's Personal File referred to as PPF); Victor S. Easter to FDR, 28 October 1944, PPF 200; Robert S. McElvaine, Down & Out in the Great Depression: Letters from the Forgotten Man (Chapel Hill: University of North Carolina Press, 1983), 167.

3. Raymond Moley, 27 Masters of Politics: In a Personal Perspective (New York: Funk & Wagnalls, 1949), 134; Richard Lowitt and Maurine Beasley, eds., One Third of a Nation: Lorena Hickok Reports on the Great Depression (Urbana: University of Illinois Press, 1983), 215.

4. Erik Barnouw, Tube of Plenty (New York: Oxford University Press, 1977 [1975]), 72.

5. Adviser quoted in Sherwood, Roosevelt and Hopkins, 42–43; Perkins, The Roosevelt I Knew, 72; Federal Writers' Project of the Works Progress Administration, These Are Our Lives (New York: W. W. Norton, 1975 [1939]), 210.

6. Freidel, The Triumph, 267–268, 313; Freidel, Launching the New Deal, 186 fn.; Michelson quoted in Schlesinger, Coming of the New Deal, 560. See also, Samuel I. Rosenman, Working with Roosevelt (New York: Harper & Bros., 1952).

7. The most complete treatment of FDR's relationship with the press is Graham J. White, *FDR and the Press* (Chicago: University of Chicago Press, 1979). See also White, "News Media," in Otis L. Graham, Jr., and Meghan Robinson Wander, eds., *Franklin D. Roosevelt: His Life and Times, An Encyclopedic View* (Boston: G.K. Hall & Co., 1985), 92–93.

8. John Gunther, *Roosevelt in Retrospect: A Profile in History* (New York: Harper & Bros., 1950), 22–23; newsman quoted in Miller, *FDR*, 353–54.

9. Gunther, *Roosevelt in Retrospect*, 23.

10. Betty Houchin Winfield, "F.D.R.'s Pictorial Image, Rule and Boundaries," *Journalism History* 5 (Winter 1978–79): 110–114, 136. On FDR's attempts to conceal his disability from the press and public, see also Goldberg, *The Making of Franklin D. Roosevelt* and Gallagher, *FDR's Splendid Deception*.

11. Stephen B. Oates, *With Malice Toward None: The Life of Abraham Lincoln* (New York: New American Library, 1977), 265–66.

12. Rosenman, *Working with Roosevelt*, 15–27.

13. For an excellent discussion of Roosevelt's use of biblical imagery and its relationship to charismatic leadership, see Ann R. Willner, *The Spellbinders: Charismatic Political Leadership* (New Haven: Yale University Press, 1984), 151–171. For a provocative discussion of how southern Americans viewed the depression and Roosevelt within a biblical context, see Pete Daniel, "The New Deal, Southern Agriculture, and Economic Change," in James C. Cobb and Michael V. Namorato, eds., *The New Deal and the South* (Jackson: University Press of Mississippi, 1984), 37–61.

14. Kansas man quoted in McElvaine, *Down & Out in the Great Depression*, 220; Texas congressman quoted in Freidel, *Launching the New Deal*, 445; Alfred Lemire, from New Hampshire, to FDR, 23 August 1944, PPF 200; O'Connell quoted in Schlesinger, *Coming of the New Deal*, 13. For a discussion of civil religion see Robert N. Bellah, "Civil Religion in America," *Daedalus* 96 (Winter 1967): 1–21. Curiously, Bellah and other students of civil religion neglect to mention Roosevelt. See also in this connection John William Ward, *Andrew Jackson: Symbol for an Age* (New York: Oxford University Press, 1962).

15. Marquis Childs, "They Hate Roosevelt," in Frank Freidel, ed., *The New Deal and the American People* (Englewood Cliffs, N.J.: Prentice-Hall, 1964), 98–104.

16. George Wolfskill and John A. Hudson, *All But the People* (New York: Macmillan, 1969), 6, 13, 22–23; For the stamp stealing story I am indebted to Jane Simons who frequently heard the tale as she was growing up in New England.

17. Quoted in Schlesinger, *Coming of the New Deal*, 567.

18. Burns, *The Lion and the Fox*, 236.

19. Quoted in Miller, *FDR*, 384–85.

20. One of the more unusual manuscript collections at the Franklin D. Roosevelt Library contains thousands of letters that people wrote to Roosevelt's dog Fala.

21. See, for example, Geoffrey Hellman, "Roosevelt: From Breakfast to Bed," *Life* (20 January 1941).

22. Schlesinger, *Coming of the New Deal*, 585–86; Leuchtenburg, *Roosevelt and the New Deal*, 167.

23. Perkins, *The Roosevelt I Knew*, 144–45; Eleanor Roosevelt, *This I Remember*, 149–50.

24. James Roosevelt and Sidney Shalett, *Affectionately, F.D.R.*, 87; Sherwood,

Roosevelt and Hopkins, 9. Rexford Tugwell believed that religion gave Roosevelt "a sense of balance and perspective capable of supporting him firmly when grave decisions had to be made and when counsels were confused. It enabled him, moreover, to sleep long and restfully at night, when he felt that the day had been given to the service of men—who, along with him, were God's children." See *The Democratic Roosevelt,* 31.

25. *Public Papers,* vol. 7: 74. In 1935, on the four hundreth anniversary of the printing of the first English Bible, FDR said: "Where we have been truest and most consistent in obeying its precepts we have attained the greatest measure of contentment and prosperity; where it has been to us as the words of a book that is sealed, we have faltered in our way, lost our range-finders and found our progress checked." See *Public Papers,* vol. 4: 420.

26. Ward, *Before the Trumpet,* 186, 200.

27. For an example of FDR citing converstations with Wilson, see FDR to Robert W. Bingham, 29 September 1931, in *Personal Letters,* vol. 3: 219.

28. For the details of his relationship with Lucy Mercer, see Lash, *Eleanor and Franklin.*

29. The note read: "This is the original manuscript of the Inaugural Address as written at Hyde Park on Monday, February 27th, 1933. I started it about 9:00 P.M. and ended at 1:30 A.M. A number of minor changes were made in subsequent drafts but the final draft is substantially the same as this original." Freidel, *Launching the New Deal,* 186.

30. Quoted in Schlesinger, *Coming of the New Deal,* 584.

31. Perkins, *The Roosevelt I Knew,* 3; Morgenthau quoted in Sherwood, *Roosevelt and Hopkins,* 9; Phillips quoted in Leuchtenburg. *Roosevelt and the New Deal,* 167. Most historians agreed with this assessment. He had, said Arthur Schlesinger, Jr., expressing the widely held view, an "infinitely complex mind." "Origins of the Cold War," *Foreign Affairs* 46 (October 1967), 22–52.

32. "What's to Become of Us?" *Fortune* (December 1933): 24.

33. Quoted in Schlesinger, *Coming of the New Deal,* 583–84.

34. Lash, *Eleanor and Franklin,* 638.

35. Quoted in Miller, *FDR,* 361. On Eleanor Roosevelt's activities on behalf of blacks, see Lash, *Eleanor and Franklin,* 668–97.

36. Alsop, *A Centenary Remembrance,* 96; Miller, *FDR,* 361.

37. FDR quoted in Miller, *FDR,* 381; Landon quoted in Schlesinger, *Politics of Upheaval,* 607.

38. Burns, *The Lion and the Fox,* 280.

39. The Committee for Industrial Organization (1935-1938) was the forerunner of the Congress of Industrial Organizations (1938).

40. FDR quoted in Schlesinger, *Politics of Upheaval,* 590; Early quoted in Burns, *The Lion and the Fox,* 268–69.

41. Schlesinger, *Politics of Upheaval,* 630.

42. FDR quoted in Burns, *The Lion and the Fox,* 282–83; Raymond Moley, *After Seven Years: A Political Analysis of the New Deal* (New York: Harper & Brothers, 1939), 351–52.

43. Schlesinger, *Politics of Upheaval,* 581–82.

44. Leuchtenburg, *Roosevelt and the New Deal,* 189–90. For sources on the New Deal coalition, see the bibliographic essay.

CHAPTER 6

1. *Public Papers,* vol. 6: 1–6.

2. The sources that supply the information upon which the following account is based are discussed in the bibliographic essay.

3. Quoted in Burns, *The Lion and the Fox,* 297.

4. Quoted in Leuchtenburg, *Roosevelt and the New Deal,* 234.

5. Quoted in Joseph Alsop and Turner Catledge, *The 168 Days* (Garden City, N.Y.: Doubleday, Doran, 1938), 74.

6. Ibid., 82–83.

7. Burton K. Wheeler, "My Years with Roosevelt," in Rita James Simon, ed., *As We Saw the Thirties* (Urbana: University of Illinois Press, 1967), 190–215; Miller, *FDR,* 398; Alsop and Catledge, *168 Days,* 192; Farley, *Jim Farley's Story,* 88.

8. Alsop, *A Centenary Remembrance,* 101.

9. Quoted in Miller, *FDR,* 401.

10. Alsop and Catledge, *168 Days,* 153.

11. On Howe's relationship with FDR, see Schlesinger, *Coming of the New Deal,* 514. Eleanor Roosevelt quoted in *This I Remember,* 167–68.

12. Alsop and Catledge, *168 Days,* 228–33.

13. Ibid., 270–71.

14. On executive reorganization, see Barry D. Karl, *Executive Reorganization and Reform in the New Deal: The Genesis of Administrative Management, 1900-1939* (Cambridge, Mass: Harvard University Press, 1963) and Richard Polenberg, *Reorganizing Roosevelt's Government: The Controversy Over Executive Reorganization, 1936–1939* (Cambridge, Mass.: Harvard University Press, 1966).

15. See, for example, Morgenthau diaries, 18 May 1939, 22 May 1939, Roosevelt Library.

16. Morgenthau diaries, 25 July 1939.

17. Harold D. Smith diary, 31 May 1939, Roosevelt Library.

18. Burns, *The Lion and the Fox,* 328–29.

19. Quotations in Schlesinger, *Coming of the New Deal,* 535, 543.

20. Gunther, *Roosevelt in Retrospect,* 127. Gunther describes this incident as having taken place early during his first term. The Morgenthau diaries, cited earlier, make clear that it occurred during the second term.

21. Quoted in Burns, *The Lion and the Fox,* 344.

22. W. Elliot Brownlee, "Recession of 1937–38," in Graham and Robinson, *Franklin D. Roosevelt: His Life and Times, An Encyclopedic View,* 346–47; *The Gallup Poll,* vol. 1: 1, 12, 45, 55, 80, 89.

23. For an overview of the recession see Kenneth D. Roose, *The Economics of Recession and Revival, An Interpretation of 1937–38* (New Haven: Yale University Press, 1954).

24. Morgenthau diary, 12 April 1938, 13 April 1938.

25. On the purge, see Vernon A. Fagin, "Franklin D. Roosevelt, Liberalism in the Democratic Party, and the 1938 Congressional Elections: The Urge to Purge" (Ph.D. dissertation, University of California, Los Angeles, 1979). For other sources, see the bibliographic essay.

26. James F. Byrnes, *All in One Lifetime* (New York: Harper & Bros., 1958), 103.

27. Quoted in Leuchtenburg, *Roosevelt and the New Deal,* 272.

28. "Franklin D. Roosevelt," *Current Biography: 1942* (New York: The H.W. Wilson Company, 1942), 711; Lash, *Eleanor and Franklin*, 617.

29. Morgenthau diaries, 18 May 1939; 22 May 1939; 12 April 1938; and 16 May 1939; Burns, *The Lion and the Fox*, 316.

30. On the legislative output of these years, see David L. Porter, *Congress and the Waning of the New Deal* (Port Washington, N.Y.: Kennikat Press, 1980); *The Gallup Poll*, vol. 1: 125–26; Burns, *The Lion and the Fox*, 362.

31. Burns, *The Lion and the Fox*, 375–80; James MacGregor Burns and Michael R. Beschloss, "The Forgotten FDR," *The New Republic* (7 April 1982): 19–22; Alonzo L. Hamby, ed., *The New Deal: Analysis and Interpretation* (New York: Weybright and Talley, 1969), 7–8.

CHAPTER 7

1. Davis, *Beckoning of Destiny*, 60–62, 76–80, 148–49, 158–59, 194–97; Burner, *Herbert Hoover*, 25–62; Isaiah Berlin, *Personal Impressions* (New York: Viking, 1981), 17.

2. Quoted in Robert Dallek, *Franklin D. Roosevelt and American Foreign Policy* (New York: Oxford University Press, 1979), 13. On the evolution of FDR's foreign policy, see Freidel, *The Ordeal*, ch. 8, and Dallek, *Roosevelt and Americam Foreign Policy*, prolog.

3. Quoted in Hofstadter, *The American Political Tradition*, 343.

4. Moley, *After Seven Years*, 113–14; Dallek, *Roosevelt and American Foreign Policy*, 55.

5. *Gallup Poll*, vol. 1: 54.

6. This summary of the isolationist rationale is based in part on four studies by Wayne S. Cole: *America First: The Battle Against Intervention, 1940–1941* (Madison: University of Wisconsin Press, 1953); *Senator Gerald P. Nye and American Foreign Relations* (Minneapolis: University of Minnesota Press, 1962); *Charles A. Lindbergh and the Battle against American Intervention in World War II* (New York: Harcourt Brace Jovanovich, 1974); and *Roosevelt and the Isolationists, 1932–1945* (Lincoln: University of Nebraska Press, 1983).

7. Robert A. Divine, *Roosevelt and World War II* (Baltimore: Johns Hopkins University Press, 1969), 1–23; Cole, *Roosevelt and the Isolationists*, 149.

8. Arnold A. Offner, *American Appeasement: United States Foreign Policy and Germany 1933–1938* (New York: W. W. Norton, 1976 [1969]), 155–160, 162, 277; Robert A. Divine, *The Reluctant Belligerent: American Entry into World War II* (New York: John Wiley & Sons, 1965), 31–34.

9. Quoted in Freidel, *The Apprenticeship*, 356; Miller, *FDR*, 423.

10. For a description of Roosevelt's later accounts of his World War I experience see Freidel, *The Apprenticeship*, 336–72.

11. *Public Papers*, vol. 6: 406–411; Divine, *Roosevelt and World War II*, 17; Dallek, *Roosevelt and American Foreign Policy*, 147–49.

12. Cordell Hull, *The Memoirs of Cordell Hull*, 2 vols. (New York: Macmillan, 1948), vol. 1: 580.

13. Hull, *Memoirs*, vol. 1: 582; William L. Langer and S. Everett Gleason, *The Challenge to Isolation, 1937–1940* (New York: Harper, 1952), 29–35.

14. Roosevelt's efforts to mediate an end to the European crisis are discussed in Langer and Gleason, *The Challenge to Isolation*, 160–201.

15. Geoffrey Perrett, *A Country Made By War: From the Revolution to Vietnam—The Story of America's Rise to Power* (New York: Random House, 1989), 360. The unemployment rate in 1939 was 17.2 percent.

16. FDR quoted in Freidel, *The Apprenticeship,* 6; and in Miller, *FDR,* 428–29.

17. On the fate of the Wagner-Rogers bill, see David S. Wyman, *Paper Walls* (Amherst: University of Massachusetts Press, 1968).

18. Wyman, *Paper Walls;* "Yet for all this," writes Robert Dallek, "it is difficult to escape the feeling that a sustained call by FDR for allowing Nazi victims to come to the United States in greater numbers might have mobilized the country's more humane instincts." See *Roosevelt and American Foreign Policy,* 168.

19. *Public Papers,* vol. 8: 460–64.

20. Dallek, *Roosevelt and American Foreign Policy,* 199–204.

21. *Public Papers,* vol. 9: 85–94.

22. Dallek, *Roosevelt and American Foreign Policy,* 215; Schlesinger, *Politics of Unheaval,* 117. On the Welles mission, see Dallek, *Roosevelt and American Foreign Policy* 216–18; David Reynolds, *The Creation of the Anglo-American Alliance 1937–1941* (Chapel Hill: University of North Carolina Press, 1982), 19–22.

23. *Public Papers,* vol. 9: 263; Dallek, *Roosevelt and American Foreign Policy,* 218–32, 243–47.

24. Richard Rhodes, *The Making of the Atomic Bomb* (New York: Simon & Schuster, 1986), 305–317.

25. Forrest C. Pogue, *George C. Marshall: Ordeal and Hope 1939–1942* (New York: Viking, 1966), 56–63; Langer and Gleason, *The Challenge to Isolation,* 474–75.

26. Quoted in Maney, *"Young Bob" La Follette,* 56–57.

27. On the third term, see Herbert S. Parmet and Marie B. Hecht, *Never Again: A President Runs for a Third Term* (New York: Macmillan, 1968) and Bernard F. Donahoe, *Private Plans and Public Dangers* (Notre Dame: University of Notre Dame Press, 1965).

28. Eleanor Roosevelt, *This I Remember,* 212; Farley, *Jim Farley's Story,* 180–191; Parmet, *Never Again,* 36.

29. Eleanor Roosevelt, *This I Remember,* 213; Farley, *Jim Farley's Story,* 180–191; Parment, *Never Again,* 7.

30. John Gunther, *Roosevelt In Retrospect,* 309.

31. Miller, *FDR,* 451–453.

32. On Willkie, see Ellsworth Barnard, *Wendell Willkie: Fighter for Freedom* (Marquette: Northern Michigan University Press, 1966).

33. Sherwood, *Roosevelt and Hopkins,* 193–94, 198.

34. Dallek, *Roosevelt and American Foreign Policy,* 250–51.

35. Roosevelt "Four Freedoms" speech, 6 January 1941, and Lend-Lease Act, 11 March 1941, in Henry Steele Commager, ed., *Documents of American History* (New York: Appleton-Century-Crofts, 1968), vol. 2: 446, 449; Cole, *Roosevelt and the Isolationists,* 409–422.

36. Sherwood quoted in Cole, *Charles A. Lindbergh,* 147; Ickes quoted in Cole, *Roosevelt and the Isolationists,* 461. On Roosevelt and the FBI, see Kenneth O'Reilly, "A New Deal for the FBI: The Roosevelt Administration, Crime Control, and National Security," *Journal of American History* 69 (December 1982): 638–58.

37. Quoted in Burns, *Soldier of Freedom,* 44.

38. Reynolds, *Creation of the Anglo-American Alliance,* 347, fn 38.

39. Henry L. Stimson and McGeorge Bundy, *On Active Service in Peace and War* (New York: Harper & Bros., 1947, 1948), 364–76.; and Elting E. Morison, *Turmoil and Tradition: A Study of the Life and Times of Henry L. Stimson* (Boston: Houghton Mifflin, 1960), 517–21.

40. Ibid.

41. Morison, *Turmoil and Tradition*, 520; Waldo Heinrichs, *Threshold of War: Franklin D. Roosevelt and American Entry into World War II* (New York: Oxford University Press, 1988), 102. See also FDR to William D. Leahy, 26 June 1941, in *Personal Letters*, vol. 2: 1177.

42. Reynolds, *Creation of the Anglo-American Alliance*, 214–15.

43. Dallek, *Roosevelt and American Foreign Policy*, 287–89.

44. Quoted in Cole, *Roosevelt and the Isolationists*, 447; Reynolds, *Creation of the Anglo-American Alliance*, 219.

45. Burns, *Soldier of Freedom*, 111–12; Cole, *Roosevelt and the Isolationists*, 433; Dallek, *Roosevelt and American Foreign Policy*, 297–98.

46. Dallek, *Roosevelt and American Foreign Policy*, 295–96.

47. Stimson and Bundy, *On Active Service*, 364–76. The last Gallup poll taken on the subject before Pearl Harbor asked, "Which of these two things do you think is the more important—that this country keep out of war, or that Germany be defeated?" 32 percent favored keeping out of war, 68 percent defeating Germany. *Gallup Poll*, vol. 1: 311.

48. This discussion of U.S.-Japanese relations is based primarily on information in Reynolds, *Creation of the Anglo-American Alliance* and Heinrichs, *Threshold of War.*

49. Irvine H. Anderson, Jonathan G. Utley, and David Reynolds have argued that Roosevelt, hoping to avoid a showdown with the Japanese, did not intend to stop all shipments of oil to Japan but that second-echelon bureaucrats, most notably Assistant Secretary of State Dean Acheson, acting on their own initiative and without the president's approval, made the embargo complete. "Because of F.D.R.'s casual administrative habits and the lack of an adequate White House secretariat to ensure that decisions were properly executed," writes Reynolds, "U.S. diplomatic and commercial policies were badly out of line." On the other hand, Waldo Heinrichs argues that Roosevelt must have known of and approved the embargo. While the evidence is not entirely conclusive, Heinrichs seems to have the better of the argument and on this point I have followed his interpretation. For a discussion of the issue, see Irvine H. Anderson, "The 1941 De Facto Embargo on Oil to Japan: A Bureaucratic Reflex," *Pacific Historical Review*, 44 (May 1975): 201–31; Jonathan G. Utley, "Upstairs, Downstairs at Foggy Bottom: Oil, Exports, and Japan, 1930–41," *Prologue*, 8 (Spring 1976): 17–28; Reynolds, *Creation of the Anglo-American Alliance*, 235–36; Heinrichs, *Threshold of War*, n. 68, 246–47.

50. Sherwood, *Roosevelt and Hopkins*, 431. On the attack on Pearl Harbor and the events leading up to it, see Gordon W. Prange, *At Dawn We Slept: The Untold Story of Pearl Harbor* (New York: McGraw-Hill, 1981).

51. *Public Papers*, vol. 10: 514–15.

52. Dallek, *Roosevelt and American Foreign Policy*, 312.

53. The most persuasive refutation of the conspiracy theory is Roberta Wohlstetter, *Pearl Harbor: Warning and Decision* (Stanford, Calif.: Stanford University Press, 1962). See also Prange, *At Dawn We Slept*, esp. 725–38. On the underestimation of the Japanese, see John W. Dower, *War Without Mercy: Race and Power in the Pacific War* (New York: Pantheon, 1986).

CHAPTER 8

1. Burns, *Soldier of Freedom*, 178–79; David Brinkley, *Washington Goes to War* (New York: Alfred A. Knopf, 1988), 103–104.

2. *Public Papers*, vol. 11: 32–42; Burns, *Soldier of Freedom*, 178–85.

3. *Public Papers*, vol. 11: 105–16; Dallek, *Roosevelt and American Foreign Policy*, 333.

4. Burns, *Soldier of Freedom*, 176, 644. Although the memo was written by FDR's secretary, Burns argues that internal evidence suggests that FDR was the author.

5. Hassett, *Off the Record with F.D.R.*, 145.

6. Ibid., 45.

7. Burns, *Soldier of Freedom*, 255–56.

8. Morgenthau diaries, 25 August 1942.

9. Kent R. Greenfield, *American Strategy in World War II: A Reconsideration* (Baltimore: Johns Hopkins University Press, 1963), 49–84.

10. Dill quoted in Burns, *Soldier of Freedom*, 182, and in Pogue, *Ordeal and Hope*, 262; Churchill quoted in Martin Gilbert, "The Big Two," *New York Review of Books*, (14 February 1985): 34.

11. Pogue, *Ordeal and Hope*, 283, 298.

12. On Marshall, see Forrest C. Pogue, *Marshall*, 4 vols. (New York: Viking Press, 1964–85). On King, see Thomas Buell, *Master of Sea Power* (Boston: Little, Brown, 1979), Eric Larrabee, *Commander in Chief: Franklin Delano Roosevelt, His Lieutenants and Their War* (New York: Harper & Row, 1987), 153–205, and Ronald H. Spector, *Eagle Against the Sun*, (New York: Free Press, 1985), 126–27.

13. For a discussion of the debate over strategy, see Pogue, *Ordeal and Hope*, esp. 261–349.

14. FDR to Churchill, 9 March, 1942, Warren F. Kimball, ed., *Churchill and Roosevelt: The Complete Correspondence* (Princeton: Princeton University Press, 1984), vol. 1: 398.

15. Pogue, *Ordeal and Hope*, 305–306; Stimson and Bundy, *On Active Service*, 416–18.

16. FDR to Churchill, 1 and 3, April 1942, in Kimball, *Churchill and Roosevelt*, vol. 1: 437–41.

17. FDR to Churchill via Hopkins, 17 April 1942 and editor's notes, ibid, 460.

18. Ibid., 494, 592; Pogue, *Ordeal and Hope*, 327, 334; Stimson and Bundy, *On Active Service*, 419; Dallek, *Roosevelt and American Foreign Policy*, 348.

19. On Marshall and Stimson, see Dallek, *Roosevelt and American Foreign Policy*, 348, and Pogue, *Ordeal and Hope*, 329–30. Historical works that would seem to suggest that FDR was in control of events include Greenfield, *American Strategy in World War II*; Dallek, *Roosevelt and American Foreign Policy*; and Larrabee, *Commander in Chief*.

20. Pogue, *Ordeal and Hope*, 342–43.

21. Quoted in Larrabee, *Commander in Chief*, 136.

22. Sherwood, *Roosevelt and Hopkins*, 600–605; Eisenhower quoted in Pogue, *Ordeal and Hope*, 347.

23. Quoted in Burns, *Soldier of Freedom*, 351.

24. Actually, Roosevelt did not pull the higher figures out of thin air. They were

based on more optimistic projections of American productive capacity by economists associated with the War Production Board. See Bruce Catton, *The War Lords of Washington* (New York: Harcourt Brace, 1948), 188.

25. Quotations in Sherwood, *Roosevelt and Hopkins*, 473–74, and Burns, *Soldier of Freedom*, 177.

26. Richard Polenberg, *War and Society: The United States, 1941–1945* (Philadelphia: Lippincott, 1972), 73–98.

27. Ibid., 99–130; Jervis Anderson, *A. Philip Randolph: A Biographical Portrait* (New York: Harcourt Brace Jovanovich, 1972), 241–261; Sitkoff, *A New Deal For Blacks*, 298–325.

28. Quoted in Polenberg, *War and Society*, 110.

29. Ibid, 110; Stimson quoted in Burns, *Soldier of Freedom*, 266.

30. Roy Wilkins, *Standing Fast: The Autobiography of Roy Wilkins* (New York: Penguin, 1982), 127–28.

31. FDR quoted in Burns, *Soldier of Freedom*, 214; press conference No. 796, 2 January 1942 in *The Complete Presidential Press Conferences of Franklin D. Roosevelt* (New York: Da Capo Press, 1972).

32. Peter Irons, *Justice at War: The Story of the Japanese American Internment Cases* (New York: Oxford University Press, 1983), 3–74. See also Polenberg, *War and Society*, 37–72.

33. Burns, *Soldier of Freedom*, 216; Irons, *Justice at War*, ix.

34. Smith diary, 13 July 1944; 1 January 1945.

35. Miller, *FDR*, 490.

36. Burns, *Soldier of Freedom*, 292–98; Robert F. Burk, *Dwight D. Eishenhower: Hero and Politician* (Boston: Twayne Publishers, 1986), 64–67.

37. Steel, *Walter Lippmann*, 400–403.

38. Burns, *Soldier of Freedom*, 295–98; Burk, *Eisenhower*, 64–67.

39. Burns, *Soldier of Freedom*, 316.

40. Sherwood, *Roosevelt and Hopkins*, 671–74.

41. Burns, *Soldier of Freedom*, 316–17; Sherwood, *Roosevelt and Hopkins*, 671–74.

42. Eliot Janeway, *The Struggle for Survival: A Chronicle of Economic Mobilization* (New Haven: Yale University Press, 1951), 194.

43. U.S. Bureau of the Census, *Historical Statistics of the United States, Colonial Times to 1970*, part 2 (Washington, D.C.: U.S. Government Printing Office, 1975), 768.

44. John Ellis, *Brute Force: Allied Strategy and Tactics in the Second World War* (New York: Viking, 1990), 334–35.

45. See A.J.P. Taylor, *The War Lords* (New York: Penguin, 1979).

CHAPTER 9

1. *Public Papers*, vol. 13: 32–42; Stimson, *On Active Service*, 480–84. On the labor situation during the war, see Zieger, *American Workers, American Unions*, 85–86.

2. *Public Papers*, vol. 13: 32–42.

3. Robert M. La Follette to Philip F. La Follette, 8 July 1943, Philip F. La Follette

Papers, State Historical Society of Wisconsin, Madison; Allen Drury, *A Senate Journal, 1943–1945* (New York: McGraw-Hill, 1963), 4.

4. Burns, *Soldier of Freedom,* 273–81.

5. Polenberg, *War and Society,* 197–99; Alben W. Barkley, *That Reminds Me* (Garden City, N.Y.: Doubleday, 1954), 167–82.

6. On the GI Bill, see Keith W. Olson, *The G.I. Bill, the Veterans, and the Colleges* (Lexington: University of Kentucky Press, 1974) and Davis R. B. Ross, *Preparing for Ulysses: Politics and Veterans During World War II* (New York: Columbia University Press, 1969).

7. Burns, *Soldier of Freedom,* 503–507. On the manuevering over a vice-presidential candidate, see Robert L. Messer, *The End of an Alliance; James F. Byrnes, Roosevelt, Truman, and the Origins of the Cold War* (Chapel Hill: University of North Carolina Press, 1982).

8. On Dewey, see Richard Norton Smith, *Thomas E. Dewey and His Times* (New York: Simon & Schuster, 1982). See also Polenberg, *War and Society,* 201–212.

9. Burns, *Soldier of Freedom,* 448–50.

10. For a different interpretation, see Gallagher, *FDR's Splendid Deception,* 178–91, which attributes FDR's lack of inquisitiveness about his condition to mental depression.

11. Morganthau diaries, 25 August 1944. The day after the dinner, Morgenthau wrote: "I called on the President this morning, and I really was shocked for the first time because he is a very sick man and seems to have wasted away."

12. Burns, *Soldier of Freedom,* 508, 521–24; Alsop, *A Centenary Remembrance,* 153. Judging from an extended excerpt from the speech in a documentary produced by the American Broadcasting Company in 1982, the speech holds up well over time.

13. On the effects of the Fala speech, see Burns, *Soldier of Freedom,* 524.

14. Polenberg, *War and Society,* 210–12.

15. Tape, "The Democratic Program," 6 November 1944, in possession of the author; R. LeRoy Bannerman, *Norman Corwin and Radio* (University, Ala.: University of Alabama Press, 1986), 140–42; Norman Corwin, "The Radio," in Jack Goodman, ed., *While You Were Gone* (New York: Simon & Schuster, 1946), 389–90.

16. *Historical Statistics,* vol. 2: 1071–73; Burns, *Soldier of Freedom,* 532–34.

17. Divine, *Roosevelt and World War II,* 63–64; Charles de Gaulle, *The Complete Memoirs of Charles de Gaulle, 1940–1946* (New York: Da Capo Press, 1967 [1964]), 573; Dallek, *Roosevelt and American Foreign Policy,* 472–75, 477–79.

18. Dallek, *Roosevelt and American Foreign Policy,* 479; Robert A. Divine, *Roosevelt and World War II* (Baltimore: Johns Hopkins Press, 1969), 60.

19. *Public Papers,* vol. 13: 99.

20. Freidel, *Franklin D. Roosevelt: A Rendezvous with Destiny,* 466.

21. Quoted in J. William Fulbright, *The Arrogance of Power* (New York: Vintage, 1966), 115.

22. David S. Wyman, *The Abandonment of the Jews: America and the Holocaust, 1941–1945* (New York: Pantheon Books, 1984), 72, 311. Wyman's concluding chapter (pp. 311–40) contains an excellent and persuasive analysis of Roosevelt's responsibity for the Holocaust.

23. Quoted in Arthur M. Schlesinger, Jr., "The Cold War Revisited," *New York Review of Books* (25 October 1979), 47.

24. For the main works on Yalta, see the bibliographic essay.

25. Quoted in Burns, *Soldier of Freedom,* 572.

26. Kennan's views are presented in his *Memoirs,* 198–264. Bohlen's assessment of Yalta is contained in his *Witness to History, 1929–1969* (New York: W. W. Norton, 1973), 200–201.

27. *Public Papers,* vol. 13: 570.

28. Grace Tully, *F.D.R.: My Boss* (New York: Charles Scribner's Sons, 1949), 357; General Albert C. Wedemeyer, *Wedemeyer Reports!* (New York: Henry Holt, 1958), 340.

29. Elizabeth Shoumatoff, "FDR: The Last Photo," *American Heritage,* 38 (July/August 1987): 102–103. On FDR's last days, see Burns, *Soldier of Freedom,* 595–600, and Hassett, *Off the Record with FDR,* 327–36.

30. Drury, *Senate Journal,* 414–15.

CHAPTER 10

1. Robert K. Murray and Tim H. Blessing, "The Presidential Performance Study: A Progress Report," *Journal of American History* 70 (December 1983): 535–55.

2. Allan Nevins, "The Place of Franklin D. Roosevelt in History," *American Heritage* 17 (June 1966): 12.

3. Tugwell, *The Democratic Roosevelt,* 96; Nevins, "The Place of Franklin D. Roosevelt in History," 12–14, 101–104. Speaking to prospective staff members of his library, Roosevelt further conveyed his sense of his special place in history when he cited a recently published book chronicling the activities of Abraham Lincoln, day by day, from birth to death. One of their first tasks, he said, should be to compile a similar account of his own life. FDR's remarks on the Lincoln chronology are cited in Ward, *A First-Class Temperament,* fn. 7, 609.

4. Freidel, *Launching the New Deal,* fn. 186; Tugwell, *The Democratic Roosevelt,* 96–97.

5. Clapper and Commager quoted in Charles A. Beard, "In Defense of Congress," *Atlantic Monthly* 172 (July 1943): 91–92.

6. Theodore H. White, *The Making of the President 1960* (New York: Pocket Books, 1961), 413.

7. Clinton Rossiter, *The American Presidency* (New York: Harcourt, Brace & World, 1960 [1956]), 15, 261–62. On the celebration of the presidency that occurred during the 1950s and 1960s, see Godfrey Hodgson, *America in Our Time* (New York: Random House, 1976), 99–110.

8. On the impact of Roosevelt on his successors, see William E. Leuchtenburg, *In the Shadow of FDR: From Harry Truman to Ronald Reagan* (Ithaca: Cornell University Press, 1983).

9. Rossiter, *The American Presidency,* 146; Ted Morgan, *FDR: A Biography* (New York: Simon & Schuster, 1985), 379; JFK quoted in Godfrey Hodgson, *All Things to All Men: The False Promise of the Modern American Presidency* (New York: Simon & Schuster, 1980), 60.

10. On FDR and Vietnam, see Walter La Feber, "Roosevelt, Churchill, and Indochina: 1942–1945," *American Historical Review* 80 (December 1975): 1277–95, and George C. Herring, *America's Longest War: The United States and Vietnam 1950–1975,* 2d ed. (New York: Alfred A. Knopf, 1986), 7–8.

11. Quoted in Leuchtenburg, *Roosevelt and the New Deal,* 47.

12. David M. Potter, *People of Plenty: Economic Abundance and the American Character* (Chicago: University of Chicago Press, 1954), 120–21.

13. Cole, *Roosevelt and the Isolationists,* 530.

14. Hodgson, *All Things to All Men.* See also Theodore J. Lowi, *The Personal President* (Ithaca: Cornell University Press, 1985).

15. John Milton Cooper, Jr., "Book Reviews," *Wisconsin Magazine of History* 74 (Autumn 1990): fn 1, 49.

16. One prominent political scientist even devised a "character" test to predict whether presidents would be successes or failures. See James Barber, *The Presidential Character: Predicting Performance in the White House,* 2d. ed. (Englewood Cliffs, N.J.: Prentice-Hall, 1977).

17. Nor, did it matter very much, according to James Bryce, an English visitor to the United States in the late nineteenth century. In his classic study, Bryce observed that, because of the nature of the office, a man may lack "profundity of thought or extent of knowledge" and still make an excellent president. *The American Commonwealth* (London: Macmillan, 1889), 76.

18. Lou Cannon, *Reagan* (New York: Putnam, 1982), 32.

19. Jack W. Germond and Jules Witcover, *Wake Us When It's Over: Presidential Politics of 1984* (New York: Macmillan, 1985), 534.

BIBLIOGRAPHIC ESSAY

More books and articles have been written about Franklin Roosevelt than about any other president, including Lincoln. The vast amount of source material therefore precludes any comprehensive discussion of the literature. What follows is an attempt both to indicate the major primary and secondary sources consulted in the preparation of this study and to refer readers to some of the important books and articles that contain additional information on particular topics.

Biographies and General Assessments

For his biographers, Roosevelt has proved a daunting subject. The length and importance of his tenure in office and the sheer volume of material relating to his life have prevented any one biographer from mastering the relevant sources for Roosevelt as, say, historian Dumas Malone did for another daunting figure in American history, Thomas Jefferson. Consequently, historians have written about segments of Roosevelt's life. With some distinguished exceptions, those who have written most authoritatively about his early life and domestic presidency have not extensively studied his foreign policy or war leadership. By the same token, those who have written about "Dr. Win-the-War," have not examined "Dr. New Deal." There is, then, a certain disjointedness to the Roosevelt literature.

Although many aspects of his life and career remain controversial, the bulk of the scholarly literature, like public opinion during his lifetime, is favorable. Three superior multivolume works, the first installments of which appeared in the 1950s, continue to dominate the biographical literature. The dean of Roosevelt biographers is Frank Freidel, who began research on his subject during World War II, before Roosevelt's death, and whose four-volume *Franklin D. Roosevelt: The Apprenticeship; The Ordeal; The Triumph;* and *Launching the New Deal* (Boston: Little, Brown, 1952-73), follows Roosevelt from boyhood through the first half of his first year in the presidency. The first three volumes remain indispensable for the pre-presidential years. In the most recently completed volume of the series, which covers the interregnum between Hoover and Roosevelt and the first five months of the Roosevelt presidency, the author implicitly challenges Roosevelt's critics, especially those who have argued that Roosevelt lacked a coherent approach to fighting the depression. Although this multivolume work remains incomplete, Freidel has produced a useful one-volume biography, *Franklin D. Roosevelt: A Rendezvous with Destiny* (Boston: Little, Brown, 1990).

The second major work on Roosevelt is Arthur M. Schlesinger, Jr., *The Age of Roosevelt: The Crisis of the Old Order; The Coming of the New Deal*; and *The Politics of Upheaval* (Boston: Houghton Mifflin, 1957–60), which carries Roosevelt through the 1936 election. Brilliantly written, frankly partisan, and rich in pithy quotations, telling anecdotes, and vivid character sketches, Schlesinger's is the single most influential work on Roosevelt. With a knack for transforming Roosevelt's apparent weaknesses into great strengths, Schlesinger argues that Roosevelt saved capitalism from self-destruction and preserved democracy from authoritarian threats of the right and the left.

The most analytically satisfying and, of the multivolume works, the only complete biography, is James MacGregor Burns, *Roosevelt: The Lion and the Fox* and *Roosevelt: The Soldier of Freedom* (New York: Harcourt Brace Jovanovich, 1956, 1970). Although sympathetic to his subject, Burns faults Roosevelt for such things as failing to act sooner to transform the Democratic party into a more reliable vehicle for liberal action, failing to recognize the value of deficit spending as a recovery measure, and, most tellingly, failing to consider the long-term consequences of his actions. Burns's biography, especially the more critical first volume, is not only the best work on Roosevelt but also one of the best modern American biographies.

Several other biographies are noteworthy. Rexford G. Tugwell, *The Democratic Roosevelt* (Baltimore: Penguin, 1969 [1957]) is a full-scale life study that emphasizes the missed opportunities of the Roosevelt presidency. Tugwell's analysis of Roosevelt's personality and character strongly influenced my own view of Roosevelt. Joseph P. Lash's grand *Eleanor and Franklin* (New York: W. W. Norton, 1971) focuses on Eleanor but presents an indispensable and largely unflattering personal portrait of Franklin. Kenneth S. Davis's multivolume work, *F.D.R.: The Beckoning of Destiny, 1882–1928* (New York: Putnam, 1971); *The New York Years, 1928–1933*; and *The New Deal Years, 1933–1937* (New York: Random House, 1985, 1986) presents a detailed and highly sympathetic account of Roosevelt's life through the first term.

Geoffrey C. Ward, *Before the Trumpet: Young Franklin Roosevelt, 1882–1905* (New York: Harper & Row, 1985) and *A First-Class Temperament: The Emergence of Franklin Roosevelt* (New York: Harper & Row, 1989) provide the most extensive coverage of Roosevelt's personal and family life before he became governor.

In footnotes throughout both volumes, Ward revealingly demonstrates how the adult Roosevelt constantly revised accounts of his early life to meet the needs of the moment. Edgar E. Robinson, *The Roosevelt Leadership, 1933–1945* (Philadelphia: Lippincott, 1955), although not a biography, is a sharply critical general appraisal of Roosevelt's presidency from a constitutionalist's perspective. It contains an excellent bibliographic essay on early works on Roosevelt.

In addition to the previously mentioned works by Freidel and Tugwell, three one-volume biographies aim for a more general audience: Nathan Miller, *FDR: An Intimate History* (Garden City, N.Y.: Doubleday, 1983), a sound, well-written study; Ted Morgan, *FDR: A Biography* (New York: Simon & Schuster, 1985), a lively work packed with colorful anecdotes and quotations; and Joseph Alsop, *FDR, 1882–1945: A Centenary Remembrance* (New York: Viking, 1982), an excellent, concise biography-memoir by a prominent journalist and Roosevelt kinsman.

Other important assessments include, on the critical side, Richard Hofstadter's brilliant "Franklin D. Roosevelt: The Patrician as Opportunist," in *The American Political Tradition* (New York: Alfred A. Knopf, 1948) and Paul K. Conkin's devastating, but insightful, biographical sketch in his *The New Deal* (Arlington Heights, Ill.: AHM Publishing Corp., 1975 [1967]), especially ch. 1; and on the positive side, Clinton Rossiter in *The American Presidency* (New York: Harcourt, Brace & World, 1960 [1956]) and Isaiah Berlin's superb essays on Roosevelt and Winston Churchill in *Personal Impressions* (New York: Viking, 1981), 1–31. See also Eric F. Goldman, *Rendezvous with Destiny* (New York: Vintage, 1955), 248–326; John Morton Blum, *The Progressive Presidents* (New York: W. W. Norton, 1980), 107–162; Robert S. McElvaine, "Franklin D. Roosevelt, 1933–1945," in Frank N. Magill, ed., *The American Presidents* (Pasadena, CA: Salem Press, 1986), 3: 576–624. Otis L. Graham, Jr., and Meghan Robinson Wander, eds., *Franklin D. Roosevelt: His Life and Times, An Encyclopedic View* (Boston: G. K. Hall & Co., 1985) contains a treasure trove of scholarly essays on many aspects of Roosevelt's life and career. Also useful is James S. Olson, ed., *Historical Dictionary of the New Deal: From Inauguration to Preparation for War* (Westport, Conn.: Greenwood, 1985).

Personal Writings and Addresses

Roosevelt's personal papers are at the Roosevelt Library in Hyde Park, New York. Several thousand of his letters—a fairly representative sample, as it turns out—are conveniently collected in Elliott Roosevelt, ed., *F.D.R., His Personal Letters*, 4 vols. (New York: Duell, 1947–50). Anyone expecting dramatic disclosures or deep personal insights from the letters will be disappointed, for they are straightforward and cautiously worded. In Roosevelt's case, the public record provides a far better guide to his political views than his personal correspondence. His most important speeches and state papers are contained in Samuel I. Rosenman, ed., *The Public Papers and Addresses of Franklin D. Roosevelt*, 13 vols. (New York: 1938–50), which must be consulted with caution, for some of the addresses underwent editing after they were delivered but before publication. Another excellent source of his views is *The Complete Presidential Press Conferences of Franklin D. Roosevelt*, 25 vols. (New York: Da Capo Press, 1972).

Memoirs and Diaries

Roosevelt generated more memoirs than any other president. Almost everyone who knew him, it seems, from cabinet secretaries to the White House usher, set down his recollections. Because Roosevelt's own writings are so cautious and noncommittal, the remembrances of those around him are indispensible. The best of these works are Rexford Tugwell's biography-memoir, *The Democratic Roosevelt*, previously mentioned, and Raymond Moley, *After Seven Years* (New York: Harper Brothers, 1939). Although Tugwell and Moley worked for Roosevelt for relatively short periods of time, they spent the rest of their lives reflecting upon the Roosevelt leadership. Among their other important works are Tugwell's *The Brains Trust* (New York: Viking, 1967) and *In Search of Roosevelt* (Cambridge, Mass.: Harvard University Press, 1972); and Moley's *The First New Deal* (New York: Harcourt, Brace & World, 1966) and a fascinating biographical sketch of FDR in *27 Masters of Politics* (New York: Funk & Wagnalls, 1949), 30–45.

Other important memoirs or diaries are Eleanor Roosevelt's remarkably candid *This Is My Story* (New York: Harper, 1937) and *This I Remember* (Harper, 1949); Harold Ickes, *The Secret Diary of Harold Ickes*, 3 vols. (New York: Simon & Schuster, 1953–54), a revealing account of the inner workings of the administration by one of its key members; Frances Perkins, *The Roosevelt I Knew* (New York: Viking, 1946), especially good for its contrast between the young, arrogant state senator and the mature, seasoned politician; William D. Hassett, *Off the Record with F.D.R.: 1942–1945* (New Brunswick, N. J.: Rutgers University Press, 1958), a diary by FDR's correspondence secretary, which conveys, better than any other source, what Roosevelt was like personally on a daily basis; John M. Blum, *From the Morgenthau Diaries*, 3 vols. (Boston: Houghton, Mifflin, 1959–67); and Henry L. Stimson and McGeorge Bundy, *On Active Service in Peace and War* (New York: Harper, 1948).

A third tier of remembrances are useful, but not essential. They include Samuel I. Rosenman, *Working with Roosevelt* (New York: Harper & Bros., 1952) by FDR's longtime speechwriter; Marriner S. Eccles, *Beckoning Frontiers: Public and Personal Recollections* (New York: Alfred A. Knopf, 1951); William O. Douglas, *Go East Young Man* (New York: Random House, 1974), which records some colorful and, if accurate, revealing anecdotes about the president; Douglas's less useful *The Court Years* (New York: Random House, 1980); James A. Farley, *Jim Farley's Story: The Roosevelt Years* (New York: Whittlesey House, 1948), a bitter story of betrayal at the president's hands; Dean Acheson, *Morning and Noon* (Boston: Houghton Mifflin, 1965), esp. 162–94, which contains a revealing discussion of Roosevelt's personality; Michael F. Reilly, *Reilly of the White House* (New York: Simon & Schuster, 1947), a surprisingly insightful memoir by the head of the White House Secret Service detail, which, among other things, describes the elaborate measures Roosevelt had to take to function with his disability and which chronicles the president's dangerous and daring trips overseas during World War II; Ed Flynn, *You're the Boss* (New York: Viking, 1947); Grace Tully, *F.D.R.: My Boss* (New York: Charles Scribner's Sons, 1949), by FDR's secretary; Francis Biddle, *In Brief Authority* (New York: Doubleday, 1962), the author of which served in various positions in the Roosevelt administration, including in the attorney generalship; Elliott Roosevelt, *As He Saw It* (New York: Duell, 1946) and with James Brough, *An Untold Story: The Roosevelts of Hyde Park* (New York: G. P. Putnam's Sons, 1973), and *A Rendevous with Destiny: The Roosevelts of the White House* (New York: G. P. Putnam's Sons, 1975); and James Roosevelt and Sidney Shallett, *Affectionately, F.D.R.* (New York: Avon Books, 1959).

Two unpublished diaries, both at the Roosevelt Library, were consulted for this study: that of Henry Morgenthau, Jr., which contains material not included in the previously mentioned published versions; and that of Harold D. Smith, Roosevelt's budget director from 1939 to 1945. Smith's diary, which has received less attention from scholars than Morgenthau's, provides revealing material on Roosevelt's administrative style and economic views, and on the budget process in general.

Preparation for Politics, 1882–1910

Curiously, Roosevelt's early life has received more thorough coverage than some of the important aspects of his presidency. We know more, for example, about his boyhood than we do about his economic views in the later stages of the New Deal and during the war; we know more about his relationship with Eleanor (or Lucy Mercer) than we do about his relationship with Congress. The most detailed accounts of his early life are contained in Freidel, *The Apprenticeship*, 3–96; Davis, *Beckoning of Destiny*, 16–223; and Ward, *Before the Trumpet*. Ward presents the most complete portraits of Roosevelt's parents and of half-brother James Roosevelt Roosevelt (Rosy) and cousin James Roosevelt, Jr. (Taddy). Tugwell, *The Democratic Roosevelt*, contains a suggestive analysis of Roosevelt's psycological development. The Roosevelt Family Papers Donated by the Children, a collection of letters at the Roosevelt Library that was unavailable to Roosevelt's early biographers, sheds light on James and Sara and their relationship with Franklin.

Among the many good works on Eleanor Roosevelt, Joseph Lash, *Eleanor and Franklin*, is the most thorough. It is also essential for an understanding of the relationship between Eleanor and Franklin, although it views that relationship from Eleanor's perspective. A useful corrective in this regard is Joseph Alsop, *FDR, 1882–1945: A Centenary Remembrance.* Ward, *A First-Class Temperament*, also presents a detailed and subtle account of that complex relationship. See also Kenneth S. Lynn, "The First Lady's Lady Friend," *The Air-line to Seattle* (Chicago: University of Chicago Press, 1983), 152–62.

Rise to Power, 1910–1928

The standard biographies provide full accounts of Roosevelt's career as state senator, assistant secretary of the navy, and vice-presidential candidate, which, had he not gone on to be president, would have merited but a small footnote in the history of these years. Especially useful are Ernest K. Lindley, *Franklin D. Roosevelt: A Career in Progressive Democracy* (New York: Blue Ribbon Books, 1931), a campaign biography by a sympathetic journalist that exaggerates Roosevelt's importance and overstates his commitment to liberalism but nevertheless contains information nowhere else available; Freidel, *The Apprenticeship*, 97–156, a thoroughly balanced account; and Perkins, *The Roosevelt I Knew*, 9–37, with its revealing depiction of Roosevelt as an aloof state senator, indifferent to the needs of ordinary people. Two works on Louis Howe, who first came into Roosevelt's life during this period, are helpful: Lela Stiles, *The Man Behind Roosevelt: The Story of Louis McHenry Howe* (Cleveland and New York: World Publishing Co., 1954) and especially Alfred B. Rollins, Jr., *Roosevelt and Howe* (New York: Alfred A. Knopf, 1962). The political-intellectual milieu that formed the setting for Roosevelt's early career is skillfully delineated in John Milton Cooper, Jr., *The Warrior and the Priest: Woodrow Wilson and Theodore Roosevelt* (Cambridge, Mass.: Belknap Press, Harvard University Press, 1983), and Ellis Hawley, *The Great War and the Search for a Modern World Order: A History of the American People and Their Institutions, 1917–1933* (New York: St. Martin's Press, 1979), 9–11.

On the Roosevelt–Lucy Mercer relationship and its impact on Roosevelt's marriage and career, the previously mentioned works by Lash, Alsop, and Ward recount the basic story. Alsop accords it the most importance, arguing that the personal crisis precipitated by the affair toughened and matured Roosevelt.

Two excellent works vividly describe Roosevelt's struggle with polio: Richard T. Goldberg, *The Making of Franklin D. Roosevelt: Triumph Over Disability* (Cambridge, Mass.: Abt Books, 1981) and Hugh Gregory Gallagher, *FDR's*

Splendid Deception (New York: Dodd, Mead, 1985). Unlike virtually all previous commentators on the subject, Goldberg and Gallagher (himself a polio victim) correctly view polio not as a single episode in Roosevelt's life but as a lifelong ordeal. Ward, *A First-Class Temperament,* nicely weaves together into narrative form the findings of Goldberg, Gallagher, and others who have written on the subject. On the paradoxically positive impact of polio on Roosevelt's career, Alsop, *A Centenary Remembrance* is persuasive. Theo Lippman, *The Squire of Warm Springs* (New York: Playboy Press, 1977) contains information on Roosevelt's involvement with Warm Springs.

On Roosevelt's business dealings during the 1920s, Freidel, *The Ordeal,* 138–59, is the basic source. That same volume also chronicles Roosevelt's political comeback, as does David Burner, *The Politics of Provincialism: The Democratic Party in Transition, 1918–1932* (New York: Alfred A. Knopf, 1968).

Governor and Presidential Candidate, 1929–1932

On Roosevelt's governorship, the two standard accounts are Bernard Bellush, *Franklin D. Roosevelt as Governor of New York* (New York: Columbia University Press, 1955) and Freidel, *The Triumph,* 3–240. The most recent work is Kenneth Davis, *FDR: The New York Years 1928–1933* (New York: Random House, 1985). Less complimentary are the relevant sections in Hofstadter's "Franklin D. Roosevelt: Patrician as Opportunist," and John T. Flynn, *Country Squire in the White House* (New York: Doubleday, Doran, 1940). The first volume of Samuel I. Rosenman, ed., *The Public Papers and Addresses of Franklin D. Roosevelt,* which contains Roosevelt's major speeches as governor, is the best guide to his political views during this stage of his career.

The causes and consequences of the Great Depression are clearly discussed in Lester V. Chandler, *America's Greatest Depression, 1929–1941* (New York: Harper & Row, 1970); Charles P. Kindleberger, *The World in Depression, 1929–1939* (London: Penguin, 1973); John A. Garraty, *The Great Depression* (San Diego and New York: Harcourt Brace Jovanovich, 1986); Broadus Mitchell, *Depression Decade: From New Era through New Deal, 1929–1941* (New York: Holt, Rinehart & Winston, 1947); Robert S. McElvaine, *The Great Depression: America 1929–41* (New York: New York Times Books, 1984); and Susan Previant Lee and Peter Passell, *A New Economic View of American History* (New York: W. W. Norton, 1979), 362–99.

In recent years, Herbert Hoover has stimulated a more vigorous and productive scholarly debate than Roosevelt. The most balanced biography is David Burner, *Herbert Hoover: A Public Life* (New York: Alfred A. Knopf, 1979). Two other important interpretive biographies, both sympathetic to the subject, are Joan Hoff Wilson, *Herbert Hoover: Forgotten Progressive* (Boston: Little, Brown, 1975) and Martin L. Fausold, *The Presidency of Herbert C. Hoover* (Lawrence:

University of Kansas Press, 1985). Albert U. Romasco, *The Poverty of Abundance: Hoover, the Nation and the Depression* (New York: Oxford University Press, 1965) is a penetrating analysis of Hoover's unsuccessful efforts to combat the depression. Well-reasoned rebuttals to recent interpretations that see Hoover as a precursor of the New Deal are Robert H. Zieger, "Herbert Hoover: A Reinterpretation," *American Historical Review* 81 (October 1976): 800–810; Arthur M. Schlesinger, Jr., *The Cycles of American History* (Boston: Houghton Mifflin, 1986), 374–87; and Elliot A. Rosen, *Hoover, Roosevelt, and the Brains Trust: From Depression to New Deal* (New York: Columbia University Press, 1977).

Full accounts of the 1932 nomination fight and presidential campaign can be found in Freidel, *The Triumph*, 241–372; Davis, *FDR: The New York Years*, 195–376; Burner, *The Party of Provincialism*; and in most of the major biographies of Roosevelt. In addition, Rosen, *Hoover, Roosevelt, and the Brains Trust*, 26–38, 212–75, emphasizes the ideological stakes involved in the battle for the Democratic nomination. Rosen also provides an arresting reinterpretation of the nomination fight that diminishes the images of key Roosevelt aides James Farley and Louis Howe and enhances Roosevelt's image as a politician. On the tendency to underestimate Roosevelt and the reasons for it, see Ronald Steel, *Walter Lippmann and the American Century* (Boston: Little, Brown, 1980), 285–98. A revealing contemporary portrait in this regard is Milton MacKaye, "Profiles: The Governor," *New Yorker* (15 and 22 August 1931).

The fullest account of the interregnum is contained in Freidel, *Launching the New Deal*, 3–195, which generally defends Roosevelt for declining to cooperate with Hoover, as does Rosen, *Hoover, Roosevelt, and the Brains Trust*, 361–79. Robinson, *The Roosevelt Leadership*, 81–103, makes the case against Roosevelt.

Birth of the New Deal, 1933–1936

This author's basic perspective on the legislative history of the New Deal, which emphasizes the role of Congress, derives in large part from research done in the preparation of an earlier study of Robert M. La Follette, Jr. Because La Follette had a hand in most of the legislation of the New Deal, his papers at the Library of Congress contain a wealth of information on nearly all of the legislative enactments of the 1930s. Published works detailing the contributions of individual legislators to the New Deal include: on relief and public works, the NIRA, Social Security, and labor legislation, J. Joseph Huthmacher, *Senator Robert F. Wagner and the Rise of Urban Liberalism* (New York: Atheneum, 1968); on relief and public works, Fred Greenbaum, *Fighting Progressive: A Biography of Edward P. Costigan* (Washington, D.C.: Public Affairs Press, 1971); on the TVA, Richard Lowitt, *George W. Norris: The Persistence of a Progressive, 1913–1933* (Urbana: University of Illinois Press, 1971) and *George W. Norris: The Triumph of a Progressive, 1933–1944* (Urbana: University of Illinois Press, 1978); on relief, public works, labor legislation, and taxation, Patrick J. Maney, *"Young Bob" La Follette: A Biography of Robert M. La Follette, Jr., 1895–1953* (Columbia: University of Missouri Press, 1978); and Alfred Steinberg, *Sam Rayburn: A Biography* (New York: Hawthorn, 1975). Lawrence H. Chamberlain, *The President, Congress and Legislation* (New York: Columbia University Press, 1946), is an important study that weighs the relative contributions of the president and Congress to important legislation between 1870s and 1940 and concludes that Congress played a more important role in the legislative process than has been generally supposed. Detailed examination of the above-mentioned studies of individual legislators bolsters Chamberlain's conclusion.

The absence of any general study on the relationship between Roosevelt and Congress is one of the conspicuous gaps in the literature, although James T. Patterson, *Congressional Conservatism and the New Deal: The Growth of the Conservative Coalition in Congress, 1933–1939* (Lexington: University of Kentucky Press, 1967) is an excellent study that provides much useful information on and many insights into the subject. Ronald L. Feinman, *Twilight of Progressivism: The Western Republican Senators and the New Deal* (Baltimore: Johns Hopkins University Press, 1981) and Ronald A. Mulder, *The Insurgent Progressives in the United States Senate and the New Deal, 1933–1939* (New York: Garland, 1979) describe the activities of the so-called progressive bloc in the Senate.

Works on the New Deal abound. Two fine overviews are William E. Leuchtenburg, *Franklin D. Roosevelt and the New Deal, 1933–1940* (New York: Harper & Row, 1963) and Anthony J. Badger, *The New Deal: The Depression Years, 1933–40* (New York: Farrar, Straus & Giroux, 1989). Badger not only incorporates into the narrative an impressive amount of recent scholarship, but in a detailed bibliographic essay, he provides the most up-to-date guide to the literature. Useful overviews of the New Deal in a broad context also include Robert S. McElvaine, *The Great Depression: America 1929–41* (New York: New York Times Books, 1984) and Richard S. Kirkendall, *The United States, 1929–1945: Years of Crisis and Change* (New York: McGraw-Hill, 1973). Provocative and important interpretations are contained in Carl Degler, *Out of Our Past: The Forces that Shaped Modern America* (New York: Harper & Row, 1970 [1959]), 379–413, which describes the New Deal as the "Third American Revolution" and Richard Hofstadter, *The Age of Reform* (New York: Alfred A. Knopf, 1955), 302–328. For an introduction to the scholarly debates on the New Deal, see Richard Kirkendall, "The New Deal as Watershed: The Recent Literature," *Journal of American History* 54 (March 1968): 839–52; and Jerold Auerbach, "New Deal, Old Deal, or Raw Deal: Some Thoughts on New Left Historiography," *Journal of Southern History* 35 (February 1969): 18–30. An important collection of essays is John Braeman, Robert H. Bremner, and David Brody, editors, *The New Deal*: vol. 1, *The National Level*; vol. 2, *State and Local Levels* (Columbus, Ohio, 1975).

Other essential works include Freidel, *Launching the New Deal*; Burns, *The Lion and the Fox*; Ellis W. Hawley, *The New Deal and the Problem of Monopoly, 1933–39* (Princeton: Princeton University Press, 1966); Tugwell, *The Democratic Roosevelt*; Raymond Moley, *After Seven Years*; and Schlesinger, *The Coming of the New Deal* and *The Politics of Upheaval.* Important critiques of the New Deal are Paul Conkin, *The New Deal*, and Barton J. Bernstein, "The New Deal: The Conservative Achievements of Liberal Reform," in Bernstein, ed., *Towards a New Past: Dissenting Essays in American History* (New York: Pantheon, 1967). On the New Deal as broker state, see Burns, *The Lion and the Fox*, 191–208; Leuchtenburg, *Roosevelt and the New Deal*, 87–89; and John Braeman, "The New Deal and the 'Broker State': A Review of the Recent Scholarly Literature," *Business History Review* 46 (1972): 409–20.

Important works of a more recent vintage include Susan Ware, *Beyond Suffrage: Women in the New Deal* (Cambridge: Harvard University Press, 1981); Albert U. Romasco, *The Politics of Recovery: Roosevelt's New Deal* (New York: Oxford University Press, 1983); and Mark Leff, *The Limits of Symbolic Reform: The New Deal and Taxation, 1933–1939* (Cambridge: Cambridge University Press, 1984). Leff, who points to the disparity between the rhetoric and reality of New Deal tax policy, not only provides a much needed examination of fiscal practices during the 1930s, but, with his emphasis on symbolism, suggests a richly rewarding way of viewing the Roosevelt leadership. Alan Brinkley's *Voices of Protest: Huey Long, Father Coughlin and the Great Depression* (New York: Alfred A. Knopf, 1982), provides an excellent overview of the careers of two of Roosevelt's main foes and also helps illuminate the ideological climate of the 1930s. A recent collection of essays assessing the impact of the New Deal on politics, the economy, race relations, social welfare, the cities, women, culture, and foreign policy is Harvard Sitkoff, ed., *Fifty Years Later: The New Deal Evaluated* (New York: Alfred A. Knopf, 1985). Two of the most recent works to appear depict Roosevelt as a serious thinker and place him at the center of the economic and ideological debates of the 1930s. They are Richard P. Adelstein, "'The Nation as an Economic Unit'": Keynes, Roosevelt, and the Managerial Ideal," *Journal of American History*, vol. 78 (June 1991): 160–187; and Philip Abbott, *The Exemplary Presidency: Franklin D. Roosevelt and the American Political Tradition* (Amherst: University of Massachusetts Press, 1990).

Although Roosevelt occasionally seemed indifferent to the fate of organized labor, labor played a critical role in the events of his administration. A concise authoritative overview of the subject is contained in Robert H. Zieger, *American Workers, American Unions, 1920–1985* (Baltimore: Johns Hopkins University Press, 1985), 26–61. The standard work remains Irving Bernstein, *The Turbulent Years: A History of the American Worker, 1933–1941* (Boston: Houghton Mifflin, 1969).

On blacks and the New Deal, see Nancy J. Weiss, *Farewell to the Party of Lincoln: Black Politics in the Age of FDR* (Princeton: Princeton University Press, 1983), which traces the movement of blacks from the Republican to the Democratic party and which points out that blacks gave to FDR and the Democratic party more than they received. Other important works on the subject include Harvard Sitkoff, *A New Deal for Blacks: The Emergence of Civil Rights as a National Issue* (New York: Oxford University Press, 1978); Raymond Wolters, *Negroes and the Great Depression: The Problem of Economic Recovery* (Westport, Conn.: Greenwood, 1970); and John B. Kirby, *Black Americans in the Roosevelt Era; Liberalism and Race* (Knoxville: University of Tennessee Press, 1980).

A recent thrust in the New Deal literature is the renewed interest in the pivotal role of the state—its structure and functionings—in shaping history. Challenging interpretions along these lines are contained in various works authored and co-authored by Theda Skocpol, including "Political Response to Capitalist Crisis: Neo-Marxist Theories of the State and the Case of the New Deal," *Politics and Society* 10 (1980): 155–201, and, with John Ikenberry, "Expanding Social Benefits: The Role of Social Security," *Political Science Quarterly* 102 (1987): 389–416. See also Ellis W. Hawley, "The New Deal and the Anti-Bureaucratic Tradition," in Robert Eden, ed., *The New Deal and Its Legacy: Critique and Reappraisal,* (Westport, Conn.: Greenwood, 1989); and Barry Karl, *The Uneasy State* (Chicago: University of Chicago Press). Hawley and Karl point out that the New Deal failed to establish anything approaching a centralized mechanism for economic and social planning. But also see on the subject of planning Otis L. Graham, Jr. *Toward a Planned Society: From Roosevelt to Nixon* (New York: Oxford University Press, 1976).

Studies of Roosevelt "team" members, most of them highly sympathetic to their subjects, include, on Harry Hopkins: Robert E. Sherwood, *Roosevelt and Hopkins: An Intimate History* (New York: Grosset & Dunlap, 1950 [1948]); Searle F. Charles, *Minister of Relief: Harry Hopkins and the Depression* (Syracuse: Syracuse University Press, 1963); Henry W. Adams, *Harry Hopkins: A Biography* (New York: Putnam, 1977); and especially illuminating about the FDR-Hopkins relationship, George McJimsay, *Harry Hopkins: Ally of the Poor and Defender of Democracy* (Cambridge: Harvard University Press, 1987). On Harold Ickes: Linda J. Lear, *Harold L. Ickes: The Aggressive Progressive, 1874–1933* (New York: Garland, 1981), the first volume in a projected multivolume study; Graham White and John Maze, *Harold Ickes of the New Deal: His Private Life and Public Career* (Cambridge: Harvard University Press, 1985); and T. H. Watkins, *Righteous Pilgrim: The Life and Times of Harold L. Ickes, 1874–1952* (New York: Henry Holt, 1990). On Frances Perkins: George Martin, *Madam Secretary: Frances Perkins* (Boston: Houghton Mifflin, 1976). On the underrated Jesse Jones: Bascom M. Timmons, *Jesse H. Jones: The Man and the Statesman* (New York: Henry Holt, 1956); and James S. Olson, *Saving Capitalism: The Reconstruction Finance*

Corporation and the New Deal, 1933–1940 (Princeton: Princeton University Press, 1989). On Adolf A. Berle: Jordan A. Schwarz, *Liberal: Adolf A. Berle and the Vision of an American Era* (New York: Free Press, 1987). A contemporary source with colorful sketches of prominent New Dealers is The Unofficial Observer [J. Franklin Carter], *The New Dealers* (New York: Simon & Schuster, 1934). This last work also contains a shrewd early assessment of Roosevelt's role in the New Deal.

The New Deal: The Roosevelt Presence, 1933–1936

An excellent source for understanding how Roosevelt was perceived by the public is the letters that people wrote to the Roosevelts. Among several collections of such letters at the Roosevelt Library, two in particular contain rich material. One contains thousands of songs about, or in honor of, the president written for the most part by ordinary people, not by professional composers. This collection also contains the letters that accompanied the songs. The other collection contains letters that accompanied gifts that people sent to the president. An excellent published collection of letters to and about Roosevelt is Robert S. McElvaine, *Down & Out in the Great Depression: Letters from the Forgotten Man* (Chapel Hill: University of North Carolina Press, 1983).

On Roosevelt's relationship with the press, the most detailed work is Graham J. White, *FDR and the Press* (Chicago: University of Chicago Press, 1979), an important work that is broader in scope than the title suggests. White concludes that Roosevelt was much more ideological than most historians have supposed. White's "News Media," in Graham and Wander, eds., *Franklin D. Roosevelt: His Life and Times, An Encyclopedic View*, 92–93, is a concise summary of the subject. *The Complete Presidential Press Conferences of Franklin D. Roosevelt* includes transcripts of most of his formal news conferences and has an adequate, though not complete, index. *Public Papers and Addresses* also contains excerpts from some news conferences as well as from some of the most important fireside chats. Betty Houchin Winfield, "F.D.R.'s Pictorial Image, Rules and Boundaries," *Journalism History* 5 (Winter 1978–79): 110–14, 136, describes the steps Roosevelt and Press Secretary Stephen Early took to control White House photographers, while Gallagher, *FDR's Splendid Deception*, describes Roosevelt's efforts to conceal the extent of his disability from the press and the public.

Roosevelt's frequent use of biblical imagery seems to have tapped a rich vein of religious sentiment in the American public, which may help explain the intensity of feelings toward him. An excellent discussion of Roosevelt's use of biblical imagery and its relationship to charismatic leadership is contained in Ann R. Willner, *The Spellbinders: Charismatic Political Leadership* (New Haven: Yale University Press, 1984), 151–71. Pete Daniel, "The New Deal, Southern

Agriculture, and Economic Change," in James C. Cobb and Michael V. Na-morato, eds., *The New Deal and the South* (Jackson: University Press of Missis-sippi, 1984), 37–61, describes how southerners viewed the depression and Roosevelt within a biblical context. A good introduction to the subject of civil religion is Robert N. Bellah, "Civil Religion in America," *Daedalus* 96 (Winter 1967): 1–21. The symbolic and mythical nature of the Roosevelt presidency remains largely unexamined. John William Ward's classic study, *Andrew Jackson: Symbol for an Age* (New York: Oxford University Press, 1962), suggests what might be done for Roosevelt.

Roosevelt's foes were as intense in their feelings as his friends. On his extreme critics, the classic piece is Marquis Childs, "They Hate Roosevelt," in Frank Freidel, ed., *The New Deal and the American People* (Englewood Cliffs, N.J.: Prentice-Hall, 1964), 98–104. See also George Wolfskill and John A. Hudson, *All But the People: Roosevelt and His Critics, 1933–1939* (Toronto: Mac-millan, 1969), a rich source of anti-Roosevelt material; and George Wolfskill, *The Revolt of the Conservatives* (Boston: Houghton Mifflin, 1962), a study of the American Liberty League, one of the leading organizations opposed to Roosevelt.

Scholars have delved deeply into the origins, nature, and composition of the New Deal coalition. Two lucid introductions to the complex subject are John M. Allswang, *The New Deal and American Politics* (New York: John Wiley & Sons, 1978) and John Braeman, "The Making of the Roosevelt Coalition: Some Reconsiderations," *Canadian Review of American Studies* 11 (Fall 1980): 233–53, which reviews important literature on the New Deal coalition and, with admirable clarity, explains some of the complicated issues at stake. Other key works include Samuel Lubell, *The Future of American Politics* (Garden City, N.Y.: Doubleday, 1956 [1952]), 29–60, which sees the origins of the coalition in the vote for Al Smith in 1928; Allan J. Lichtman, *Prejudice and the Old Politics: The Presidential Election of 1928* (Chapel Hill: University of North Ca-rolina Press, 1979), which casts doubt on the Lubell thesis; Kristi Andersen, *The Creation of a Democratic Majority, 1928–1936* (Chicago: University of Chi-cago Press, 1979), which argues that the political realignment that took place during the Roosevelt era resulted not from the conversion of voters who had previously voted Republican but from the mobilization of newly eligible or pre-viously inactive voters; and James L. Sundquist, *Dynamics of the Party System: Alignment and Realignment of Political Parties in the United States* (Washington, D.C.: Brookings Institution, 1973), which stresses the importance of the depres-sion in creating a Democratic majority; John W. Jeffries, *Testing the Roosevelt Coalition: Connecticut Society and Politics in the Era of World War II* (Knoxville: University of Tennessee Press, 1979), a sophisticated analysis of the emergence and course of the New Deal coalition in a state with social and economic char-acteristics similar to other coalition states. See also, Bernard Sternsher, "The

New Deal Party System: A Reappraisal," *Journal of Interdisciplinary History* 15 (Summer 1984): 53–81; and Otis L. Graham, Jr., "The Democratic Party, 1932–1942," in Arthur M. Schlesinger, Jr., ed., *History of U.S. Political Parties* (New York: Chelsea House Publishers, 1973), 3: 1939–2066.

Time of Troubles, 1937–1938

On the court-packing controversy, the starting point is Joseph Alsop and Turner Catledge, *The 168 Days* (Garden City, N.Y.: Doubleday, Doran, 1938). Despite a deceptively "breezy" journalistic style and some inaccuracies, this first-class piece of reportage remains the best account of the political struggle for Court reform. It is less successful at delineating the judicial issues at stake in the struggle. Two excellent essays by William E. Leuchtenburg succinctly tell the basic story: "The Origins of Franklin D. Roosevelt's 'Court-Packing' Plan," in Philip B. Kurland, ed., *The Supreme Court Review: 1966* (Chicago: University of Chicago Press, 1966) and "Franklin D. Roosevelt's Supreme Court 'Packing' Plan," in Harold M. Hollingsworth and William F. Holmes, eds., *Essays on the New Deal* (Austin: University of Texas Press, 1969). Alpheus T. Mason, *Harlan Fiske Stone: Pillar of the Law* (New York: Viking Press, 1956), a model biography, discusses the controversy from the perspective of one of the key members of the Supreme Court. A succinct overview of the subject is Michael E. Parrish, "The Supreme Court," in Graham and Wander, eds., *Franklin D. Roosevelt: His Life and Times, An Encyclopedic View*, 409–12. The political consequences of court-packing are described in James T. Patterson, *Congressional Conservatism and the New Deal*.

There are two basic works on executive reorganization. Barry D. Karl, *Executive Reorganization and Reform in the New Deal: The Genesis of Administrative Management, 1900–1939* (Cambridge: Harvard University Press, 1963) discusses the diverse intellectual origins of attempts to rationalize the workings of government and analyzes the ideas of the three men—Louis D. Brownlow, Charles E. Merriam, and Luther Gulick—who formulated Roosevelt's reorganization plans. Richard Polenberg, *Reorganizing Roosevelt's Government: The Controversy Over Executive Reorganization, 1936–1939* (Cambridge: Harvard University Press, 1966), which is sympathetic to the cause of reorganization, describes the political course of Roosevelt's proposal.

The pros and cons of Roosevelt's administrative style are discussed in Schlesinger, *Coming of the New Deal*, 520–22, 533–52, which summarizes the case for his unorthodox management methods; Leuchtenburg, *Roosevelt and the New Deal*, 328–29; Burns, *The Lion and the Fox*, 371–75, a balanced treatment; *The Secret Diaries of Harold L. Ickes*, which is critical; and at the Roosevelt Library, the Morgenthau and Harold Smith diaries. John Gunther, *Roosevelt in*

Retrospect: A Profile in History (New York: Harper & Bros., 1950), 125–34, is also useful.

Detailed accounts of the causes and consequences of the recession of 1937–38 are contained in Leuchtenburg, *Roosevelt and the New Deal*, 244–54, and Kenneth D. Roose, *The Economics of Recession and Revival: An Interpretation of 1937–38* (New Haven: Yale University Press, 1954). For the effects of the recession on liberal thought, see Alan Brinkley, "The New Deal and the Idea of the State," in Steve Fraser and Gary Gerstle, *The Rise and Fall of the New Deal Order, 1930–1980* (Princeton: Princeton University Press, 1989), 85–121, an excellent discussion that illuminates economic policies in the later stages of the New Deal. Roosevelt, however, is conspicuous by his absence from Brinkley's account. See also Dean L. May, *From New Deal to New Economics: An American Liberal Response to the Recession of 1937* (New York: Garland, 1981) and Robert M. Collins, *The Business Response to Keynes, 1929–1964* (New York: Columbia University Press, 1981).

On Roosevelt's unsuccessful purge attempt, see Leuchtenburg, *Roosevelt and the New Deal*, 267–74; Burns, *The Lion and the Fox*, 358–80; and Patterson, *Congressional Conservatism and the New Deal*, 250–87, all of which—especially Patterson—emphasize the obstacles to party purification that were beyond Roosevelt's control. Martha H. Swain, *Pat Harrison: The New Deal Years* (Jackson: University of Mississippi Press, 1978), 168–94, describes the purge attempt from the vantage point of conservatives, but one who does not easily fit the image of ardent foe of the New Deal; while A. Cash Koeniger, "The New Deal and the States: Roosevelt versus the Byrd Organization in Virginia," *Journal of American History* 68 (March 1982): 876–96, describes the purge from the vantage point of one who does fit the image. Vernon A. Fagin, "Franklin D. Roosevelt, Liberalism in the Democratic Party, and the 1938 Congressional Elections: The Urge to Purge" (Ph.D. dissertation, University of California, Los Angeles, 1979) emphasizes Roosevelt's tactical errors and seems to suggest that, with better planning and execution, the purge attempt could have been successful. A recent positive assessment of Roosevelt as party leader is Sean Savage, *Roosevelt: The Party Leader, 1932–1945* (Lexington: University of Kentucky Press, 1991).

Historians have accorded the domestic events of Roosevelt's second term, including court-packing, executive reorganization, the recession, and the purge, much less attention than events before and after. In most accounts, this period seems to be a brief interlude between the successes of the first term and the coming of World War II. Three works that make the case for the second term as an important period in its own right are Barry Karl, *The Uneasy State*, 131–81; Ellis W. Hawley, "The New Deal and the Anti-Bureaucratic Tradition," in Robert Eden, ed., *The New Deal and Its Legacy: Critique and Reappraisal*; and James MacGregor Burns and Michael R. Beschloss, "The Forgotten FDR," *New Republic* (7 April 1982): 19–22.

A Third Term and the Road to War, 1938–1941

Roosevelt's conduct of foreign policy in the years before Pearl Harbor has sparked even more controversy than his domestic policies. Works that have been particularly useful in the preparation of this study are Burns, *Soldier of Freedom*; William L. Langer and S. Everett Gleason, *The Challenge to Isolation, 1937–1940* and *The Undeclared War, 1940–1941* (New York: Harper & Row, 1952, 1953), which remain a rich source of information; Henry L. Stimson and McGeorge Bundy, *On Active Service in Peace and War* (New York: Harper, 1948), the most incisive critique of Roosevelt from an interventionist perspective; Elting E. Morison, *Turmoil and Tradition: A Study of the Life and Times of Henry L. Stimson* (Boston: Houghton Mifflin, 1960); David Reynolds, *The Creation of the Anglo-American Alliance 1937–1941* (Chapel Hill: University of North Carolina Press, 1982), a surperb study that sheds light on virtually all of the key issues; Arnold A. Offner, *American Appeasement: United States Foreign Policy and Germany, 1933–1938* (Cambridge: Belknap Press, Harvard University Press, 1969); Cordell Hull, *Memoirs*, 2 vols. (New York: Macmillan, 1948); Robert A. Divine, *Roosevelt and World War II* (Baltimore: Johns Hopkins Press, 1969); Robert Dallek, *Franklin D. Roosevelt and American Foreign Policy* (New York: Oxford University Press, 1979), an influential work that, although not uncritical, resolves the major issues in Roosevelt's favor; Waldo Heinrichs, *Threshold of War: Franklin D. Roosevelt & American Entry into World War II* (New York: Oxford University Press, 1988), which nicely demonstrates the interrelationship of developments in Europe and Asia and emphasizes the constraints to bolder action that Roosevelt faced; and Frederick W. Marks III, *Wind Over Sand: The Diplomacy of Franklin Roosevelt* (Athens: University of Georgia Press, 1988), a detailed indictment of nearly all aspects of Roosevelt's diplomacy.

On the isolationists, four books by Wayne S. Cole provide balanced coverage: *America First: The Battle Against Intervention 1940–1941* (Madison: University of Wisconsin Press, 1953); *Senator Gerald P. Nye and American Foreign Relations* (Minneapolis: University of Minnesota Press, 1962); *Charles A. Lindbergh and the Battle against American Intervention in World War II* (New York: Harcourt Brace Jovanovich, 1974); and *Roosevelt and the Isolationists, 1932–45* (Lincoln: University of Nebraska Press, 1983). On Roosevelt's use of the FBI to combat critics of his foreign policy, see Kenneth O'Reilly, "A New Deal for the FBI: The Roosevelt Administration, Crime Control, and National Security," *Journal of American History* 69 (December 1982): 638–58; and Richard Gid Powers, *Secrecy and Power: The Life of J. Edgar Hoover* (New York: Free Press, 1987).

Critical but fair accounts of the Roosevelt's handling of the German-Jewish refugee issue are David S. Wyman, *Paper Walls* (Amherst: University of Massachusetts Press, 1968) and Henry L. Feingold, *The Politics of Rescue* (New Brunswick: Rutgers University Press, 1970). See also Saul Friedman, *No Haven for the Oppressed: United States Policy Toward Jewish Refugees, 1938–1945* (Detroit: Wayne State University Press, 1973). Two books treat Roosevelt's quest for a third term: Bernard F. Donahoe, *Private Plans and Public Dangers* (South Bend: University of Notre Dame Press, 1965); and Herbert S. Parmet and Marie B. Hecht, *Never Again: A President Runs for a Third Term* (New York: Macmillan, 1968).

Although conspiracy theories linger in the popular literature, scholars have long since rejected charges that Roosevelt knew in advance of the attack on Pearl Harbor but allowed it to proceed in order to involve a reluctant nation in war. Persuasive refutations of the charges are Roberta Wohlstetter, *Pearl Harbor: Warning and Decision* (Stanford: Stanford University Press, 1962) and Gordon W. Prange, *At Dawn We Slept: The Untold Story of Pearl Harbor* (New York: McGraw-Hill, 1981). On the underestimation of the Japanese by the American high command, see John W. Dower, *War Without Mercy: Race and Power in the Pacific War* (New York: Pantheon, 1986). A recent example of the conspiratorial view of Pearl Harbor is John Toland, *Infamy: Pearl Harbor and Its Aftermath* (Garden City: Doubleday, 1982).

World War II, 1941–1945

The best work on Roosevelt's wartime presidency is Burns, *Soldier of Freedom*, which, although generally favorable to FDR, sharply criticizes certain aspects of his leadership, especially on the home front. The earliest works on the war depicted Roosevelt as a relatively inactive commander in chief who left military matters to the military experts. "He picked a first-class military team, and never interfered with it," wrote John Gunther in *Roosevelt in Retrospect*. Two works that effectively counter this impression of passivity are William R. Emerson, "F.D.R. (1941–1945)," in Ernest R. May, ed., *The Ultimate Decision: The President as Commander in Chief* (New York: Braziller, 1960), 133–77; and Kent R. Greenfield, *American Strategy in World War II: A Reconsideration* (Baltimore: Johns Hopkins University Press, 1963), 49–84. Other important works on Roosevelt's military leadership include the second and third volumes of Forrest Pogue's first-rate biography of George C. Marshall, *George C. Marshall: Ordeal and Hope* and *Organizer of Victory* (New York: Viking, 1966, 1973), which, despite Marshall's retrospective praise for Roosevelt, cast the president in a critical light; Stimson and Bundy, *On Active Service in Peace and War*; Sherwood, *Roosevelt and Hopkins*; and Warren F. Kimball, ed., *Churchill and Roosevelt: The Complete Correspondence*, 3 vols. (Princeton: Princeton University Press, 1984), an indispensable source that, among other things, documents Roosevelt's crooked path to the second front. See also Eric Larrabee's highly sympathetic *Commander in Chief: Franklin Delano Roosevelt, His Lieutenants and Their War* (New York: Harper & Row, 1987), especially the first and last chapters.

On the home front, key studies, in addition to that of Burns, include John M. Blum, *V Was for Victory* (New York: Harcourt Brace Jovanovich, 1977); Richard Polenberg, *War and Society: The United States, 1941–1945* (Philadelphia: Lippincott, 1972); Geoffrey Perrett, *Days of Sadness, Years of Triumph* (New York: Coward, McCann & Geoghegan, 1973); Bruce Catton, *The War Lords of Washington* (New York: Harcourt Brace, 1948), an enduring critique of the mobilization effort; Eliot Janeway, *The Struggle for Survival: A Chronicle of Economic Mobilization* (New Haven: Yale University Press, 1951); and Paul A. C. Koistinen, "Mobilizing the World War II Economy: Labor and the Industrial-Military Alliance," *Pacific Historical Review* 42 (November 1973): 443–78.

Numerous works deal with specific aspects of the war at home. A revealing account of Roosevelt's relationship with labor leader John L. Lewis and with labor in general is contained in Robert H. Zieger, *John L. Lewis: Labor Leader* (Boston: Twayne Publishers, 1988), 132–49. On Roosevelt's role in the internment of Japanese Americans, Peter Irons, *Justice at War: The Story of Japanese American Internment Cases* (New York: Oxford University Press, 1983) is excellent. On Roosevelt and blacks, useful works include Polenberg, *War and Society*, 99–130; Sitkoff, *A New Deal for Blacks*, 298–325; Jervis Anderson, *A. Philip Randolph: A Biographical Portrait* (New York: Harcourt Brace Jovanovich, 1972), 241–61; and Blum, *V Was for Victory*, 182–220. The troubled wartime relationship between the executive and legislative branches of government is described in Roland Young, *Congressional Politics in the Second World War* (New York: Columbia University Press, 1956); James T. Patterson, *Mr. Republican: A Biography of Robert A. Taft* (Boston: Houghton Mifflin, 1972); Maney, *"Young Bob" La Follette*, 250–75; Polly A. Davis, *Alben W. Barkley: Senate Majority Leader and Vice President* (New York: Garland, 1979); and Allen Drury, *A Senate Journal, 1943–1945* (New York: McGraw-Hill, 1963). Roosevelt's inattention to Democratic party matters is detailed in Robert E. Ficken, "Political Leadership in Wartime: Franklin D. Roosevelt and the Elections of 1942," *Mid-America* 57 (January 1975): 20–37.

The 1944 presidential campaign is described in Burns, *Soldiers of Freedom*, 497–531; Polenberg, *War and Society*, 184–214; and Richard Norton Smith, *Thomas E. Dewey and His Times* (New York: Simon & Schuster, 1982), 393–437, an excellent biography of the GOP contender. John W. Partin, "Roosevelt, Byrnes, and the 1944 Vice-Presidential Nomination," *Historian* 42 (November 1979): 85–100, describes the elaborate maneuvers involved in Roosevelt's selection of a running mate. On Roosevelt's deteriorating health, Burns, *Soldier of Freedom* is authoritative. Burns cites technical information from a then-unpublished manuscript written by Roosevelt's physician, Howard G. Bruenn. The manuscript was later published as "Clinical Notes on the Illness and Death of President Franklin D. Roosevelt," *Annals of Internal Medicine* 72 (April 1970): 579–91. Detailed works on Roosevelt's wartime diplomacy include Dallek,

Franklin D. Roosevelt and American Foreign Policy; Divine, *Roosevelt and World War II*; and Gaddis Smith, *American Diplomacy during the Second World War, 1941–1945* (New York: John Wiley & Sons, 1965). The most recent study, Warren F. Kimball, *The Juggler: Franklin Roosevelt as Wartime Statesman* (Princeton: Princeton University Press, 1991), which appeared as this work was in press, discerns in Roosevelt a consistent and coherent plan for the postwar world. Together with the previously mentioned, recent works by Sean Savage on FDR's party leadership, Philip Abbott on FDR's political philosophy, and Eric Larrabee on FDR as military leader, Kimball underscores the durability of Roosevelt's historical reputation.

The works of diplomat-historian George F. Kennan offer a particularly challenging perspective against which to measure Roosevelt's diplomacy: *American Diplomacy, 1900–1950* (Chicago: University of Chicago Press, 1951); *Russia and the West under Lenin and Stalin* (Boston: Little, Brown, 1961); and his brilliant *Memoirs: 1925–1950* (Boston: Little Brown, 1967). Roosevelt's views toward colonialism are discussed in Walter La Feber, "Roosevelt, Churchill, and Indochina: 1942–1945," *American Historical Review* 80 (December 1975): 1277–95 and Christopher Thorne, *Allies of a Kind: The United States, Britain, and the War against Japan, 1941–1945* (New York: Oxford University Press, 1978). David S. Wyman, *The Abandonment of the Jews: America and the Holocaust, 1941–1945* (New York: Pantheon, 1984), assesses the Roosevelt administration's responsibility for the Holocaust.

Just as they reject conspiracy theories concerning Pearl Harbor, most scholars reject claims by Roosevelt's extreme critics that at Yalta he sold out Poland and Eastern Europe to the Russians. On the Yalta Conference, Burns, *Soldier of Freedom*, 557–80 and Dallek, *Roosevelt and American Foreign Policy*, 506–25 provide succinct summaries. More detailed treatments include Diane Shaver Clemens, *Yalta* (New York: Oxford University Press, 1970) and more recently, Russell D. Buhite, *Decisions at Yalta: An Appraisal of Summit Diplomacy* (Wilmington, Del.: Scholarly Resources, 1986), a concise, clear-headed introduction to the subject and to the literature on it. Charles E. Bohlen, *Witness to History, 1929–1969* (New York: W. W. Norton, 1973) is an important eyewitness account. Also useful is Walter Lippmann, "The Yalta Papers," 3 parts, *Washington Post and Times—Herald*, 31 March, 5 April, and 7 April 1955.

Reputation and Legacies

Works dealing with Roosevelt's historical reputation and legacies are William E. Leuchtenburg, *In the Shadow of FDR: From Harry Truman to Ronald Reagan* (Ithaca: Cornell University Press, 1983), which assesses Roosevelt's impact on his successors; Allan Nevins, "The Place of Franklin D. Roosevelt in History,"

American Heritage 17 (June 1966): 12–14, 101–104; Rossiter, *The American Presidency*; Godfrey Hodgson, *America in Our Time* (New York: Random House, 1976), 99–110, and *All Things to All Men: The False Promise of the Modern American Presidency* (New York: Simon & Schuster, 1980); and Theodore J. Lowi, *The Personal President: Power Invested, Promise Unfulfilled* (Ithaca: Cornell University Press, 1985), 44–66.

INDEX